# Poems of Grace

Texts of The Hymnal 1982

# Poems of Grace

Texts of The Hymnal 1982

 CHURCH

Church Publishing Incorporated, New York

Copyright © 1998, The Church Pension Fund. All rights reserved.

Church Publishing Incorporated
445 Fifth Avenue
New York, NY 10016

5 4 3 2 1

ISBN 978-089869-158-0

## Publisher's Dedication

*Poems of Grace* represents an accomplishment for the publisher, but far more importantly, it represents the fulfillment of a dream for a fine and dedicated priest of the church. From almost the moment *The Hymnal 1982* arrived from the bindery, Archdeacon Frederic Williams believed that the church needed a text-only edition. He understood in a profound way, certainly long before the rest of us, that the hymn texts he shepherded through General Convention 1982, as Chair of the Standing Commission on Church Music which produced the new hymnal, constituted very significant religious poetry.

Alec Wyton once commented that, "Episcopalians would sing any heresy to a good tune." One key element then, in the preparation of hymn texts, is that they be theologically sound. These are; but, they must be more. They must be theologically sound and

be great poetry. And, these are. Thanks in no
small part to the vigilant effort and tireless
dedication of Archdeacon Williams and his
colleagues.

*Poems of Grace* is commended to our church and
dedicated to Archdeacon Williams by the
publisher to be exactly what Father Williams
hoped and trusted that it would be—a source of
beauty, a guide in meditation, and most impor-
tantly, a means of prayer.

New York
October 3, 1998

The 90th Birthday of
The Venerable Frederic P. Williams

# Table of Contents

|  | Hymns |
|---|---|
| **The Daily Office** | **1–46** |
| Daily Morning Prayer | 1–11 |
| Noonday | 12–23 |
| Order of Worship for the Evening and Daily Evening Prayer | 24–37 |
| Compline | 38–46 |
| **The Church Year** | **47–293** |
| Sunday | 47–52 |
| Advent | 53–76 |
| Christmas Season | 77–115 |
| Epiphany Season | 116–139 |
| Lent | 140–152 |
| Holy Week | 153–173 |
| Easter | 174–213 |
| Ascension Day | 214–222 |
| The Day of Pentecost | 223–230 |
| Holy Days, The Common of Saints, and Various Occasions | 231–293 |
| **Holy Baptism** | **294–299** |
| **Holy Eucharist** | **300–347** |

| | |
|---|---|
| **Confirmation** | 348–349 |
| **Marriage** | 350–353 |
| **Burial of the Dead** | 354–358 |
| **Ordination** | 359 |
| **Consecration of a Church** | 360–361 |
| **General Hymns** | 362–634 |
|     The Holy Trinity | 362–371 |
|     Praise to God | 372–433 |
|     Jesus Christ our Lord | 434–499 |
|     The Holy Spirit | 500–516 |
|     The Church | 517–527 |
|     The Church's Mission | 528–544 |
|     Christian Vocation and Pilgrimage | 545–565 |
|     Christian Responsibility | 566–612 |
|     The Kingdom of God | 613–617 |
|     The Church Triumphant | 618–625 |
|     Holy Scripture | 626–634 |
| **The Christian Life** | 635–709 |
| **Rounds and Canons** | 710–715 |
| **National Songs** | 716–720 |
| *Copyright Index* | *Page 599* |
| *Index of First Lines* | *Page 613* |

**1, 2**

Father, we praise thee, now the night is over,
active and watchful, stand we all before thee;
singing we offer prayer and meditation:
    thus we adore thee.

Monarch of all things, fit us for thy mansions;
banish our weakness, health and wholeness sending;
bring us to heaven, where thy saints united
    joy without ending.

All-holy Father, Son, and equal Spirit,
Trinity blessèd, send us thy salvation;
thine is the glory, gleaming and resounding
    through all creation.

<sub>Latin, 10th cent.; tr. Percy Dearmer (1867–1936)</sub>

**3, 4**

Now that the daylight fills the sky,
we lift our hearts to God on high,
that he, in all we do or say,
would keep us free from harm this day:

Our hearts and lips may he restrain;
keep us from causing others pain,
that we may see and serve his Son,
and grow in love for everyone.

From evil may he guard our eyes,
our ears from empty praise and lies;
from selfishness our hearts release,
that we may serve, and know his peace;

that we, when this new day is gone,
and night in turn is drawing on,
with conscience free from sin and blame,
may praise and bless his holy Name.

To God the Father, heavenly Light,
to Christ, revealed in earthly night,
to God the Holy Ghost we raise
our equal and unceasing praise.

Sts. 1–4, Latin, 6th cent.; st.1, tr. John Mason Neale (1818–1866); sts. 2–4, tr. Peter Scagnelli (b. 1949). St. 5, Charles Coffin (1676–1749); tr. John Chandler (1806–1876)

## 5

O splendor of God's glory bright,
thou that bringest light from light,
Light of Light, light's living spring,
O Day, all days illumining,

O thou true Sun of heavenly love,
pour down thy radiance from above:
the Spirit's sanctifying beam
upon our earthly senses stream.

With prayer the Father we implore:
O Father, glorious evermore,

we plead with thee for grace and power
to conquer in temptation's hour,

to guide whate'er we nobly do,
with love all envy to subdue,
to give us grace our wrongs to bear,
to make ill fortune turn to fair.

All laud to God the Father be;
all praise, eternal Son, to thee;
all glory to the Spirit raise
in equal and unending praise.

Ambrose of Milan (340–397), tr. Robert Seymour Bridges (1844–1930), alt.

**6, 7**

Christ, whose glory fills the skies,
    Christ, the true, the only Light,
Sun of Righteousness, arise!
    Triumph o'er the shades of night:
Dayspring from on high, be near;
Daystar, in my heart appear.

Dark and cheerless is the morn
    unaccompanied by thee;
joyless is the day's return,
    till thy mercy's beams I see,
till they inward light impart,
glad my eyes, and warm my heart.

Visit then this soul of mine!
    Pierce the gloom of sin and grief!
Fill me, radiancy divine;
    scatter all my unbelief;
more and more thyself display,
shining to the perfect day.

Charles Wesley (1707–1788)

## 8

Morning has broken
like the first morning,
blackbird has spoken
    like the first bird.
        Praise for the singing!
        Praise for the morning!
        Praise for them, springing
            fresh from the Word!

Sweet the rain's new fall
sunlit from heaven,
like the first dewfall
    on the first grass.
        Praise for the sweetness
        of the wet garden,
        sprung in completeness
            where his feet pass.

Mine is the sunlight!
Mine is the morning
born of the one light
   Eden saw play!
      Praise with elation,
      praise every morning,
      God's re-creation
         of the new day!

Eleanor Farjeon (1881–1965), alt.

**9**

Not here for high and holy things
   we render thanks to thee,
but for the common things of earth,
   the purple pageantry
of dawning and of dying days,
   the splendor of the sea,

the royal robes of autumn moors,
   the golden gates of spring,
the velvet of soft summer nights,
   the silver glistering
of all the million million stars,
   the silent song they sing,

of faith and hope and love undimmed,
   undying still through death,

the resurrection of the world,
    what time there comes the breath
of dawn that rustles through the trees,
    and that clear voice that saith:

Awake, awake to love and work!
    The lark is in the sky,
the fields are wet with diamond dew,
    the worlds awake to cry
their blessings on the Lord of life,
    as he goes meekly by.

Come, let thy voice be one with theirs,
    shout with their shout of praise;
see how the giant sun soars up,
    great lord of years and days!
So let the love of Jesus come
    and set thy soul ablaze,

to give and give, and give again,
    what God hath given thee;
to spend thyself nor count the cost;
    to serve right gloriously
the God who gave all worlds that are,
    and all that are to be.

Geoffrey Anketel Studdert-Kennedy (1883–1929)

**10**

New every morning is the love
our wakening and uprising prove;
through sleep and darkness safely brought,
restored to life and power and thought.

New mercies, each returning day,
around us hover while we pray;
new perils past, new sins forgiven,
new thoughts of God, new hopes of heaven.

If on our daily course our mind
be set to hallow all we find,
new treasures still, of countless price,
God will provide for sacrifice.

Old friends, old scenes, will lovelier be,
as more of heaven in each we see;
some softening gleam of love and prayer
shall dawn on every cross and care.

The trivial round, the common task,
will furnish all we ought to ask:
room to deny ourselves; a road
to bring us daily nearer God.

Only, O Lord, in thy dear love,
fit us for perfect rest above;
and help us, this and every day,
to live more nearly as we pray.

John Keble (1792–1866)

## 11

Awake, my soul, and with the sun
thy daily stage of duty run;
shake off dull sloth, and joyful rise
to pay thy morning sacrifice:

Lord, I my vows to thee renew;
disperse my sins as morning dew;
guard my first springs of thought and will,
and with thyself my spirit fill.

Direct, control, suggest, this day,
all I design, or do, or say;
that all my powers, with all their might,
in thy sole glory may unite.

Praise God, from whom all blessings flow;
praise him, all creatures here below;
praise him above, ye heavenly host:
praise Father, Son, and Holy Ghost.

Thomas Ken (1637–1711), alt.

## 12, 13

The golden sun lights up the sky,
imparting vigor to the day.
Amid our customary round,
we offer you our prayer and praise.

At the third hour you took your cross,
you stumbled, Lord, beneath its weight.

Now help us bear our daily load
and strive to follow where you lead.

At the third hour your faithful band
was clothed with power on Pentecost.
Bestow your Spirit on us now,
and give us strength to do your will.

O God, creation's ruling force,
O Jesus, crucified for us,
O Spirit, love's life-giving ray,
we praise and bless you every hour.

Charles P. Price (b. 1920)

**14, 15**

O God, creation's secret force,
yourself unmoved, all motion's source,
you, from the morn till evening's ray,
through all its changes guide the day:

Grant us, when this short life is past,
the glorious evening that shall last;
that, by a holy death attained,
eternal glory may be gained.

Almighty Father, hear our cry
through Jesus Christ, our Lord Most High,
whom with the Spirit we adore
for ever and for evermore.

Ambrose of Milan (340–397); tr. John Mason Neale (1818–1866), alt. St. 3, James Waring McCrady (b. 1938)

## 16, 17

> Now let us sing our praise to God
> with fervent heart and ready mind:
> each day the sun at zenith calls
> the faithful to their noonday prayers.
>
> For at this hour to all the world
> the grace of true salvation came:
> the Lamb of God restored our peace
> by virtue of his saving cross.
>
> So dazzling is its holy light,
> it puts the noonday sun in shade.
> Then let us all with joy embrace
> the flaming splendor of such grace.
>
> All glory be to you, Lord Christ,
> who, conquering death, reign gloriously
> with God, Creator of all things
> and with the Spirit, Comforter.

Latin; ver. *Hymnal 1982*. St. 4, Anne K. LeCroy (b. 1930)

## 18

> As now the sun shines down at noon,
> your light, O Lord, burns in our hearts;
> assist us to endure that light,
> and through your judgment find your grace.

*Monday and Thursday*
> The sun stood still for Joshua
> while he contended, Lord, for you;
> so may we struggle faithfully
> and seek our victory in your peace.
>
> At noon you hung upon the cross,
> betrayed, forsaken, all alone;
> help us to share your pain and grief,
> and, sharing, know life's victory won.
>
> At noon you came to Jacob's well,
> athirst and spent, you asked for aid;
> to us, like her who saw your need,
> your living water give to drink.

*Tuesday and Saturday*
> Elijah taunted Baal at noon;
> he knew you, Lord, would answer him;
> may we, too, trust your sovereign power
> when we must act in day's hard light.
>
> On Golgotha the sky turned dark;
> all shadows of the morn and eve
> converged to shield frail human eyes
> from all the woe you bore for us.
>
> At noontime Paul beheld your light,
> so bright it canceled out the sun;
> you blinded and converted him:
> O turn us now to see your face.

*Wednesday and Friday*
>By noon's bright light, destruction stalks;
>ten thousand perish at our side;
>held by your unrelenting grace,
>let us cling always to your love.
>
>The dark midday could not conceal
>your cry of awful agony;
>teach us to hear its echoes still
>in every human misery.
>
>In noonday vision Peter saw
>that all you made was pure and clean;
>grant us that same revealing light
>that we may see your world is good.

*Doxology*
>O God, creation's ruling force,
>O Jesus, crucified for us,
>O Spirit, bringing truth and love,
>we praise and bless you every hour.

Charles P. Price (b. 1920) and Carl P. Daw, Jr. (b. 1944)

## 19, 20

>Now Holy Spirit, ever One
>with God the Father and the Son,
>pour forth into our hearts, we pray,
>the fullness of your grace today.

Let mouth and tongue, mind, sense, and strength
God's mighty actions tell at length;
let love in flames of living fire
the hearts of all the world inspire.

Almighty Father, hear our cry
through Jesus Christ, our Lord Most High,
whom with the Spirit we adore
for ever and for evermore.

Ambrose of Milan (340–397); ver. *Hymnal 1982*. St. 3, James Waring McCrady (b. 1938)

## 21, 22

O God of truth, O Lord of might,
you order time and change aright,
you send the early morning ray,
and light the glow of perfect day.

Quench now on earth the flames of strife;
from passion's heat preserve our life;
and while you keep our body whole,
pour healing peace upon our soul.

Almighty Father, hear our cry
through Jesus Christ, our Lord Most High,
whom with the Spirit we adore
for ever and for evermore.

Ambrose of Milan (340–397); tr. John Mason Neale (1818–1866), alt. St. 3, James Waring McCrady (b. 1938)

## 23

The fleeting day is nearly gone;
we harvest what the morning sowed.
Now grant us undiminished strength
to stand and do what still remains.

At prayer time, near the Temple gate,
Apostles made a lame man walk.
They gave him healing in your Name;
now give us grace to walk your way.

With "It is finished" on your lips,
at that ninth hour you died for us.
Inspire us by your dying breath
to live for you and do your will.

O God, creation's ruling force,
O Jesus, crucified for us,
O Spirit, bringing power and health,
we praise and bless you every hour.

Charles P. Price (b. 1920)

## 24

The day thou gavest, Lord, is ended,
    the darkness falls at thy behest;
to thee our morning hymns ascended,
    thy praise shall sanctify our rest.

We thank thee that thy Church, unsleeping
    while earth rolls onward into light,

through all the world her watch is keeping,
   and rests not now by day or night.

As o'er each continent and island
   the dawn leads on another day,
the voice of prayer is never silent,
   nor dies the strain of praise away.

So be it, Lord; thy throne shall never,
   like earth's proud empires, pass away;
thy kingdom stands, and grows for ever,
   till all thy creatures own thy sway.

John Ellerton (1826–1893)
*This hymn may be used in the morning by omitting stanza 1.*

## 25, 26

O gracious Light, Lord Jesus Christ,
   in you the Father's glory shone.
Immortal, holy, blest is he,
   and blest are you, his holy Son.

Now sunset comes, but light shines forth,
   the lamps are lit to pierce the night.
Praise Father, Son, and Spirit: God
   who dwells in the eternal light.

Worthy are you of endless praise,
   O Son of God, Life-giving Lord;
wherefore you are through all the earth
   and in the highest heaven adored.

Greek, 3rd cent.; tr. F. Bland Tucker (1895–1984); para. of
*O Gracious Light*

## 27, 28

O blest Creator, source of light,
you gave the day with splendor bright,
when on the new and living earth
you brought all things to glorious birth.

You joined the morn and evening ray;
you found it good and called it "day."
But now the threat in darkness nears—
we pray you, Father, calm our fears.

Lest we, beset by doubt and strife,
forget your blessèd gift of life,
and anguished and in mind distressed,
be crushed by guilt, by sin oppressed.

Eternal Father, help us rise
and strive to gain the heavenly prize;
for you alone can make us strong
to turn from sin and cease from wrong.

Defend us, Father, through the night,
and with your Son, and Spirit bright—
the Trinity whom we adore—
be with us now and evermore.

Latin, 6th cent.; tr. Anne K. LeCroy (b. 1930), alt.

**29, 30**

O Trinity of blessèd light,
O Unity of princely might,
the fiery sun now goes his way;
shed thou within our hearts thy ray.

To thee our morning song of praise,
to thee our evening prayer we raise;
O grant us with thy saints on high
to praise thee through eternity.

To God the Father, heavenly Light,
to Christ revealed in earthly night,
to God the Holy Ghost we raise
our equal and unceasing praise.

Latin, 6th cent.; tr. John Mason Neale (1818–1866). St. 3,
Charles Coffin (1676–1749); tr. John Chandler (1806–1876)

**31, 32**

Most Holy God, the Lord of heaven,
who in the high arched sky has placed
the sun that flames up from the east
and brings the splendors of the dawn:

for you the dazzling star shines forth
which in its gleaming path declares
the wonders of your glorious power,
and beckons us to worship you.

The day departs, the evening stars
serenely light the darkening sky;
the moon with cool reflected glow
will bring the silences of night.

You, Holy One, Creator, Lord,
you in the primal world once set
the boundaries of the day and night
and ordered seasons in their round.

Like sun and day, shine in our hearts;
like moon and night, give loving peace.
Free us from bonds of blinding sin
and guide us on our path to you.

Latin; tr. Anne K. LeCroy (b. 1930)

## 33, 34, 35

Christ, mighty Savior, Light of all creation,
you make the daytime radiant with the sunlight
and to the night give glittering adornment,
    stars in the heavens.

Now comes the day's end as the sun is setting:
mirror of daybreak, pledge of resurrection;
while in the heavens choirs of stars appearing
    hallow the nightfall.

Therefore we come now evening rites to offer,
joyfully chanting holy hymns to praise you,

with all creation joining hearts and voices
    singing your glory.

Give heed, we pray you, to our supplication:
that you may grant us pardon for offenses,
strength for our weak hearts, rest for aching bodies,
    soothing the weary.

Though bodies slumber, hearts shall keep their vigil,
for ever resting in the peace of Jesus,
in light or darkness worshiping our Savior
    now and for ever.

Mozarabic, 10th cent.; tr. Alan G. McDougall (1895–1964); rev. Anne K. LeCroy (b. 1930)

**36**

O gladsome Light, O grace
    of God the Father's face,
the eternal splendor wearing;
    celestial, holy, blest,
    our Savior Jesus Christ,
joyful in thine appearing.

Now, ere day fadeth quite,
    we see the evening light,
our wonted hymn outpouring;
    Father of might unknown,
    thee, his incarnate Son,
and Holy Spirit adoring.

> To thee of right belongs
> all praise of holy songs,
> O Son of God, Lifegiver;
> thee, therefore, O Most High,
> the world doth glorify,
> and shall exalt for ever.

Greek, 3rd cent.; tr. Robert Seymour Bridges (1844–1930); para. of *O Gracious Light*

## 37

> O brightness of the immortal Father's face,
> most holy, heavenly, blest,
> Lord Jesus Christ, in whom his truth and grace
> are visibly expressed:
>
> the sun is sinking now, and one by one
> the lamps of evening shine;
> we hymn the eternal Father, and the Son,
> and Holy Ghost divine.
>
> Worthy art thou at all times to receive
> our hallowed praises, Lord.
> O Son of God, be thou, in whom we live,
> through all the world adored.

Greek, 3rd cent.; tr. Edward W. Eddis (1825–1905); para. of *O Gracious Light*

**38, 39**

Jesus, Redeemer of the world,
Word of the Father throned on high,
light from the light invisible,
and watchful guardian over all:

The whole creation's architect,
you set the bounds of night and day;
give to our wearied bodies rest
in night's enfolding quietness.

You broke the chains of death and hell:
Lord, free us from our ancient foe
and let him never lead astray
those you have ransomed by your blood.

Lord, while we live for this short time
as mortals clothed in earth-bound frame,
refresh us now with restful sleep
that waking we may watch with you.

All glory be to you, Lord Christ,
who, conquering death, reign gloriously
with God, Creator of all things
and with the Spirit, Comforter.

Latin, 10th cent.; ver. *Hymnal 1982.* St. 5, Anne K. LeCroy (b. 1930)

## 40, 41

O Christ, you are both light and day,
you drive away the shadowed night;
as Daystar you precede the dawn,
the Herald of the light to come.

We pray you, O most holy Lord,
to be our guardian while we sleep;
bestow on us who rest in you
the blessing of a quiet night.

Although our eyes in sleep be closed,
let hearts in constant vigil watch;
with your right hand you will protect
those who believe and trust in you.

Defender of us all, look down;
repel our dread, malicious foe;
direct your faithful household, Lord,
whom you have purchased with your blood.

O Christ, Redeemer of the world,
O God, our Maker and our end,
O Spirit, bond of peace and love,
to you be thanks and endless praise.

Latin, 6th cent.; ver. *Hymnal, 1982*. St. 5, Charles P. Price (b. 1920)

**42**

Now the day is over,
   night is drawing nigh,
shadows of the evening
   steal across the sky.

Jesus, give the weary
   calm and sweet repose;
with thy tenderest blessing
   may our eyelids close.

Grant to little children
   visions bright of thee;
guard the sailors tossing
   on the deep, blue sea.

Comfort every sufferer
   watching late in pain;
those who plan some evil
   from their sin restrain.

Through the long night watches
   may thine angels spread
their white wings above me,
   watching round my bed.

When the morning wakens,
   then may I arise
pure, and fresh, and sinless
   in thy holy eyes.

Sabine Baring-Gould (1834–1924), alt.

## 43

All praise to thee, my God, this night,
for all the blessings of the light:
keep me, O keep me, King of kings,
beneath thine own almighty wings.

Forgive me, Lord, for thy dear Son,
the ill that I this day have done;
that with the world, myself, and thee,
I, ere I sleep, at peace may be.

O may my soul on thee repose,
and with sweet sleep mine eyelids close;
sleep that shall me more vigorous make
to serve my God when I awake.

Praise God, from whom all blessings flow;
praise him, all creatures here below;
praise him above, ye heavenly host:
praise Father, Son, and Holy Ghost.

Thomas Ken (1637–1711)

## 44, 45

To you before the close of day,
Creator of all things, we pray
that in your constant clemency
our guard and keeper you would be.

Save us from troubled, restless sleep,
from terror's dreams your children keep;

so calm our minds that fears may cease
and rested bodies wake in peace.

A healthy life we ask of you,
the fire of love in us renew,
and when the dawn new light will bring
your praise and glory we shall sing.

Almighty Father, hear our cry
through Jesus Christ, our Lord Most High,
whom with the Spirit we adore
for ever and for evermore.

Latin, 6th cent.; ver. *Hymnal, 1982*. St. 4, James Waring McCrady (b. 1938)

**46**

The duteous day now closeth,
each flower and tree reposeth,
    shade creeps o'er wild and wood:
let us, as night is falling,
on God our Maker calling,
    give thanks to him, the Giver good.

Now all the heavenly splendor
breaks forth in starlight tender
    from myriad worlds unknown;
and we, this marvel seeing,
forget our selfish being
    for joy of beauty not our own.

> Though long our mortal blindness
> has missed God's loving-kindness
>     and plunged us into strife;
> yet when life's day is over,
> shall death's fair night discover
>     the fields of everlasting life.

Paul Gerhardt (1607–1676); tr. Robert Seymour Bridges (1844–1930) and others

## 47

> On this day, the first of days,
> God the Father's Name we praise,
> who, creation's Lord and spring,
> did the world from darkness bring.
>
> On this day the eternal Son
> over death his triumph won;
> on this day the Spirit came
> with his gifts of living flame.
>
> Maker, who didst fashion me
> image of thyself to be,
> fill me with thy love divine,
> let my every thought be thine.
>
> Holy Jesus, may I be
> dead and buried here with thee;
> and, by love inflamed, arise
> unto thee a sacrifice.

Thou, who dost all gifts impart,
shine, blest Spirit, in my heart;
best of gifts, thyself bestow;
make me burn thy love to know.

God, the blessèd Three in One,
dwell within my heart alone;
thou dost give thyself to me:
help me give myself to thee.

<sub>Latin; tr. Henry Williams Baker (1821–1877), alt.</sub>

**48**

O day of radiant gladness,
　O day of joy and light,
O balm of care and sadness,
　most beautiful, most bright;
this day the high and lowly,
　through ages joined in tune,
sing, "Holy, holy, holy,"
　to the great God Triune.

This day at the creation,
　the light first had its birth;
this day for our salvation
　Christ rose from depths of earth;
this day our Lord victorious
　the Spirit sent from heaven,
and thus this day most glorious
　a triple light was given.

This day, God's people meeting,
   his Holy Scripture hear;
his living presence greeting,
   through Bread and Wine made near.
We journey on, believing,
   renewed with heavenly might,
from grace more grace receiving
   on this blest day of light.

That light our hope sustaining,
   we walk the pilgrim way,
at length our rest attaining,
   our endless Sabbath day.
We sing to thee our praises,
   O Father, Spirit, Son;
the Church her voice upraises
   to thee, blest Three in One.

Sts. 1–2, Christopher Wordsworth (1807–1835), alt.; st. 3, Charles P. Price (b. 1920); st. 4, ver. *Hymnal 1982*

## 49

Come, let us with our Lord arise,
our Lord who made both earth and skies,
who died to save the world he made
and rose triumphant from the dead;
he rose, the prince of life and peace,
and stamped the day for ever his.

This is the day the Lord hath made
that all may see his love displayed,
may feel his resurrection's power
and rise again to fall no more,
in perfect righteousness renewed
and filled with all the life of God.

Then let us render him his own,
with solemn prayer approach the throne,
with meekness hear the gospel word,
with thanks his dying love record;
our joyful hearts and voices raise
and fill his courts with songs of praise.

Charles Wesley (1707–1788)

**50**

This is the day the Lord hath made,
   he calls the hours his own;
let heaven rejoice, let earth be glad,
   and praise surround the throne.

Today he rose and left the dead,
   and Satan's empire fell;
today the saints his triumphs spread,
   and all his wonders tell.

Hosanna to the anointed King,
   to David's holy Son!
Make haste to help us, Lord, and bring
salvation from thy throne.

Blest be the Lord, who comes to us
    with messages of grace!
Who comes, in God his Father's name,
    to save our sinful race.

Hosanna in the highest strains
    the Church on earth can raise;
the highest heavens in which he reigns
    shall give him nobler praise.

Isaac Watts (1674–1748), alt.

## 51

We the Lord's people, heart and voice uniting,
praise him who called us out of sin and darkness
into his own light, that he might anoint us
    a royal priesthood.

This is the Lord's house, home of all his people,
school for the faithful, refuge for the sinner,
rest for the pilgrim, haven for the weary;
    all find a welcome.

This is the Lord's day, day of God's own making,
day of creation, day of resurrection,
day of the Spirit, sign of heaven's banquet,
    day for rejoicing.

In the Lord's service bread and wine are offered,
that Christ may take them, bless them, break,
          and give them
to all his people, his own life imparting,
    food everlasting.

John E. Bowers (b. 1923), alt.

**52**

This day at thy creating word
first o'er the earth the light was poured;
O Lord, this day upon us shine
and fill our souls with light divine.

This day the Lord for sinners slain
in might victorious rose again;
O Jesus, may we lifted be
from death of sin to life in thee!

This day the Holy Spirit came
with fiery tongues of cloven flame;
O Spirit, fill our hearts this day
with grace to hear and grace to pray.

All praise to God the Father be,
all praise, eternal Son, to thee,
whom, with the Spirit, we adore
for ever and for evermore.

William Walsham How (1823–1897), alt.

## 53

Once he came in blessing,
all our ills redressing;
came in likeness lowly,
Son of God most holy;
bore the cross to save us,
hope and freedom gave us.

Still he comes within us,
still his voice would win us
from the sins that hurt us,
would to Truth convert us:
not in torment hold us,
but in love enfold us.

Thus, if thou canst name him,
not ashamed to claim him,
but wilt trust him boldly
nor dost love him coldly,
he will then receive thee,
heal thee, and forgive thee.

One who thus endureth
bright reward secureth.
Come, then, O Lord Jesus,
from our sins release us;
let us here confess thee
till in heaven we bless thee.

Jan Roh (1485?–1547); tr. Catherine Winkworth (1827–1878), alt.

**54**

Savior of the nations, come!
Virgin's Son, make here your home.
Marvel now, both heaven and earth,
that the Lord chose such a birth.

Wondrous birth! Oh, wondrous child
of the Virgin undefiled!
Mighty God and Mary's son,
eager now his race to run!

Thus on earth the Word appears,
gracing his created spheres;
hence to death and hell descends,
then the heavenly throne ascends.

Come, O Father's saving Son,
who o'er sin the victory won.
Boundless shall your kingdom be;
grant that we its glories see.

Martin Luther (1483–1546) after Ambrose of Milan (340–397); tr. William M. Reynolds (1812–1876) and James Waring McCrady (b. 1938)

## 55

Redeemer of the nations, come;
reveal yourself in virgin birth,
the birth which ages all adore,
a wondrous birth, befitting God.

From human will you do not spring,
but from the Spirit of our God;
O Word of God, come; take our flesh
and grow as child in Mary's womb.

You came forth from the eternal God,
and you returned to that same source.
You suffered death and harrowed hell,
and reigned once more from God's high throne.

With God the Father you are one,
and one with us in human flesh.
Oh, fill our weak and dying frame
with godly strength which never fails.

Your cradle shines with glory's light;
its splendor pierces all our gloom.
Our faith reflects those radiant beams;
no night shall overcome it now.

All praise, O unbegotten God,
all praise to you, eternal Word,
all praise, life-giving Spirit, praise,
all glory to our God Triune.

Att. to Ambrose of Milan (340–397); tr. Charles P. Price (b. 1920)

**56**

*December 23*
>O come, O come, Emmanuel,
>and ransom captive Israel,
>that mourns in lonely exile here
>until the Son of God appear.
>
>>*Rejoice! Rejoice! Emmanuel*
>>*shall come to thee, O Israel!*

*December 17*
>O come, thou Wisdom from on high,
>who orderest all things mightily;
>to us the path of knowledge show,
>and teach us in her ways to go.
>
>*Refrain*

*December 18*
>O come, O come, thou Lord of might,
>who to thy tribes on Sinai's height
>in ancient times didst give the law,
>in cloud, and majesty, and awe.
>
>*Refrain*

*December 19*
>O come, thou Branch of Jesse's tree,
>free them from Satan's tyranny
>that trust thy mighty power to save,
>and give them victory o'er the grave.
>
>*Refrain*

*December 20*
> O come, thou Key of David, come,
> and open wide our heavenly home;
> make safe the way that leads on high,
> and close the path to misery.
>
> *Refrain*

*December 21*
> O come, thou Dayspring from on high,
> and cheer us by thy drawing nigh;
> disperse the gloomy clouds of night,
> and death's dark shadow put to flight.
>
> *Refrain*

*December 22*
> O come, Desire of nations, bind
> in one the hearts of all mankind;
> bid thou our sad divisions cease,
> and be thyself our King of Peace.
>
> *Refrain*

*December 23*
> O come, O come, Emmanuel,
> and ransom captive Israel,
> that mourns in lonely exile here
> until the Son of God appear.
>
> *Refrain*

*The stanzas may be used as antiphons with "The Song of Mary" on the dates given.*

Latin, ca. 9th cent.; ver. *Hymnal 1940,* alt.

**57, 58**

Lo! he comes, with clouds descending,
   once for our salvation slain;
thousand thousand saints attending
   swell the triumph of his train:
   Alleluia!
   Christ the Lord returns to reign.

Every eye shall now behold him,
   robed in dreadful majesty;
those who set at nought and sold him,
   pierced, and nailed him to the tree,
   deeply wailing,
   shall the true Messiah see.

Those dear tokens of his passion
   still his dazzling body bears,
cause of endless exultation
   to his ransomed worshipers;
   with what rapture
   gaze we on those glorious scars!

Yea, amen! let all adore thee,
   high on thine eternal throne;
Savior, take the power and glory;
   claim the kingdom for thine own:
   Alleluia!
   Thou shalt reign, and thou alone.

Charles Wesley (1707-1788)

## 59

Hark! a thrilling voice is sounding:
　　"Christ is nigh," it seems to say;
"Cast away the works of darkness,
　　O ye children of the day."

Wakened by the solemn warning,
　　from earth's bondage let us rise;
Christ, our sun, all sloth dispelling,
　　shines upon the morning skies.

Lo! the Lamb, so long expected,
　　comes with pardon down from heaven;
let us haste, with tears of sorrow,
　　one and all to be forgiven;

so when next he comes with glory,
　　and the world is wrapped in fear,
may he with his mercy shield us,
　　and with words of love draw near.

Honor, glory, might, and blessing
　　to the Father and the Son,
with the everlasting Spirit
　　while unending ages run.

Latin, ca. 6th cent.; tr. *Hymns Ancient and Modern*, 1861, alt.

**60**

Creator of the stars of night,
your people's everlasting light,
O Christ, Redeemer of us all,
we pray you hear us when we call.

In sorrow that the ancient curse
should doom to death a universe,
you came, O Savior, to set free
your own in glorious liberty.

When this old world drew on toward night,
you came; but not in splendor bright,
not as a monarch, but the child
of Mary, blameless mother mild.

At your great Name, O Jesus, now
all knees must bend, all hearts must bow:
all things on earth with one accord,
like those in heaven, shall call you Lord.

Come in your holy might, we pray,
redeem us for eternal day;
defend us while we dwell below
from all assaults of our dread foe.

To God the Father, God the Son,
and God the Spirit, Three in One,
praise, honor, might, and glory be
from age to age eternally.

Latin, 9th cent.; ver. *Hymnal 1940*, alt.

## 61, 62

"Sleepers, wake!" A voice astounds us,
the shout of rampart guards surrounds us:
   "Awake, Jerusalem, arise!"
Midnight's peace their cry has broken,
their urgent summons clearly spoken:
   "The time has come, O maidens wise!
Rise up, and give us light;
the Bridegroom is in sight.
   Alleluia!
     Your lamps prepare
     and hasten there,
that you the wedding feast may share."

Zion hears the watchmen singing;
her heart with joyful hope is springing,
   she wakes and hurries through the night.
Forth he comes, her Bridegroom glorious
in strength of grace, in truth victorious:
   her star is risen, her light grows bright.
Now come, most worthy Lord,
God's Son, Incarnate Word,
   Alleluia!
     We follow all
     and heed your call
to come into the banquet hall.

Lamb of God, the heavens adore you;
let saints and angels sing before you,
 as harps and cymbals swell the sound.
Twelve great pearls, the city's portals:
through them we stream to join the immortals
 as we with joy your throne surround.
No eye has known the sight,
no ear heard such delight:
 Alleluia!
  Therefore we sing
  to greet our King;
 for ever let our praises ring.

Philip Nicolai (1556–1608); tr. Carl P. Daw, Jr. (b. 1944)

## 63, 64

O heavenly Word, eternal Light,
begotten of the Father's might,
who in these latter days wast born
for blessing to a world forlorn;

pour light upon us from above,
and fire our hearts with ardent love,
that, as we hear thy truth today,
all wrong desires may burn away;

and when, as judge, thou drawest nigh
the secrets of our hearts to try,
to recompense each hidden sin
and bid the saints their reign begin;

O let us not, for evil past,
be driven from thy face at last,
but with thy saints for evermore
behold thee, love thee, and adore.

To God the Father, God the Son,
and God the Spirit, ever One,
praise, honor, might, and glory be
from age to age eternally.

Latin, ca. 7th cent.; tr. *Hymnal 1982*

## 65

Prepare the way, O Zion,
    your Christ is drawing near!
Let every hill and valley
    a level way appear.
Greet One who comes in glory,
foretold in sacred story.

> *Oh, blest is Christ that came*
> *in God's most holy Name.*

He brings God's rule, O Zion;
    he comes from heaven above.
His rule is peace and freedom,
    and justice, truth, and love.
Lift high your praise resounding,
for grace and joy abounding.

*Refrain*

Fling wide your gates, O Zion;
   your Savior's rule embrace.
His tidings of salvation
   proclaim in every place.
All lands will bow before him,
their voices will adore him.

*Refrain*

Frans Mikael Franzen (1772–1847); tr. composite; adapt. Charles P. Price (b. 1920)

**66**

Come, thou long-expected Jesus,
   born to set thy people free;
from our fears and sins release us,
   let us find our rest in thee.

Israel's strength and consolation,
   hope of all the earth thou art:
dear desire of every nation,
   joy of every longing heart.

Born thy people to deliver,
   born a child, and yet a king,
born to reign in us for ever,
   now thy gracious kingdom bring.

By thine own eternal Spirit
   rule in all our hearts alone;
by thine all-sufficient merit
   raise us to thy glorious throne.

Charles Wesley (1707–1788)

## 67

Comfort, comfort ye my people,
    speak ye peace, thus saith our God;
comfort those who sit in darkness
    mourning 'neath their sorrows' load.
Speak ye to Jerusalem
of the peace that waits for them;
tell her that her sins I cover,
and her warfare now is over.

Hark, the voice of one that crieth
    in the desert far and near,
calling us to new repentance
    since the kingdom now is here.
Oh, that warning cry obey!
Now prepare for God a way;
let the valleys rise to meet him
and the hills bow down to greet him.

Make ye straight what long was crooked,
    make the rougher places plain;
let your hearts be true and humble,
    as befits his holy reign.
For the glory of the Lord
now o'er earth is shed abroad;
and all flesh shall see the token
that the word is never broken.

Johann G. Olearius (1611–1684); tr. Catherine Winkworth (1827–1878), alt.

# 68

Rejoice! rejoice, believers,
    and let your lights appear!
The evening is advancing,
    and darker night is near.
The Bridegroom is arising,
    and soon he will draw nigh;
up, watch in expectation!
    at midnight comes the cry.

See that your lamps are burning,
    replenish them with oil;
look now for your salvation,
    the end of sin and toil.
The marriage-feast is waiting,
    the gates wide open stand;
rise up, ye heirs of glory,
    the Bridegroom is at hand!

Our hope and expectation,
    O Jesus, now appear;
arise, thou Sun so longed for,
    above this darkened sphere!
With hearts and hands uplifted,
    we plead, O Lord, to see
the day of earth's redemption,
    and ever be with thee!

Laurentius Laurenti (1660–1722); tr. Sarah B. Findlater (1823–1907), alt.

## 69

What is the crying at Jordan?
 Who hears, O God, the prophecy?
Dark is the season, dark our hearts
 and shut to mystery.

Who then shall stir in this darkness,
 prepare for joy in the winter night?
Mortal in darkness we lie down,
 blind-hearted, seeing no light.

Lord, give us grace to awake us,
 to see the branch that begins to bloom;
in great humility is hid
 all heaven in a little room.

Now comes the day of salvation,
 in joy and terror the Word is born!
God gives himself into our lives;
 O let salvation dawn!

Carol Christopher Drake (b. 1933), alt.

## 70

Herald, sound the note of judgment,
 warning us of right and wrong,
turning us from sin and sadness
 till once more we sing the song.

> *Sound the trumpet! Tell the message!*
> *Christ, the Savior King, has come!*

Herald, sound the note of gladness;
   tell the news that Christ is here;
make a pathway through the desert
   for the one who brings God near.

*Refrain*

Herald, sound the note of pardon—
   those repenting are forgiven;
God receives his wayward children,
   and to them new life is given.

*Refrain*

Herald, sound the note of triumph;
   Christ has come to share our life,
bringing God's own love and power,
   granting victory in our strife.

*Refrain*

Moir A. J. Waters (1906–1980), alt.

## 71, 72

Hark! the glad sound! the Savior comes,
   the Savior promised long:
let every heart prepare a throne,
   and every voice a song.

He comes, the prisoners to release
   in Satan's bondage held;
the gates of brass before him burst,
   the iron fetters yield.

He comes, the broken heart to bind,
    the bleeding soul to cure;
and with the treasures of his grace
    to enrich the humble poor.

Our glad hosannas, Prince of Peace,
    thy welcome shall proclaim;
and heaven's eternal arches ring
    with thy beloved Name.

Philip Doddridge (1702–1751)

## 73

The King shall come when morning dawns
    and light triumphant breaks;
when beauty gilds the eastern hills
    and life to joy awakes.

Not, as of old, a little child,
    to bear, and fight, and die,
but crowned with glory like the sun
    that lights the morning sky.

The King shall come when morning dawns
    and earth's dark night is past;
O haste the rising of that morn,
    the day that e'er shall last;

and let the endless bliss begin,
    by weary saints foretold,
when right shall triumph over wrong,
    and truth shall be extolled.

The King shall come when morning dawns
    and light and beauty brings:
Hail, Christ the Lord! Thy people pray,
    come quickly, King of kings.

Greek; tr. John Brownlie (1859–1925), alt.

**74**

Blest be the King whose coming
    is in the name of God!
For him let doors be opened,
    no hearts against him barred!
Not robed in royal splendor,
    in power and pomp, comes he;
but clad as are the poorest,
    such his humility!

Blest be the King whose coming
    is in the name of God!
By those who truly listen
    his voice is truly heard;
pity the proud and haughty,
    who have not learned to heed
the Christ who is the Promise,
    who has atonement made.

Blest be the King whose coming
    is in the name of God!
He only to the humble
    reveals the face of God.

All power is his, all glory!
　　All things are in his hand,
all ages and all peoples,
　　till time itself shall end!

Blest be the King whose coming
　　is in the name of God!
He offers to the burdened
　　the rest and grace they need.
Gentle is he and humble!
　　And light his yoke shall be,
for he would have us bear it
　　so he can make us free!

Federico J. Pagura (b. 1923); tr. F. Pratt Green (b. 1903), alt.

## 75

There's a voice in the wilderness crying,
　　a call from the ways untrod:
Prepare in the desert a highway,
　　a highway for our God!
The valleys shall be exalted,
　　the lofty hills brought low;
make straight all the crooked places
　　where the Lord our God may go!

O Zion, that bringest good tidings,
　　get thee up to the heights and sing!
Proclaim to a desolate people
　　the coming of their King.

Like the flowers of the field they perish,
    like grass our works decay,
the power and pomp of nations
    shall pass like a dream away;

but the word of our God endureth,
    the arm of the Lord is strong;
he stands in the midst of nations,
    and he will right the wrong.
He shall feed his flock like a shepherd,
    the lambs he'll gently hold;
to pastures of peace he'll lead them,
    and bring them safe to his fold.

James Lewis Milligan (1876–1961), alt.

**76**

On Jordan's bank the Baptist's cry
announces that the Lord is nigh;
awake and hearken, for he brings
glad tidings of the King of kings.

Then cleansed be every breast from sin;
make straight the way for God within,
and let each heart prepare a home
where such a mighty guest may come.

For thou art our salvation, Lord,
our refuge, and our great reward;
without thy grace we waste away
like flowers that wither and decay.

To heal the sick stretch out thine hand,
and bid the fallen sinner stand;
shine forth, and let thy light restore
earth's own true loveliness once more.

All praise, eternal Son, to thee,
whose advent doth thy people free;
whom with the Father we adore
and Holy Spirit evermore.

Charles Coffin (1676–1749); tr. Charles Winfred Douglas (1867–1944), after John Chandler (1806–1876); alt.

## 77

From east to west, from shore to shore,
    let every heart awake and sing
the holy child whom Mary bore,
    the Christ, the everlasting King.

Behold, the world's creator wears
    the form and fashion of a slave;
our very flesh our Maker shares,
    his fallen creatures all to save.

For this how wondrously he wrought!
    A maid in lowly human place became,
in ways beyond all thought,
    the chosen vessel of his grace.

And while the angels in the sky
    sang praise above the silent field,

to shepherds poor the Lord Most High,
    the one great Shepherd, was revealed.

All glory for this blessèd morn
    to God the Father ever be;
all praise to thee, O Virgin-born,
    all praise, O Holy Ghost, to thee.

Caelius Sedilius (5th cent.); tr. John Ellerton (1826–1893), alt.

**78, 79**

O little town of Bethlehem,
    how still we see thee lie!
Above thy deep and dreamless sleep
    the silent stars go by;
yet in thy dark streets shineth
    the everlasting Light;
the hopes and fears of all the years
    are met in thee tonight.

For Christ is born of Mary;
    and gathered all above,
while mortals sleep, the angels keep
    their watch of wondering love.
O morning stars, together
    proclaim the holy birth!
and praises sing to God the King,
    and peace to men on earth.

How silently, how silently,
    the wondrous gift is given!
So God imparts to human hearts
    the blessings of his heaven.
No ear may hear his coming,
    but in this world of sin,
where meek souls will receive him, still
    the dear Christ enters in.

Where children pure and happy
    pray to the blessèd Child,
where misery cries out to thee,
    Son of the mother mild;
where charity stands watching
    and faith holds wide the door,
the dark night wakes, the glory breaks,
    and Christmas comes once more.

O holy Child of Bethlehem,
    descend to us, we pray;
cast out our sin and enter in,
    be born in us today.
We hear the Christmas angels
    the great glad tidings tell;
O come to us, abide with us,
    our Lord Emmanuel!

Phillips Brooks (1835–1893)

**80**

From heaven above to earth I come
to bring good news to everyone!
Glad tidings of great joy I bring
to all the world, and gladly sing:

to you this night is born a child
of Mary, chosen virgin mild;
this newborn child of lowly birth
shall be the joy of all the earth.

This is the Christ, God's Son most high,
who hears your sad and bitter cry;
he will himself your Savior be
and from all sin will set you free.

The blessing which the Father planned
the Son holds in his infant hand,
that in his kingdom bright and fair,
you may with us his glory share.

Martin Luther (1483–1546); tr. *Lutheran Book of Worship*, 1978

**81**

Lo, how a Rose e'er blooming
   from tender stem hath sprung!
Of Jesse's lineage coming
   as seers of old have sung.
It came, a blossom bright,
   amid the cold of winter,
when half spent was the night.

Isaiah 'twas foretold it,
 the Rose I have in mind,
with Mary we behold it,
 the Virgin Mother kind.
To show God's love aright,
 she bore to us a Savior,
when half spent was the night.

O Flower, whose fragrance tender
 with sweetness fills the air,
dispel in glorious splendor
 the darkness everywhere;
true man, yet very God,
 from sin and death now save us,
and share our every load.

St. 1–2 German, 15th cent.; tr. Theodore Baker (1851–1934). St. 3, Friedrich Layritz (1808–1859): tr. Harriet Reynolds Krauth Spaeth (1845–1925); ver. *Hymnal 1940*

## 82

Of the Father's love begotten,
 ere the worlds began to be,
he is Alpha and Omega,
 he the source, the ending he,
of the things that are, that have been,
 and that future years shall see,
 evermore and evermore!

O that birth for ever blessèd,
    when the Virgin, full of grace,
by the Holy Ghost conceiving,
    bore the Savior of our race;
and the Babe, the world's Redeemer,
    first revealed his sacred face,
    evermore and evermore!

Let the heights of heaven adore him;
    angel hosts, his praises sing;
powers, dominions, bow before him,
    and extol our God and King;
let no tongue on earth be silent,
    every voice in concert ring,
    evermore and evermore!

Christ, to thee with God the Father,
    and, O Holy Ghost, to thee,
hymn and chant and high thanksgiving,
    and unwearied praises be;
honor, glory and dominion,
    and eternal victory,
    evermore and evermore!

Marcus Aurelius Clemens Prudentius (348–410?); tr. John Mason Neale (1818–1866) and Henry Williams Baker (1821–1877), alt.

## 83

O come, all ye faithful,
joyful and triumphant,
O come ye, O come ye to Bethlehem;
come, and behold him,
born the King of angels;

> *O come, let us adore him,*
> *Christ the Lord.*

God from God,
Light from Light eternal,
lo! he abhors not the Virgin's womb;
only-begotten
Son of God the Father;

*Refrain*

Sing, choirs of angels,
sing in exultation,
sing, all ye citizens of heaven above;
glory to God,
glory in the highest;

*Refrain*

See how the shepherds,
summoned to his cradle,
leaving their flocks, draw nigh to gaze;
we too will thither
bend our joyful footsteps;

*Refrain*

Child, for us sinners
poor and in the manger,
we would embrace thee, with love and awe;
who would not love thee,
loving us so dearly?

*Refrain*

Yea, Lord, we greet thee,
born this happy morning;
Jesus, to thee be glory given;
Word of the Father,
now in flesh appearing;

*Refrain*

John Francis Wade (1711–1786); tr. Frederick Oakeley (1802–1880) and others

**84**

Love came down at Christmas,
love all lovely, love divine;
love was born at Christmas:
star and angels gave the sign.

Worship we the Godhead,
love incarnate, love divine;
worship we our Jesus,
but wherewith for sacred sign?

Love shall be our token;
> love be yours and love be mine,
love to God and neighbor,
> love for plea and gift and sign.

Christina Rossetti (1830–1894), alt.

## 85, 86

O Savior of our fallen race,
O Brightness of the Father's face,
O Son who shared the Father's might
before the world knew day or night,

O Jesus, very Light of Light,
our constant star in sin's deep night;
now hear the prayers your people pray
throughout the world this holy day.

Remember, Lord of life and grace,
how once, to save our fallen race,
you put our human vesture on
and came to us as Mary's son.

Today, as year by year its light
bathes all the world in radiance bright,
one precious truth outshines the sun:
salvation comes from you alone.

For from the Father's throne you came,
his banished children to reclaim;
and earth and sea and sky revere
the love of him who sent you here.

O Christ, Redeemer virgin-born,
let songs of praise your Name adorn,
whom with the Father we adore
and Holy Spirit evermore.

Latin, ca. 6th cent.; tr. Gilbert E. Doan (b. 1930)

**87**

Hark! the herald angels sing
glory to the newborn King!
Peace on earth and mercy mild,
God and sinners reconciled!
Joyful, all ye nations, rise,
join the triumph of the skies;
with the angelic host proclaim
Christ is born in Bethlehem!

> *Hark! the herald angels sing*
> *glory to the newborn King!*

Christ, by highest heaven adored;
Christ, the everlasting Lord;
late in time behold him come,
offspring of the Virgin's womb.
Veiled in flesh the Godhead see;
hail the incarnate Deity.
Pleased as man with man to dwell;
Jesus, our Emmanuel!

*Refrain*

Mild he lays his glory by,
born that we no more may die,
born to raise us from the earth,
born to give us second birth.
Risen with healing in his wings,
light and life to all he brings,
hail, the Sun of Righteousness!
hail, the heaven-born Prince of Peace!

*Refrain*

Charles Wesley (1707–1788), alt.

## 88

Sing, O sing, this blessèd morn,
unto us a child is born,
unto us a son is given,
God himself comes down from heaven.

> *Sing, O sing, this blessed morn,*
> *Jesus Christ today is born.*

God from God, and Light from Light,
comes with mercies infinite,
from high heaven he comes to earth,
one with us in human birth.

*Refrain*

God with us, Emmanuel,
deigns for ever now to dwell;

he on Adam's fallen race
sheds the fullness of his grace.

*Refrain*

God comes down that we may rise,
lifted by him to the skies;
Christ is born for us that we
born again in him may be.

*Refrain*

O renew us, Lord, we pray,
with thy Spirit day by day,
that we ever one may be
with the Father and with thee.

*Refrain*

Christopher Wordsworth (1807–1885), alt.

## 89, 90

It came upon the midnight clear,
    that glorious song of old,
from angels bending near the earth
    to touch their harps of gold:
"Peace on the earth, good will to men,
    from heaven's all-gracious King."
The world in solemn stillness lay
    to hear the angels sing.

Still through the cloven skies they come
    with peaceful wings unfurled,
and still their heavenly music floats
    o'er all the weary world;
above its sad and lowly plains
    they bend on hovering wing,
and ever o'er its Babel-sounds
    the blessed angels sing.

Yet with the woes of sin and strife
    the world has suffered long;
beneath the heavenly hymn have rolled
    two thousand years of wrong;
and warring humankind hears not
    the tidings which they bring;
O hush the noise and cease your strife
    and hear the angels sing!

For lo! the days are hastening on,
    by prophets seen of old,
when with the ever-circling years
    shall come the time foretold,
when peace shall over all the earth
    its ancient splendors fling,
and all the world give back the song
    which now the angels sing.

Edmund H. Sears (1810–1876), alt.

## 91

Break forth, O beauteous heavenly light,
and usher in the morning;
O shepherds, greet that glorious sight,
our Lord a crib adorning.
This child, this little helpless boy,
shall be our confidence and joy,
the power of Satan breaking,
our peace eternal making.

Johann Rist (1607–1667); ver. *Hymnal 1982*

## 92

On this day earth shall ring
with the song children sing
to the Lord, Christ our King,
> born on earth to save us;
> him the Father gave us.
> *Ideo gloria in excelsis Deo!*

His the doom, ours the mirth;
when he came down to earth
Bethlehem saw his birth;
> ox and ass beside him
> from the cold would hide him.
> *Ideo gloria in excelsis Deo!*

God's bright star, o'er his head,
Wise Men three to him led;
kneel they low by his bed,

lay their gifts before him,
praise him and adore him.
*Ideo gloria in excelsis Deo!*

On this day angels sing;
with their song earth shall ring,
praising Christ, heaven's King,
    born on earth to save us;
    peace and love he gave us.
    *Ideo gloria in excelsis Deo!*

*"Ideo gloria in excelsis Deo!" is Latin for "Therefore, glory to God in the highest!"*

Piae Cantiones, 1582; tr. Jane M. Joseph (1894–1929)

## 93

Angels, from the realms of glory,
    wing your flight o'er all the earth;
ye, who sang creation's story,
    now proclaim Messiah's birth:

    *come and worship, come and worship,*
    *worship Christ, the newborn King.*

Shepherds in the field abiding,
    watching o'er your flocks by night,
God with you is now residing;
    yonder shines the infant Light:

*Refrain*

Sages, leave your contemplations;
    brighter visions beam afar:
seek the great Desire of nations;
    ye have seen his natal star:

*Refrain*

Saints before the altar bending,
    watching long in hope and fear,
suddenly the Lord, descending,
    in his temple shall appear:

*Refrain*

James Montgomery (1771–1854), alt.

## 94, 95

While shepherds watched their flocks by night,
    all seated on the ground,
the angel of the Lord came down,
    and glory shone around.

"Fear not," said he, for mighty dread
    had seized their troubled mind;
"Glad tidings of great joy I bring
    to you and all mankind.

"To you, in David's town, this day
    is born of David's line
the Savior, who is Christ the Lord;
    and this shall be the sign:

"The heavenly Babe you there shall find
    to human view displayed,
all meanly wrapped in swathing bands,
    and in a manger laid."

Thus spake the seraph, and forthwith
    appeared a shining throng
of angels praising God, who thus
    addressed their joyful song:

"All glory be to God on high
    and on the earth be peace;
good will henceforth from heaven to men
    begin and never cease."

Nahum Tate (1625–1715)

## 96

Angels we have heard on high,
    singing sweetly through the night,
and the mountains in reply
    echoing their brave delight.
      *Gloria in excelsis Deo.*

Shepherds, why this jubilee?
    Why these songs of happy cheer?
What great brightness did you see?
    What glad tidings did you hear?
      *Gloria in excelsis Deo.*

Come to Bethlehem and see
　　him whose birth the angels sing;
come, adore on bended knee
　　Christ, the Lord, the newborn King.
　　　*Gloria in excelsis Deo.*

See him in a manger laid
　　whom the angels praise above;
Mary, Joseph, lend your aid,
　　while we raise our hearts in love.
　　　*Gloria in excelsis Deo.*

French carol; tr. James Chadwick (1813–1882), alt.

**97**

Dost thou in a manger lie,
　　who hast all created,
stretching infant hands on high,
　　Savior, long awaited?
If a monarch, where thy state?
Where thy court on thee to wait?
　　Scepter, crown, and sphere?
Here no regal pomp we see,
nought but need and penury:
　　why thus cradled here?

"For the world a love supreme
　　brought me to this stable;
all creation to redeem
　　I alone am able.

By this lowly birth of mine,
sinner, riches shall be thine,
   matchless gifts and free;
willingly this yoke I take,
and this sacrifice I make,
   heaping joys for thee."

Christ we praise with voices bold,
   laud and honor raising;
for these mercies manifold
   join the hosts in praising:
Father, glory be to thee
for the wondrous charity
   of thy Son, our Lord.
Better witness to thy worth,
purer praise than ours on earth,
angels' songs afford.

Jean Mauburn (1460–1503); tr. Elizabeth Rundle Charles (1828–1896) and others

## 98

Unto us a boy is born!
   The King of all creation,
came he to a world forlorn,
   the Lord of every nation.

Cradled in a stall was he
   with sleepy cows and asses;
but the very beasts could see
   that he all men surpasses.

Herod then with fear was filled;
 "A prince," he said, "in Jewry!"
All the little boys he killed
 at Bethlehem in his fury.

Now may Mary's son, who came
 so long ago to love us,
lead us all with hearts aflame
 unto the joys above us.

Latin carol, 15th cent., tr. Percy Dearmer (1867–1936), alt.

**99**

*Go tell it on the mountain,*
 *over the hills and everywhere;*
*go tell it on the mountain,*
 *that Jesus Christ is born!*

While shepherds kept their watching
 o'er silent flocks by night,
behold, throughout the heavens
 there shone a holy light.

*Refrain*

The shepherds feared and trembled
 when lo! above the earth
rang out the angel chorus
 that hailed our Savior's birth.

*Refrain*

Down in a lowly manger
   the humble Christ was born,
and God sent us salvation
   that blessèd Christmas morn.

*Refrain*

African-American spiritual 19th cent.; adapt. John W. Work (b. 1901)

## 100

Joy to the world! the Lord is come:
   let earth receive her King;
let every heart prepare him room,
   and heaven and nature sing.

Joy to the world! the Savior reigns;
   let us our songs employ,
while fields and floods, rocks, hills and plains,
   repeat the sounding joy.

No more let sins and sorrows grow,
   nor thorns infest the ground;
he comes to make his blessings flow
   far as the curse is found.

He rules the world with truth and grace,
   and makes the nations prove
the glories of his righteousness,
   and wonders of his love.

Isaac Watts (1674–1748), alt.

## 101

Away in a manger, no crib for his bed,
the little Lord Jesus laid down his sweet head.
The stars in the bright sky looked down where he lay,
the little Lord Jesus asleep on the hay.

The cattle are lowing, the baby awakes,
but little Lord Jesus no crying he makes.
I love thee, Lord Jesus! Look down from the sky,
and stay by my side until morning is nigh.

Be near me, Lord Jesus; I ask thee to stay
close by me for ever, and love me I pray.
Bless all the dear children in thy tender care,
and fit us for heaven to live with thee there.

Traditional carol

## 102

Once in royal David's city
   stood a lowly cattle shed,
where a mother laid her baby
   in a manger for his bed:
Mary was that mother mild,
Jesus Christ her little child.

He came down to earth from heaven,
   who is God and Lord of all,
and his shelter was a stable,
   and his cradle was a stall;

with the poor, the scorned, the lowly,
lived on earth our Savior holy.

We, like Mary, rest confounded
    that a stable should display
heaven's Word, the world's creator,
    cradled there on Christmas Day,
yet this child, our Lord and brother,
brought us love for one another.

For he is our lifelong pattern;
    daily, when on earth he grew,
he was tempted, scorned, rejected,
    tears and smiles like us he knew.
Thus he feels for all our sadness,
and he shares in all our gladness.

And our eyes at last shall see him,
    through his own redeeming love;
for that child who seemed so helpless
    is our Lord in heaven above;
and he leads his children on
to the place where he is gone.

Not in that poor lowly stable,
    with the oxen standing round,
we shall see him; but in heaven,
    where his saints his throne surround:
Christ, revealed to faithful eye,
set at God's right hand on high.

Sts. 1–2, 4–6, Cecil Francis Alexander (1818–1895), alt.; st. 3, James Waring McCrady (b. 1938)

# 103

A child is born in Bethlehem, Alleluia!
therefore rejoice Jerusalem, Alleluia, alleluia!

> *Come, join the angel throng*
> *in songs of joy,*
> *in one accord*
> *adoring Christ the Lord.*

The babe within a manger poor, Alleluia!
will rule the world for evermore, Alleluia, alleluia!

*Refrain*

Upon this joyful holy night, Alleluia!
we bless your Name, O Lord of Light,
                Alleluia, alleluia!

*Refrain*

We praise you, Holy Trinity, Alleluia!
adoring you eternally. Alleluia, alleluia!

*Refrain*

Latin, 14th cent.; tr. Ruth Fox Hume (1922–1980), alt.

## 104

A stable lamp is lighted
Whose glow shall wake the sky;
The stars shall bend their voices,
And every stone shall cry.
And every stone shall cry,
And straw like gold shall shine;
A barn shall harbor heaven,
A stall become a shrine.

This child through David's city
Shall ride in triumph by;
The palm shall strew its branches,
And every stone shall cry.
And every stone shall cry,
Though heavy, dull, and dumb,
And lie within the roadway
To pave his kingdom come.

Yet he shall be forsaken,
And yielded up to die;
The sky shall groan and darken,
And every stone shall cry.
And every stone shall cry,
For stony hearts of men:
God's blood upon the spearhead,
God's love refused again.

But now, as at the ending,
The low is lifted high;

The stars shall bend their voices,
And every stone shall cry.
And every stone shall cry,
In praises of the Child
By whose descent among us
The worlds are reconciled.

©Richard Wilbur (b. 1921)

**105**

God rest you merry, gentlemen,
   let nothing you dismay;
remember Christ our Savior
   was born on Christmas Day,
to save us all from Satan's power
   when we were gone astray.

> *O tidings of comfort and joy,*
> *   comfort and joy;*
> *O tidings of comfort and joy!*

From God our heavenly Father
   a blessèd angel came
and unto certain shepherds
   brought tidings of the same:
how that in Bethlehem was born
   the Son of God by name.

*Refrain*

"Fear not, then," said the angel,
    "Let nothing you affright;
this day is born a Savior
    of a pure virgin bright,
to free all those who trust in him
    from Satan's power and might."

*Refrain*

Now to the Lord sing praises,
    all you within this place,
and with true love and charity
    each other now embrace;
this holy tide of Christmas
    doth bring redeeming grace.

*Refrain*

London carol, 18th cent.

## 106

Christians, awake, salute the happy morn
whereon the Savior of the world was born;
rise to adore the mystery of love,
which hosts of angels chanted from above;
with them the joyful tidings first begun
of God Incarnate and the Virgin's Son.

Then to the watchful shepherds it was told,
who heard the angelic herald's voice:
"Behold, I bring good tidings of a Savior's birth

to you and all the nations on the earth:
this day hath God fulfilled his promised word,
this day is born a Savior, Christ the Lord."

He spoke, and straightway the celestial choir
in hymns of joy, unknown before, conspire;
the praises of redeeming love they sang,
and heaven's whole orb with alleluias rang;
God's highest glory was their anthem still,
peace on the earth, and unto men good will.

In Bethlehem the happy shepherds sought
to see the wonder God for us had wrought,
and found, with Joseph and the blessèd maid,
her Son, the Savior, in a manger laid;
amazed, the wondrous story they proclaim,
the earliest heralds of the Savior's name.

Let us, like these good shepherds, then employ
our grateful voices to proclaim the joy;
trace we the Babe, who hath retrieved our loss,
from his poor manger to his bitter cross;
treading his steps, assisted by his grace,
till our first heavenly state again takes place.

Then may we hope, the angelic thrones among,
to sing, redeemed, a glad triumphal song;
he that was born upon this joyful day
around us all his glory shall display;
saved by his love, incessant we shall sing
eternal praise to heaven's almighty King.

John Byrom (1692–1763), alt.

## 107

Good Christian friends, rejoice
with heart and soul and voice;
   give ye heed to what we say:
   Jesus Christ is born today;
ox and ass before him bow,
and he is in the manger now.
   Christ is born today!

Good Christian friends, rejoice
with heart and soul and voice;
   now ye hear of endless bliss;
   Jesus Christ was born for this!
He hath opened heaven's door,
and we are blest for evermore.
   Christ was born for this!

Good Christian friends, rejoice
with heart and soul and voice;
   now ye need not fear the grave:
   Jesus Christ was born to save!
Calls you one and calls you all
to gain his everlasting hall.
   Christ was born to save!

John Mason Neale (1818–1866), alt.

**108**

Now yield we thanks and praise
   to Christ enthroned in glory,
and on this day of days
   tell out redemption's story,
who truly have believed
   that on this blessèd morn,
in holiness conceived
   the Son of God was born.

What tribute shall we pay
   to him who came in weakness,
and in a manger lay
   to teach his people meekness?
Let every house be bright;
   let praises never cease;
with mercies infinite
   our Christ hath brought us peace.

Howard Chandler Robbins (1876–1952)

**109**

The first Nowell the angel did say
was to certain poor shepherds in fields as they lay;
in fields as they lay, keeping their sheep,
on a cold winter's night that was so deep.

> *Nowell, Nowell, Nowell, Nowell,*
> *born is the King of Israel.*

They looked up and saw a star
shining in the east beyond them far,
and to the earth it gave great light,
and so it continued both day and night.

*Refrain*

And by the light of that same star
three wise men came from country far;
to seek for a king was their intent,
and to follow the star wherever it went.

*Refrain*

This star drew nigh to the northwest,
o'er Bethlehem it took its rest,
and there it did both stop and stay
right over the place where Jesus lay.

*Refrain*

Then entered in those wise men three
full reverently upon their knee,
and offered there in his presence
their gold, and myrrh, and frankincense.

*Refrain*

Then let us all with one accord
sing praises to our heavenly Lord;
that hath made heaven and earth of nought,
and with his blood our life hath bought.

*Refrain*

English Carol, 18th cent.

# 110

The snow lay on the ground,
    the stars shone bright,
when Christ our Lord was born
    on Christmas night.

*Venite adoremus Dominum.*

'Twas Mary, daughter pure
    of holy Anne,
that brought into this world
    the God made man.
She laid him in a stall
    at Bethlehem;
the ass and oxen shared
    the roof with them.

*Refrain*

Saint Joseph, too, was by
    to tend the child;
to guard him, and protect
    his mother mild;
the angels hovered round,
    and sang this song,
Venite adoremus
    Dominum.

*Refrain*

And thus that manger poor
    became a throne;
for he whom Mary bore
    was God the Son.
O come, then, let us join
    the heavenly host,
to praise the Father, Son,
    and Holy Ghost.

*Refrain*

Source unknown, 19th cent.

## 111

Silent night, holy night,
all is calm, all is bright
round yon virgin mother and child.
Holy infant, so tender and mild,
sleep in heavenly peace.

Silent night, holy night,
shepherds quake at the sight,
glories stream from heaven afar,
heavenly hosts sing alleluia;
Christ, the Savior, is born!

Silent night, holy night,
Son of God, love's pure light
radiant beams from thy holy face,

with the dawn of redeeming grace,
Jesus, Lord, at thy birth.

Joseph Mohr (1792–1848); tr. John Freeman Young (1820–1885)

## 112

In the bleak midwinter,
frosty wind made moan,
earth stood hard as iron,
water like a stone;
snow had fallen, snow on snow,
snow on snow,
in the bleak midwinter,
   long ago.

Our God, heaven cannot hold him,
nor earth sustain;
heaven and earth shall flee away
when he comes to reign:
in the bleak midwinter
a stable-place sufficed
the Lord God incarnate,
   Jesus Christ.

Angels and archangels
may have gathered there,
cherubim and seraphim
throngèd the air;
but his mother only,

in her maiden bliss,
worshiped the belovèd
    with a kiss.

What can I give him,
poor as I am?
If I were a shepherd,
I would bring a lamb;
if I were a wise man,
I would do my part;
yet what I can I give him –
    give my heart.

Christina Rossetti (1830–1894)

## 113

Oh, sleep now, holy baby,
    with your head against my breast;
meanwhile the pangs of my sorrow
    are soothed and put to rest.

> *A la ru, a la mè,*
> *A la ru, a la mè,*
> *a la ru, a la ru, a la ru, a la mè.*

You need not fear King Herod,
    he will bring no harm to you;
so rest in the arms of your mother
    who sings you a la ru.

*Refrain*

Hispanic folk song; tr. John Donald Robb (1892–1989), alt.

Duérmete, Niño lindo,
   en los brazos del amor
mientras que duerme y descansa
   la pena de mi dolor.

> *A la ru, a la mè,*
> *a la ru, a la mè,*
> *a la ru, a la ru, a la mè.*

No temas al rey Herodes
   que nada te ha de hacer;
en los brazos de tu madre
   y ahí nadie te ha de ofender.

*Refrain*

Hispanic folk song

**114**

'Twas in the moon of wintertime,
   when all the birds had fled,
that God the Lord of all the earth
   sent angel-choirs instead;
before their light the stars grew dim,
and wondering hunters heard the hymn:

> *Jesus your King is born, Jesus is born,*
> *in excelsis gloria.*

Within a lodge of broken bark
   the tender babe was found,
a ragged robe of rabbit skin
   enwrapped his beauty round;

but as the hunter braves drew nigh,
the angel-song rang loud and high:

*Refrain*

The earliest moon of winter-time
    is not so round and fair
as was the ring of glory on
    the helpless infant there.
The chiefs from far before him knelt
with gifts of fox and beaver-pelt.

*Refrain*

O children of the forest free,
    the angel song is true;
the holy child of earth and heaven
    is born today for you.
Come kneel before the radiant boy,
who brings you beauty, peace, and joy.

*Refrain*

Jesse Edgar Middleton (1872–1960), alt.

## 115

What child is this, who, laid to rest,
    on Mary's lap is sleeping?
Whom angels greet with anthems sweet,
    while shepherds watch are keeping?

> *This, this is Christ the King,*
> *whom shepherds guard and angels sing;*
> *haste, haste to bring him laud,*
> *the babe, the son of Mary.*

Why lies he in such mean estate
 where ox and ass are feeding?
Good Christian, fear: for sinners here
 the silent Word is pleading.

*Refrain*

So bring him incense, gold, and myrrh,
 come, peasant, king, to own him;
the King of kings salvation brings,
 let loving hearts enthrone him.

*Refrain*

William Chatterton Dix (1837–1898)

**116**

"I come," the great Redeemer cries,
 "to do thy will, O Lord!"
At Jordan's stream, behold! He seals
 the sure prophetic word.

"Thus it becomes us to fulfill
 all righteousness," he said.
Then, faithful to the Lord's commands,
 through Jordan's flood was led.

Hark, a glad voice! The Father speaks
 from heaven's exalted height:
"This is my Son, my well-beloved,
 in whom I take delight."

Jesus, the Savior, well-beloved!
 His Name we will profess,
like him desirous to fulfill
 God's will in righteousness.

No more we'll count ourselves our own
 but his in bonds of love.
Oh, may such bonds for ever draw
 our souls to things above!

*Christian Hymnbook*, 1865, alt.

## 117, 118

Brightest and best of the stars of the morning,
 dawn on our darkness, and lend us thine aid;
star of the east, the horizon adorning,
 guide where our infant Redeemer is laid.

Cold on his cradle the dew-drops are shining,
 low lies his head with the beasts of the stall;
angels adore him in slumber reclining,
 Maker and Monarch and Savior of all.

Shall we then yield him, in costly devotion,
 odors of Edom, and offerings divine,

gems of the mountain, and pearls of the ocean,
    myrrh from the forest, and gold from the mine?

Vainly we offer each ample oblation,
    vainly with gifts would his favor secure,
richer by far is the heart's adoration,
    dearer to God are the prayers of the poor.

Brightest and best of the stars of the morning,
    dawn on our darkness, and lend us thine aid;
star of the east, the horizon adorning,
    guide where our infant Redeemer is laid.

Reginald Heber (1783–1826), alt.

## 119

As with gladness men of old
did the guiding star behold;
as with joy they hailed its light,
leading onward, beaming bright;
so, most gracious Lord, may we
evermore be led to thee.

As with joyful steps they sped
to that lowly manger-bed;
there to bend the knee before
him whom heaven and earth adore;
so may we with willing feet
ever seek the mercy-seat.

As they offered gifts most rare
at that manger rude and bare;
so may we with holy joy,
pure and free from sin's alloy,
all our costliest treasures bring,
Christ! to thee, our heavenly King.

Holy Jesus! every day
keep us in the narrow way;
and, when earthly things are past,
bring our ransomed souls at last
where they need no star to guide,
where no clouds thy glory hide.

In the heavenly country bright,
need they no created light;
thou its light, its joy, its crown,
thou its sun which goes not down:
there for ever may we sing
alleluias to our King.

William Chatterton Dix (1837–1898)

## 120

The sinless one to Jordan came,
and in the river shared our stain;
God's righteousness he thus fulfilled,
and chose the path his Father willed.

Uprising from the waters there,
the Father's voice did then declare
that Christ, the Son of God, had come
to lead his scattered people home.

Above him see the heavenly Dove,
the sign of God the Father's love,
now by the Holy Spirit shed
upon the Son's anointed head.

How blest that mission then begun
to heal and save a race undone!
Straight to the wilderness he goes
to wrestle with his people's foes.

O Christ, may we baptized from sin,
go forth with you a world to win:
grant us the Holy Spirit's power
to shield us in temptation's hour.

On you may all your people feed,
and know you are the Bread indeed,
who gives eternal life to those
that with you died, and with you rose.

G. B. Timms (b. 1910), alt.

## 121

Christ, when for us you were baptized,
>God's Spirit on you came,
as peaceful as a dove and yet
>as urgent as a flame.

God called you his belovèd Son,
>called you his servant true,
sent you his kingdom to proclaim,
>his holy will to do.

Straightway and steadfast until death
>you then obeyed his call
freely as Son of Man to serve
>and give your life for all.

Baptize us with your Spirit, Lord,
>your cross on us be signed,
that, likewise in God's service we
>may perfect freedom find.

F. Bland Tucker (1895-1984), rev.

## 122, 123

Alleluia, song of gladness,
>voice of joy that cannot die;
alleluia is the anthem
>ever raised by choirs on high;
in the house of God abiding
>thus they sing eternally.

Alleluia thou resoundest,
    true Jerusalem and free;
alleluia, joyful mother,
    all thy children sing with thee;
but by Babylon's sad waters
    mourning exiles now are we.

Alleluia though we cherish
    and would chant for evermore
alleluia in our singing,
    let us for a while give o'er,
as our Savior in his fasting
    pleasures of the world forbore.

Therefore in our hymns we pray thee,
    grant us, blessèd Trinity,
at the last to keep thine Easter
    with thy faithful saints on high;
there to thee for ever singing
    alleluia joyfully.

Latin, 11th cent.; tr. John Mason Neale (1818–1866), alt.

**124**

What star is this, with beams so bright,
more beauteous than the noonday light?
It shines to herald forth the King,
and Gentiles to his crib to bring.

True spake the prophet from afar
who told the rise of Jacob's star;

and eastern sages with amaze
upon the wondrous token gaze.

The guiding star above is bright;
within them shines a clearer light,
and leads them on with power benign
to seek the Giver of the sign.

O Jesus, while the star of grace
impels us on to seek thy face,
let not our slothful hearts refuse
the guidance of thy light to use.

To God the Father, heavenly Light,
to Christ, revealed in earthly night,
to God the Holy Ghost we raise
our equal and unceasing praise.

Charles Coffin (1676–1749); tr. *Hymns Ancient and Modern*, 1861, after John Chandler (1807–1876), alt.

## 125, 126

The people who in darkness walked
    have seen a glorious light;
on them broke forth the heavenly dawn
    who dwelt in death and night.

To hail thy rising, Sun of life,
    the gathering nations come,
joyous as when the reapers bear
    their harvest treasures home.

To us the promised Child is born,
  to us the Son is given;
him shall the tribes of earth obey,
  and all the hosts of heaven.

His name shall be the Prince of Peace
  for evermore adored,
the Wonderful, the Counselor,
  the mighty God and Lord.

His power increasing still shall spread,
  his reign no end shall know;
justice shall guard his throne above,
  and peace abound below.

John Morison (1749–1798), alt.; para. of Isaiah 9:2–7

**127**

Earth has many a noble city;
  Bethlehem, thou dost all excel:
out of thee the Lord from heaven
  came to rule his Israel.

Fairer than the sun at morning
  was the star that told his birth,
to the world its God announcing
  seen in fleshly form on earth.

Eastern sages at his cradle
  make oblations rich and rare;

see them give, in deep devotion,
    gold and frankincense and myrrh.

Sacred gifts of mystic meaning:
    incense doth their God disclose,
gold the King of kings proclaimeth,
    myrrh his sepulcher foreshows.

Jesus, whom the Gentiles worshiped
    at thy glad epiphany,
unto thee, with God the Father
    and the Spirit, glory be.

Marcus Aurelius Clemens Prudentius (348–410); tr. *Hymns Ancient and Modern*, 1861, alt.

## 128

We three kings of Orient are,
bearing gifts we traverse afar,
    field and fountain,
    moor and mountain,
following yonder star.

> *O star of wonder, star of night,*
> *star with royal beauty bright;*
>     *westward leading,*
>     *still proceeding,*
> *guide us to thy perfect light!*

Born a King on Bethlehem's plain,
gold I bring to crown him again,
> King for ever,
> ceasing never
over us all to reign.

*Refrain*

Frankincense to offer have I:
incense owns a Deity nigh;
> prayer and praising,
> gladly raising,
worship him, God Most High.

*Refrain*

Myrrh is mine; its bitter perfume
breathes a life of gathering gloom;
> sorrowing, sighing,
> bleeding, dying,
sealed in the stone-cold tomb.

*Refrain*

Glorious now behold him arise,
King and God and Sacrifice;
heaven sings alleluia:
alleluia the earth replies.

*Refrain*

John Henry Hopkins, Jr. (1820–1891), alt.

## 129, 130

Christ upon the mountain peak
  stands alone in glory blazing;
let us, if we dare to speak,
  with the saints and angels praise him.
  Alleluia!

Trembling at his feet we saw
  Moses and Elijah speaking.
All the prophets and the Law
  shout through them their joyful greeting.
  Alleluia!

Swift the cloud of glory came.
  God proclaiming in its thunder
Jesus as his Son by name!
  Nations cry aloud in wonder!
  Alleluia!

This is God's belovèd Son!
  Law and prophets fade before him;
first and last and only One,
  let creation now adore him!
  Alleluia!

Brian A. Wren (b. 1936)

## 131, 132

When Christ's appearing was made known,
King Herod trembled for his throne;
but he who offers heavenly birth
sought not the kingdoms of this earth.

The eastern sages saw from far
and followed on his guiding star;
by light their way to Light they trod,
and by their gifts confessed their God.

Within the Jordan's sacred flood
the heavenly Lamb in meekness stood,
that he, to whom no sin was known,
might cleanse his people from their own.

Oh, what a miracle divine,
when water reddened into wine!
He spoke the word, and forth it flowed
in streams that nature ne'er bestowed.

All glory, Jesus, be to thee
for this thy glad epiphany:
whom with the Father we adore
and Holy Ghost for evermore.

Caelius Sedulius (5th cent.); st.1, tr. *The Hymnbook of the Anglican Church of Canada and the United Church of Canada*, 1971; sts. 2–5, tr. John Mason Neale (1818–1866), alt.

## 133, 134

O Light of Light, Love given birth;
Jesus, Redeemer of the earth:
more bright than day your face did show,
your raiment whiter than the snow.

Two prophets, who had faith to see,
with your elect found company;
the heavens above your glory named,
your Father's voice his Son proclaimed.

May all who seek to praise aright
through purer lives show forth your light.
To you, the King of glory, now
all faithful hearts adoring bow.

Latin, 10th cent.; tr. Laurence Housman (1865–1959), alt.

## 135

Songs of thankfulness and praise,
Jesus, Lord, to thee we raise,
manifested by the star
to the sages from afar;
branch of royal David's stem
in thy birth at Bethlehem;
anthems be to thee addressed,
God in man made manifest.

Manifest at Jordan's stream,
Prophet, Priest, and King supreme;
and at Cana, wedding-guest,
in thy Godhead manifest;
manifest in power divine,
changing water into wine;
anthems be to thee addressed,
God in man made manifest.

Manifest in making whole
palsied limbs and fainting soul;
manifest in valiant fight,
quelling all the devil's might;
manifest in gracious will,
ever bringing good from ill;
anthems be to thee addressed,
God in man made manifest.

Manifest on mountain height,
shining in resplendent light,
where disciples filled with awe
thy transfigured glory saw.
When from there thou leddest them
steadfast to Jerusalem,
cross and Easter Day attest
God in man made manifest.

Sts. 1–3, Christopher Wordsworth (1807–1885); st. 4, F. Bland Tucker (1895–1984)

## 136, 137

O wondrous type! O vision fair
of glory that the Church may share,
which Christ upon the mountain shows,
where brighter than the sun he glows!

With Moses and Elijah nigh
the incarnate Lord holds converse high;
and from the cloud, the Holy One
bears record to the only Son.

With shining face and bright array,
Christ deigns to manifest today
what glory shall be theirs above
who joy in God with perfect love.

And faithful hearts are raised on high
by this great vision's mystery;
for which in joyful strains we raise
the voice of prayer, the hymn of praise.

O Father, with the eternal Son,
and Holy Spirit, ever One,
vouchsafe to bring us by thy grace
to see thy glory face to face.

Latin, 15th cent.; tr. *Hymns Ancient and Modern,* 1861, after John Mason Neale (1848–1866), alt.

## 138

All praise to you, O Lord,
   who by your mighty power
did manifest your glory forth
   in Cana's marriage hour.

You speak, and it is done;
   obedient to your word,
the water reddening into wine
   proclaims the present Lord.

Oh, may this grace be ours:
   in you always to live
and drink of those refreshing streams
   which you alone can give.

So, led from strength to strength,
   grant us, O Lord, to see
the marriage supper of the Lamb,
   the great epiphany.

Hyde W. Beadon (1812–1891), alt.

## 139

When Jesus went to Jordan's stream
    his Father's will obeying,
and was baptized by John, there came
    a voice from heaven saying,
"This is my dear belovèd Son
    upon whom rests my favor."
And till God's will is fully done
    he will not bend or waver,
    for he is Christ the Savior.

The Holy Spirit then was shown,
    a dove on him descending;
the Triune God is thus made known
    in Christ as love unending.
He taught, he healed, he raised the dead,
    yet, in his great endeavor
to save us, his own blood was shed;
    but death could hold him never.
    He rose, and lives for ever.

He came by water and by blood
    to heal our lost condition;
he cleanses, reconciles to God,
    and gives the Great Commission.
Then let us not heed worldly lies
    nor rest upon our merit,

> but trust in Christ who will baptize
> > with water and the Spirit
> > that we may life inherit.

Martin Luther (1483–1546); para. F. Bland Tucker (1895–1984), rev.

## 140, 141

> Wilt thou forgive that sin, where I begun,
> > which is my sin, though it were done before?
> Wilt thou forgive those sins through which I run,
> > and do run still, though still I do deplore?
> > When thou hast done, thou hast not done,
> > > for I have more.
>
> Wilt thou forgive that sin, by which I won
> > others to sin, and made my sin their door?
> Wilt thou forgive that sin which I did shun
> > a year or two, but wallowed in a score?
> > When thou hast done, thou hast not done,
> > > for I have more.
>
> I have a sin of fear that when I've spun
> > my last thread, I shall perish on the shore;
> swear by thyself, that at my death thy Son
> > shall shine as he shines now, and heretofore.
> > And having done that, thou hast done,
> > > I fear no more.

John Donne (1573–1631)

## 142

Lord, who throughout these forty days
    for us didst fast and pray,
teach us with thee to mourn our sins,
    and close by thee to stay.

As thou with Satan didst contend,
    and didst the victory win,
O give us strength in thee to fight,
    in thee to conquer sin.

As thou didst hunger bear and thirst,
    so teach us, gracious Lord,
to die to self, and chiefly live
    by thy most holy word.

And through these days of penitence,
    and through thy Passiontide,
yea, evermore, in life and death,
    Jesus! with us abide.

Abide with us, that so, this life
    of suffering overpast,
an Easter of unending joy
    we may attain at last!

Claudia Frances Hernaman (1838–1898)

# 143

The glory of these forty days
we celebrate with songs of praise;
for Christ, through whom all things were made,
himself has fasted and has prayed.

Alone and fasting Moses saw
the loving God who gave the law;
and to Elijah, fasting, came
the steeds and chariots of flame.

So Daniel trained his mystic sight,
delivered from the lions' might;
and John, the Bridegroom's friend, became
the herald of Messiah's name.

Then grant us, Lord, like them to be
full oft in fast and prayer with thee;
our spirits strengthen with thy grace,
and give us joy to see thy face.

O Father, Son, and Spirit blest,
to thee be every prayer addressed,
who art in threefold Name adored,
from age to age, the only Lord.

Latin, 6th cent.; tr. Maurice F. Bell (1862–1947), alt.

## 144

Lord Jesus, Sun of Righteousness,
shine in our hearts, we pray;
dispel the gloom that shades our minds
and be to us as day.

Give guidance to our wandering ways,
forgive us, Lord, our sin;
restore us by your loving care
to peace and joy within.

Lord, grant that we in penitence
may offer you our praise,
and through your saving sacrifice
receive your gift of grace.

Now nearer draws the day of days
when paradise shall bloom,
when we shall be at one with you,
Lord, risen from the tomb.

The universe your glory shows,
blest Father, Spirit, Son;
we shall acclaim your majesty,
eternal Three in One.

Latin; tr. Anne K. LeCroy (b. 1930)

## 145

Now quit your care
   and anxious fear and worry;
     for schemes are vain
     and fretting brings no gain.
Lent calls to prayer,
   to trust and dedication;
     God brings new beauty nigh;
       reply, reply,
     reply with love to love most high.

To bow the head
   in sackcloth and in ashes,
     or rend the soul,
     such grief is not Lent's goal;
but to be led
   to where God's glory flashes,
     his beauty to come near.
       Make clear, make clear,
     make clear where truth and light appear.

For is not this
   the fast that I have chosen?
     (The prophet spoke)
     To shatter every yoke,
of wickedness
   the grievous bands to loosen,
     oppression put to flight,
       to fight, to fight
     to fight till every wrong's set right.

For righteousness
   and peace will show their faces
     to those who feed
     the hungry in their need,
and wrongs redress,
   who build the old waste places,
     and in the darkness shine.
       Divine, divine,
     divine it is when all combine!

Then shall your light
   break forth as doth the morning;
     your health shall spring,
     the friends you make shall bring
God's glory bright,
   your way through life adorning;
     and love shall be the prize.
       Arise, arise,
     arise! and make a paradise!

Percy Dearmer (1867–1936), alt.

## 146, 147

Now let us all with one accord,
   in company with ages past,
keep vigil with our heavenly Lord
   in his temptation and his fast.

The covenant, so long revealed
   to those of faith in former time,
Christ by his own example sealed,
   the Lord of love, in love sublime.

Your love, O Lord, our sinful race
   has not returned, but falsified;
author of mercy, turn your face
   and grant repentance for our pride.

Remember, Lord, though frail we be,
   in your own image were we made;
help us, lest in anxiety,
   we cause your Name to be betrayed.

Therefore, we pray you, Lord, forgive;
   so when our wanderings here shall cease,
we may with you for ever live,
   in love and unity and peace.

Att. Gregory the Great (540–604); tr. *Praise the Lord*, 1972, alt.

**148**

Creator of the earth and skies,
   to whom the words of life belong,
grant us your truth to make us wise;
   grant us your power to make us strong.

We have not known you: to the skies
    our monuments of folly soar,
and all our self-wrought miseries
    have made us trust ourselves the more.

We have not loved you: far and wide
    the wreckage of our hatred spreads,
and evils wrought by human pride
    recoil on unrepentant heads.

For this, our foolish confidence,
    our pride of knowledge and our sin,
we come to you in penitence;
    in us the work of grace begin.

Teach us to know and love you, Lord,
    and humbly follow in your way.
Speak to our souls the quickening word,
    and turn our darkness into day.

David W. Hughes (1911–1967), alt.

## 149

Eternal Lord of love, behold your Church
walking once more the pilgrim way of Lent,
led by your cloud by day, by night your fire,
moved by your love and toward your presence bent:
far off yet here—the goal of all desire.

So daily dying to the way of self,
so daily living to your way of love,
we walk the road, Lord Jesus, that you trod,
knowing ourselves baptized into your death:
so we are dead and live with you in God.

If dead in you, so in you we arise,
you the first-born of all the faithful dead;
and as through stony ground the green shoots break,
glorious in springtime dress of leaf and flower,
so in the Father's glory shall we wake.

Thomas H. Cain (b. 1931)

**150**

Forty days and forty nights
   thou wast fasting in the wild;
forty days and forty nights
   tempted, and yet undefiled.

Should not we thy sorrow share
   and from worldly joys abstain,
fasting with unceasing prayer,
   strong with thee to suffer pain?

Then if Satan on us press,
   Jesus, Savior, hear our call!
Victor in the wilderness,
   grant we may not faint nor fall!

So shall we have peace divine:
>    holier gladness ours shall be;
> round us, too, shall angels shine,
>    such as ministered to thee.

Keep, O keep us, Savior dear,
>    ever constant by thy side;
> that with thee we may appear
>    at the eternal Eastertide.

George Hunt Smyttan (1822–1870), alt.

## 151

From deepest woe I cry to thee;
>    Lord, hear me, I implore thee!
> Bend down thy gracious ear to me;
>    I lay my sins before thee.
> If thou rememberest every sin,
> if nought but just reward we win,
>    could we abide thy presence?

Thou grantest pardon through thy love;
>    thy grace alone availeth.
> Our works could ne'er our guilt remove;
>    yea, e'en the best life faileth.
> For none may boast themselves of aught,
> but must confess thy grace hath wrought
>    whate'er in them is worthy.

And thus my hope is in the Lord,
    and not in my own merit;
I rest upon his faithful word
    to them of contrite spirit.
That he is merciful and just,
here is my comfort and my trust;
    his help I wait with patience.

Martin Luther (1483–1546); tr. Catherine Winkworth (1827–1878), alt.; based on Psalm 130

**152**

Kind Maker of the world, O hear
the fervent prayer, with many a tear
poured forth by all the penitent
who keep this holy fast of Lent!

Each heart is manifest to thee;
thou knowest our infirmity;
now we repent, and seek thy face;
grant unto us thy pardoning grace.

Spare us, O Lord, who now confess
our sins and all our wickedness,
and, for the glory of thy Name,
our weakened souls to health reclaim.

Give us the discipline that springs
from abstinence in outward things
with inward fasting, so that we
in heart and soul may dwell with thee.

Grant, O thou blessèd Trinity;
grant, O unchanging Unity;
that this our fast of forty days
may work our profit and thy praise!

St. Gregory the Great (540–604); ver. *Hymnal 1940*, alt.

## 153

Blessed is the King who comes
                    in the name of the Lord;
Peace in heaven and glory in the highest.
Blessed is he who comes in the name of the Lord.
Hosanna in the highest.

## 154, 155

*All glory, laud, and honor*
   *to thee, Redeemer, King!*
*to whom the lips of children*
   *made sweet hosannas ring.*

Thou art the King of Israel,
   thou David's royal Son,
who in the Lord's Name comest,
   the King and Blessèd One.

*Refrain*

The company of angels
   is praising thee on high;
and we with all creation
   in chorus make reply.

*Refrain*

The people of the Hebrews
   with palms before thee went;
our praise and prayers and anthems
   before thee we present.

*Refrain*

To thee before thy passion
   they sang their hymns of praise;
to thee, now high exalted,
   our melody we raise.

*Refrain*

Thou didst accept their praises;
   accept the prayers we bring,
who in all good delightest,
   thou good and gracious King.

*Refrain*

Theodulph of Orleans (d. 821); tr. John Mason Neale (1818–1866), alt.

## 156

Ride on! ride on in majesty!
Hark! all the tribes hosanna cry;
thy humble beast pursues his road
with palms and scattered garments strowed.

Ride on! ride on in majesty!
In lowly pomp ride on to die;
O Christ, thy triumphs now begin
o'er captive death and conquered sin.

Ride on! ride on in majesty!
The angel armies of the sky
look down with sad and wondering eyes
to see the approaching sacrifice.

Ride on! ride on in majesty!
Thy last and fiercest strife is nigh;
the Father on his sapphire throne
expects his own anointed Son.

Ride on! ride on in majesty!
In lowly pomp ride on to die;
bow thy meek head to mortal pain,
then take, O God, thy power, and reign.

Henry Hart Milman (1791–1868); alt.

# 157

*Hosanna in the highest.*
*Blessed is he who comes in the name of the Lord.*
*Hosanna in the highest.*

Open for me the gates of righteousness.
   I will enter them;
   I will offer thanks to the Lord.

"This is the gate of the Lord;
     he who is righteous may enter."

I will give thanks to you, for you answered me
   and have become my salvation.

The same stone which the builders rejected
   has become the chief cornerstone.

This is the Lord's doing,
   and it is marvelous in our eyes.

On this day the Lord has acted;
   we will rejoice and be glad in it.

Hosanna, Lord, hosanna!
   Lord, send us now success.

Blessed is he who comes in the name of the Lord;
   we bless you from the house of the Lord.

God is the Lord; he has shined upon us;
   form a procession with branches
             up to the horns of the altar.

"You are my God, and I will thank you;
 you are my God, and I will exalt you."

Give thanks to the Lord, for he is good;
 his mercy endures for ever.

> *Hosanna in the highest.*
> *Blessed is he who comes in the name of the Lord.*
> *Hosanna in the highest.*

## 158

Ah, holy Jesus, how hast thou offended,
that man to judge thee hath in hate pretended?
By foes derided, by thine own rejected,
 O most afflicted.

Who was the guilty? Who brought this upon thee?
Alas, my treason, Jesus, hath undone thee.
'Twas I, Lord Jesus, I it was denied thee:
 I crucified thee.

Lo, the Good Shepherd for the sheep is offered;
the slave hath sinnèd, and the Son hath suffered;
for our atonement, while we nothing heeded,
 God interceded.

For me, kind Jesus, was thy incarnation,
thy mortal sorrow, and thy life's oblation;
thy death of anguish and thy bitter passion,
 for my salvation.

Therefore, kind Jesus, since I cannot pay thee,
I do adore thee, and will ever pray thee,
think on thy pity and thy love unswerving,
    not my deserving.

Johann Heermann (1585–1647); tr. Robert Seymour Bridges (1844–1930), alt.

**159**

At the cross her vigil keeping,
stood the mournful mother weeping,
    where he hung, the dying Lord:
there she waited in her anguish,
seeing Christ in torment languish,
    in her heart the piercing sword.

With what pain and desolation,
with what grief and resignation,
    Mary watched her dying son.
Deep the woe of her affliction,
when she saw the crucifixion
    of the sole-begotten one.

Him she saw for our salvation
mocked with cruel acclamation,
    scourged, and crowned with thorns entwined;
saw him then from judgment taken,
and in death by all forsaken,
    till his spirit he resigned.

Who, on Christ's dear mother gazing,
pierced by anguish so amazing,
    born of woman, would not weep?

Who, on Christ's dear mother thinking,
such a cup of sorrow drinking,
    would not share her sorrows deep?

Jesus, may her deep devotion
stir in me the same emotion,
    Fount of love, Redeemer kind;
that my heart fresh ardor gaining,
and a purer love attaining,
    may with thee acceptance find.

Latin, 13th cent.; ver. *Hymnal 1982*

## 160

Cross of Jesus, cross of sorrow,
    where the blood of Christ was shed,
perfect Man on thee did suffer,
    perfect God on thee has bled!

Here the King of all the ages,
    throned in light ere worlds could be,
robed in mortal flesh is dying,
    crucified by sin for me.

O mysterious condescending!
    O abandonment sublime!
Very God himself is bearing
    all the sufferings of time!

Cross of Jesus, cross of sorrow,
    where the blood of Christ was shed,

perfect Man on thee did suffer,
    perfect God on thee has bled!

William J. Sparrow-Simpson (1860–1952)

**161**

The flaming banners of our King
advance through his self-offering.
He lived to rob death of its sting;
he died eternal life to bring.

A Roman soldier drew a spear
to mix his blood with water clear.
That blood retains its living power;
the water cleanses to this hour.

The crowd would have been satisfied
to see a prophet crucified.
They stumbled on a mystery:
Messiah reigning from a tree.

With what strange light the rough trunk shone,
its purple limbs a royal throne,
its load a royal treasury:
the ransom of a world set free.

The best are shamed before that wood;
the worst gain power to be good.
O grant, most blessèd Trinity,
that all may share the victory.

Venantius Honorius Fortunatus (540?–600?); tr. John Webster Grant (b. 1919)

## 162

The royal banners forward go,
the cross shines forth in mystic glow
where he through whom our flesh was made,
in that same flesh our ransom paid.

Fulfilled is all that David told
in true prophetic song of old;
how God the nations' King should be,
for God is reigning from the tree.

O tree of beauty, tree most fair,
ordained those holy limbs to bear
gone is thy shame, each crimsoned bough
proclaims the King of glory now.

Blest tree, whose chosen branches bore
the wealth that did the world restore,
the price which none but he could pay
to spoil the spoiler of his prey.

O cross, our one reliance, hail!
Still may thy power with us avail
to save us sinners from our sin,
God's righteousness for all to win.

To thee, eternal Three in One,
let homage meet by all be done;
as by the cross thou dost restore
so rule and guide us evermore.

Venantius Honorius Fortunatus (540?–600?); ver. *Hymnal 1982*

**163**

Sunset to sunrise changes now,
    for God doth make his world anew;
on the Redeemer's thorn-crowned brow
    the wonders of that dawn we view.

E'en though the sun withholds its light,
    lo! a more heavenly lamp shines here,
and from the cross on Calvary's height
    gleams of eternity appear.

Here in o'erwhelming final strife
    the Lord of life hath victory,
and sin is slain, and death brings life,
    and earth inherits heaven's key.

Clement of Alexandria (170?–220?); para. Howard Chandler Robbins (1876–1952), alt.

**164**

Alone thou goest forth, O Lord,
    in sacrifice to die;
is this thy sorrow nought to us
    who pass unheeding by?

Our sins, not thine, thou bearest, Lord;
    make us thy sorrow feel,
till through our pity and our shame
    love answers love's appeal.

This is earth's darkest hour, but thou
    dost light and life restore;
then let all praise be given thee
    who livest evermore.

Grant us with thee to suffer pain
    that, as we share this hour,
thy cross may bring us to thy joy
    and resurrection power.

<sub>Peter Abelard (1079–1142); tr. F. Bland Tucker (1895–1984)</sub>

## 165, 166

Sing, my tongue, the glorious battle;
    of the mighty conflict sing;
tell the triumph of the victim,
    to his cross thy tribute bring.
Jesus Christ, the world's Redeemer
    from that cross now reigns as King.

Thirty years among us dwelling,
    his appointed time fulfilled,
born for this, he meets his passion,
    this the Savior freely willed:
on the cross the Lamb is lifted,
    where his precious blood is spilled.

He endures the nails, the spitting,
    vinegar, and spear, and reed;
from that holy body broken
    blood and water forth proceed:
earth, and stars, and sky, and ocean,
    by that flood from stain are freed.

Faithful cross! above all other,
    one and only noble tree!
None in foliage, none in blossom,
    none in fruit thy peer may be:
sweetest wood and sweetest iron!
    sweetest weight is hung on thee.

Bend thy boughs, O tree of glory!
    Thy relaxing sinews bend;
for awhile the ancient rigor
    that thy birth bestowed, suspend;
and the King of heavenly beauty
    gently on thine arms extend.

Praise and honor to the Father,
    praise and honor to the Son,
praise and honor to the Spirit,
    ever Three and ever One:
one in might and one in glory
    while eternal ages run.

Venantius Honorius Fortunatus (540?–600?); ver. *Hymnal 1982,*
after John Mason Neale (1818–1866)

## 167

There is a green hill far away,
  outside a city wall,
where our dear Lord was crucified
  who died to save us all.

We may not know, we cannot tell,
  what pains he had to bear,
but we believe it was for us
  he hung and suffered there.

He died that we might be forgiven,
  he died to make us good,
that we might go at last to heaven,
  saved by his precious blood.

There was no other good enough
  to pay the price of sin,
he only could unlock the gate
  of heaven and let us in.

O dearly, dearly has he loved!
  And we must love him too,
and trust in his redeeming blood,
  and try his works to do.

Cecil Frances Alexander (1818–1895), alt.

**168, 169**

O sacred head, sore wounded,
    defiled and put to scorn;
O kingly head, surrounded
    with mocking crown of thorn:
what sorrow mars thy grandeur?
    Can death thy bloom deflower?
O countenance whose splendor
    the hosts of heaven adore!

Thy beauty, long-desirèd,
    hath vanished from our sight;
thy power is all expirèd,
    and quenched the light of light.
Ah me! for whom thou diest,
    hide not so far thy grace:
show me, O Love most highest,
    the brightness of thy face.

In thy most bitter passion
    my heart to share doth cry,
with thee for my salvation
    upon the cross to die.
Ah, keep my heart thus movèd
    to stand thy cross beneath,
to mourn thee, well-belovèd,
    yet thank thee for thy death.

What language shall I borrow
    to thank thee, dearest friend,
for this thy dying sorrow,
    thy pity without end?
Oh, make me thine forever!
    and should I fainting be,
Lord, let me never, never,
    outlive my love for thee.

My days are few, O fail not,
    with thine immortal power,
to hold me that I quail not
    in death's most fearful hour;
that I may fight befriended,
    and see in my last strife
to me thine arms extended
    upon the cross of life.

Paulus Gerhardt (1607–1676); sts. 1–3, 5, tr. Robert Seymour Bridges (1844–1930); st. 4, tr. James Waddell Alexander (1804–1859), alt.

## 170

To mock your reign, O dearest Lord,
    they made a crown of thorns;
set you with taunts along that road
    from which no one returns.
They did not know, as we do now,
    that glorious is your crown;
that thorns would flower upon your brow,
    your sorrows heal our own.

In mock acclaim, O gracious Lord,
    they snatched a purple cloak,
your passion turned, for all they cared,
    into a soldier's joke.
They did not know, as we do now,
    that though we merit blame
you will your robe of mercy throw
    around our naked shame.

A sceptered reed, O patient Lord,
    they thrust into your hand,
and acted out their grim charade
    to its appointed end.
They did not know, as we do now,
    though empires rise and fall,
your Kingdom shall not cease to grow
    till love embraces all.

F. Pratt Green (b. 1903), alt.

**171**

Go to dark Gethsemane,
    ye that feel the tempter's power;
your Redeemer's conflict see,
    watch with him one bitter hour;
turn not from his griefs away,
learn of Jesus Christ to pray.

Follow to the judgment hall;
    view the Lord of life arraigned;

O the wormwood and the gall!
    O the pangs his soul sustained!
Shun not suffering, shame, or loss;
learn of him to bear the cross.

Calvary's mournful mountain climb;
    there, adoring at his feet,
mark the miracle of time,
    God's own sacrifice complete;
"It is finished!" hear him cry;
learn of Jesus Christ to die.

James Montgomery (1771–1854)

## 172

Were you there when they crucified my Lord?
Oh! Sometimes it causes me to tremble,
                tremble, tremble.
Were you there when they crucified my Lord?

Were you there when they nailed him to the tree?
Oh! Sometimes it causes me to tremble,
                tremble, tremble.
Were you there when they nailed him to the tree?

Were you there when they pierced him in the side?
Oh! Sometimes it causes me to
                tremble, tremble, tremble.
Were you there when they pierced him in the side?

Were you there when they laid him in the tomb?
Oh! Sometimes it causes me to tremble,
               tremble, tremble.
Were you there when they laid him in the tomb?

African-American spiritual

**173**

O sorrow deep!
Who would not weep
with heartfelt pain and sighing!
God the Father's only Son
in the tomb is lying.

The Paschal Lamb,
like Isaac's ram,
in blood was offered for us,
pouring out his life that he
might to life restore us.

Blest shall they be
eternally
who ponder in their weeping
that the glorious Prince of Life
should in death be sleeping.

O Jesus blest,
my help and rest,
with tears I pray thee, hear me:
now, and even unto death,
dearest Lord, be near me.

St. 1, Friedrich von Spee (1591–1635); tr. Charles Winfred Douglas (1867–1944). Sts. 2–3, James Waring McCrady (b. 1938). St. 4, Johann Rist (1607–1667); tr. Charles Winfred Douglas (1867–1944)

## 174

At the Lamb's high feast we sing
praise to our victorious King,
who hath washed us in the tide
flowing from his piercèd side;
praise we him, whose love divine
gives his sacred Blood for wine,
gives his Body for the feast,
Christ the victim, Christ the priest.

Where the Paschal blood is poured,
death's dark angel sheathes his sword;
Israel's hosts triumphant go
through the wave that drowns the foe.
Praise we Christ, whose blood was shed,
Paschal victim, Paschal bread;
with sincerity and love
eat we manna from above.

Mighty victim from on high,
hell's fierce powers beneath thee lie;
thou hast conquered in the fight,
thou hast brought us life and light:
now no more can death appall,
now no more the grave enthrall;
thou hast opened paradise,
and in thee thy saints shall rise.

Easter triumph, Easter joy,
these alone do sin destroy.
From sin's power do thou set free
souls new-born, O Lord, in thee.
Hymns of glory, songs of praise,
Father, unto thee we raise:
risen Lord, all praise to thee
with the Spirit ever be.

Latin, 1632; tr. Robert Campbell (1814–1868), alt.

# 175

*Hail thee, festival day! blest day*
*that art hallowed forever,*
*day whereon Christ arose, breaking the*
*kingdom of death.*

Lo, the fair beauty of earth, from
                the death of the winter arising!
Every good gift of the year now with its
                Master returns:

*Refrain*

He who was nailed to the cross is Lord
                and the ruler of nature;
all things created on earth sing to the glory of God:

*Refrain*

Daily the loveliness grows, adorned
                with the glory of blossom;
heaven her gates unbars, flinging her increase
                of light:

*Refrain*

Rise from the grave now, O Lord, who art
                author of life and creation.
Treading the pathway of death, life thou
                bestowest on all:

*Refrain*

God the creator, the Lord, who rulest
: the earth and the heavens,
guard us from harm without, cleanse us
: from evil within:

*Refrain*

Jesus the health of the world, enlighten
: our minds, thou Redeemer,
Son of the Father supreme, only-begotten of God:

*Refrain*

Spirit of life and of power, now flow in us,
: fount of our being,
light that dost lighten all, life that in all
: dost abide:

*Refrain*

Praise to the Giver of good! Thou Love
: who art author of concord,
pour out thy balm on our souls, order our ways
: in thy peace:

*Refrain*

Venantius Honorius Fortunatus (540?–600?); tr. *The English Hymnal*, 1906, alt.

## 176, 177

Over the chaos of the empty waters
hovered the Spirit, bringing forth creation;
so from the empty tomb the Second Adam
    issued triumphant.

By the same Spirit we, regenerated
into the body of our risen Savior,
seek through the power of the new creation
    life everlasting.

By the same Spirit we are called to worship
God our Creator, Savior, Sanctifier,
of whom the glory, in both earth and heaven,
    is manifested.

Sts. 1–2, *A Monastic Breviary*, 1976; st. 3, *Hymnal 1982*

## 178

*Alleluia, alleluia!*
*Give thanks to the risen Lord.*
*Alleluia, alleluia!*
*Give Praise to his Name.*

Jesus is Lord of all the earth.
He is the King of creation.

*Refrain*

Spread the good news o'er all the earth:
Jesus has died and has risen.

*Refrain*

We have been crucified with Christ.
Now we shall live for ever.

*Refrain*

Come, let us praise the living God,
joyfully sing to our Savior.

*Refrain*

Donald Fishel (b. 1950)

## 179

"Welcome, happy morning!" age to age shall say:
hell today is vanquished, heaven is won today!
Lo! the dead is living, God for evermore!
Him their true Creator, all his works adore!
"Welcome, happy morning!" age to age shall say.

Earth her joy confesses, clothing her for spring,
all fresh gifts returned with her returning King:
bloom in every meadow, leaves on every bough,
speak his sorrow ended, hail his triumph now.
"Welcome, happy morning!" age to age shall say.

Months in due succession, days of lengthening light,
hours and passing moments praise thee in their flight.
Brightness of the morning, sky and fields and sea,
Vanquisher of darkness, bring their praise to thee.
"Welcome, happy morning!" age to age shall say.

Maker and Redeemer, life and health of all,
thou from heaven beholding human nature's fall,
of the Father's Godhead true and only Son,
mankind to deliver, manhood didst put on.
"Welcome, happy morning!" age to age shall say.

Thou, of life the author, death didst undergo,
tread the path of darkness, saving strength to show;
come then, true and faithful, now fulfill thy word,
'tis thine own third morning! rise, O buried Lord!
"Welcome, happy morning!" age to age shall say.

Loose the souls long prisoned, bound
                with Satan's chain;
all that now is fallen raise to life again;
show thy face in brightness, bid the nations see;
bring again our daylight: day returns with thee!
"Welcome, happy morning!" age to age shall say.

Venantius Honorius Fortunatus (540?–600?); tr. John Ellerton (1826–1893), alt.

## 180

He is risen, he is risen!
   Tell it out with joyful voice:
he has burst his three days' prison;
   let the whole wide earth rejoice:
death is conquered, we are free,
Christ has won the victory.

Come, ye sad and fearful-hearted,
   with glad smile and radiant brow!
Death's long shadows have departed;
   Jesus' woes are over now,
and the passion that he bore—
sin and pain can vex no more.

Come, with high and holy hymning,
   hail our Lord's triumphant day;
not one darksome cloud is dimming
   yonder glorious morning ray,
breaking o'er the purple east,
symbol of our Easter feast.

He is risen, he is risen!
   He hath opened heaven's gate:
we are free from sin's dark prison,
   risen to a holier state;
and a brighter Easter beam
on our longing eyes shall stream.

Cecil Frances Alexander (1818–1895), alt.

## 181

Awake and sing the song
of Moses and the Lamb;
wake every heart and every tongue
to praise the Savior's name.

Sing of his dying love,
his resurrection power;
sing how he intercedes above
for those whose sins he bore.

You pilgrims on the road
to Zion's city, sing,
rejoicing in the Lamb of God,
in Christ the eternal King.

Soon shall each raptured tongue
his endless praise proclaim,
and sing in sweeter notes the song
of Moses and the Lamb.

William Hammond (1719–1783), alt.

## 182

Christ is alive! Let Christians sing.
His cross stands empty to the sky.
Let streets and homes with praises ring.
His love in death shall never die.

Christ is alive! No longer bound
to distant years in Palestine,

he comes to claim the here and now
    and conquer every place and time.

Not throned above, remotely high,
    untouched, unmoved by human pains,
but daily, in the midst of life,
    our Savior with the Father reigns.

In every insult, rift, and war
    where color, scorn or wealth divide,
he suffers still, yet loves the more,
    and lives, though ever crucified.

Christ is alive! His Spirit burns
    through this and every future age,
till all creation lives and learns
    his joy, his justice, love, and praise.

Brian A. Wren (b. 1936), rev.

## 183

Christians, to the Paschal victim
offer your thankful praises!

A lamb the sheep redeemeth:
Christ, who only is sinless,
reconcileth sinners to the Father.

Death and life have contended
in that combat stupendous:
the Prince of life, who died, reigns immortal.

Speak, Mary, declaring
what thou sawest, wayfaring:

"The tomb of Christ, who is living,
the glory of Jesus' resurrection;

bright angels attesting,
the shroud and napkin resting.

Yea, Christ my hope is arisen;
to Galilee he goes before you."

Christ indeed from death is risen,
our new life obtaining,
have mercy, victor King, ever reigning!
Amen.  Alleluia!

Wigbert [Wipo of Burgundy] (d. 1050?); tr. *The Antiphoner and Grail*, 1880, alt.

## 184

Christ the Lord is risen again!
Christ has broken every chain!
Now through all the world it rings
that the Lamb is King of kings.
   Alleluia!

> *Alleluia, alleluia, alleluia!*
> *Christ, our Paschal Lamb indeed,*
> *Christ, today your people feed.*
> *Alleluia!*

He who gave for us his life,
who for us endured the strife,
takes our sin and guilt away
that with angels we may say:
> Alleluia!

*Refrain*

He who bore all pain and loss
comfortless upon the cross
is exalted now to save,
wresting victory from the grave.
> Alleluia!

*Refrain*

Michael Weisse (1480–1534); tr. Catherine Winkworth (1827–1878), alt.

## 185, 186

Christ Jesus lay in death's strong bands
> for our offenses given;
but now at God's right hand he stands
> and brings us life from heaven;
therefore let us joyful be,
and sing to God right thankfully
> loud songs of alleluia!
> Alleluia!

It was a strange and dreadful strife
    when life and death contended;
the victory remained with life,
    the reign of death was ended;
stripped of power, no more he reigns,
an empty form alone remains;
    his sting is lost for ever!
    Alleluia!

So let us keep the festival
    to which the Lord invites us;
Christ is himself the joy of all,
    the sun that warms and lights us;
by his grace he doth impart
eternal sunshine to the heart;
    the night of sin is ended!
    Alleluia!

Then let us feast this holy day
    on the true bread of heaven;
the word of grace hath purged away
    the old and wicked leaven;
Christ alone our souls will feed,
he is our meat and drink indeed;
    faith lives upon no other!
    Alleluia!

Martin Luther (1483–1564); tr. Richard Massie (1800–1887), alt.

## 187

Through the Red Sea brought at last,
Egypt's chains behind we cast.
    Deep and wide
    flows the tide
severing us from bondage past, Alleluia!

Like the cloud that overhead,
through the billows Israel led,
    by his tomb
    Christ makes room,
souls restoring from the dead, Alleluia!

In that cloud and in that sea
buried and baptized were we.
    Earthly night
    brought us light
which is ours eternally, Alleluia!

Ronald A. Knox (1888–1957)

## 188, 189

Love's redeeming work is done,
fought the fight, the battle won.
Death in vain forbids him rise;
Christ has opened paradise.
    Alleluia!

Lives again our glorious King;
where, O death, is now thy sting?
Once he died our souls to save,
where thy victory, O grave?
   Alleluia!

Soar we now where Christ has led,
following our exalted Head;
made like him, like him we rise,
ours the cross, the grave, the skies.
   Alleluia!

Charles Wesley (1707–1788), alt.

## 190

Lift your voice rejoicing, Mary,
   Christ has risen from the tomb;
on the cross a suffering victim,
   now as victor he is come.
Whom your tears in death were mourning,
welcome with your smiles returning.
   Let your alleluias rise!

Raise your weary eyelids, Mary,
   see him living evermore;
see his countenance, how gracious,
   see the wounds for you he bore.
All the glory of the morning
pales before those wounds redeeming.
   Let your alleluias rise!

Life is yours for ever, Mary,
    for your light is come once more
and the strength of death is broken;
    now your songs of joy outpour.
Ended now the night of sorrow,
love has brought the blessed morrow.
    Let your alleluias rise!

Latin; tr. Elizabeth Rundle Charles (1828–1896), alt.

**191**

Alleluia, alleluia!
    Hearts and voices heavenward raise:
sing to God a hymn of gladness,
    sing to God a hymn of praise.
He, who on the cross a victim,
    for the world's salvation bled,
Jesus Christ, the King of glory,
    now is risen from the dead.

Now the iron bars are broken,
    Christ from death to life is born,
glorious life, and life immortal,
    on his resurrection morn.
Christ has triumphed, and we conquer
    by his mighty enterprise:
we with him to life eternal
    by his resurrection rise.

Christ is risen, Christ, the first-fruits
    of the holy harvest-field,
which with all its full abundance
    at his second coming yield:
then the golden ears of harvest
    will their heads before him wave,
ripened by his glorious sunshine
    from the furrows of the grave.

Christ is risen, we are risen!
    Shed upon us heavenly grace,
rain and dew and gleams of glory
    from the brightness of thy face;
that, with hearts in heaven dwelling,
    we on earth may fruitful be,
and by angel hands be gathered,
    and be ever, Lord, with thee.

Alleluia, alleluia!
    Glory be to God on high;
Alleluia! to the Savior
    who has won the victory;
Alleluia! to the Spirit,
    fount of love and sanctity:
Alleluia, alleluia!
    to the Triune Majesty.

Christopher Wordsworth (1807–1885), alt.

**192**

This joyful Eastertide,
   away with sin and sorrow!
My Love, the Crucified,
   hath sprung to life this morrow.

> *Had Christ, that once was slain,*
>    *ne'er burst his three-day prison,*
> *our faith had been in vain;*
>    *but now is Christ arisen.*

Death's flood hath lost its chill,
   since Jesus crossed the river:
Lord of all life, from ill
   my passing life deliver.

*Refrain*

My flesh in hope shall rest,
   and for a season slumber,
till trump from east to west
   shall wake the dead in number.

*Refrain*

George R. Woodward (1848–1934), alt.

## 193

That Easter day with joy was bright,
the sun shone out with fairer light,
when, to their longing eyes restored,
the apostles saw their risen Lord.

His risen flesh with radiance glowed;
his wounded hands and feet he showed;
those scars their solemn witness gave
that Christ was risen from the grave.

O Jesus, King of gentleness,
do thou thyself our hearts possess
that we may give thee all our days
the willing tribute of our praise.

O Lord of all, with us abide
in this our joyful Eastertide;
from every weapon death can wield
thine own redeemed for ever shield.

All praise, O risen Lord, we give
to thee, who, dead, again dost live;
to God the Father equal praise,
and God the Holy Ghost, we raise.

Latin, 5th cent.; ver. *Hymnal 1940*

**194, 195**

Jesus lives! thy terrors now
    can no longer, death, appall us;
Jesus lives! by this we know
    thou, O grave, canst not enthrall us.
    Alleluia!

Jesus lives! for us he died;
    then, alone to Jesus living,
pure in heart may we abide,
    glory to our Savior giving.
    Alleluia!

Jesus lives! our hearts know well
    nought from us his love shall sever;
life, nor death, nor powers of hell
    tear us from his keeping ever.
    Alleluia!

Jesus lives! to him the throne
    over all the world is given:
may we go where he has gone,
    rest and reign with him in heaven.
    Alleluia!

Christian Furchtegott Gellert (1715–1769); tr. Frances Elizabeth Cox (1812–1897), alt.

## 196, 197

Look there! the Christ, our Brother, comes
    resplendent from the gallows tree
and what he brings in his hurt hands
    is life on life for you and me.

*Joy! joy! joy to the heart*
*and all in this good day's dawning!*

Good Jesus Christ inside his pain
    looked down from Golgotha's stony slope
and let the blood flow from his flesh
    to fill the springs of living hope.

*Refrain*

Good Jesus Christ, our Brother, died
    in darkest hurt upon the tree
to offer us the worlds of light
    that live inside the Trinity.

*Refrain*

Look there! the Christ, our Brother, comes
    resplendent from the gallows tree
and what he brings in his hurt hands
    is life on life for you and me.

*Refrain*

John Bennett (b. 1920), alt.

## 198

Thou hallowed chosen morn of praise,
    that best and greatest shinest:
fair Easter, queen of all the days,
    of seasons, best, divinest!
Christ rose from death; and we adore
for ever and for evermore.

Come, let us taste the vine's new fruit,
    for heavenly joy preparing;
today the branches with the root
    in resurrection sharing:
whom as true God our hymns adore
for ever and for evermore.

John of Damascus (8th cent.); tr. John Mason Neale (1818–1866), alt.

## 199, 200

Come, ye faithful, raise the strain
    of triumphant gladness!
God hath brought his Israel
    into joy from sadness:
loosed from Pharaoh's bitter yoke
    Jacob's sons and daughters,
led them with unmoistened foot
    through the Red Sea waters.

'Tis the spring of souls today:
    Christ hath burst his prison,
and from three days' sleep in death
    as a sun hath risen;
all the winter of our sins,
    long and dark, is flying
from his light, to whom we give
    laud and praise undying.

Now the queen of seasons, bright
    with the day of splendor,
with the royal feast of feasts,
    comes its joy to render;
comes to glad Jerusalem,
    who with true affection
welcomes in unwearied strains
    Jesus' resurrection.

Neither might the gates of death,
    nor the tomb's dark portal,
nor the watchers, nor the seal
    hold thee as a mortal:
but today amidst thine own
    thou didst stand, bestowing
that thy peace which evermore
    passeth human knowing.

John of Damascus (8th cent.); tr. John Mason Neale (1818–1866), alt.

## 201

On earth has dawned this day of days,
whereon the faithful give God praise!
For Christ is risen from the tomb,
and light and joy have conquered doom.
    Alleluia!

At early morn, with spices rare,
the women three assembled there,
all to anoint fair Mary's Son,
who over death had victory won.
    Alleluia!

"Whom seek ye here?" the angel said;
"The Lord is risen from the dead;
see where he lay; let joy begin,
the tomb is empty: enter in!"
    Alleluia!

So let our songs to heaven wing,
the vault with alleluias ring,
in praise of Christ, our risen Lord;
new life to all he doth afford.
    Alleluia!

Nikolaus Hermann (1480?–1561); tr. Charles Sanford Terry (1864–1936), alt.

## 202

The Lamb's high banquet called to share,
arrayed in garments white and fair,
the Red Sea past, we now would sing
to Jesus our triumphant King.

Protected in the Paschal night
from the destroying angel's might,
in triumph went the ransomed free
from Pharaoh's cruel tyranny.

Now Christ our Passover is slain,
the Lamb of God without a stain;
his flesh, the true unleavened bread,
is freely offered in our stead.

O all-sufficient Sacrifice,
beneath thee hell defeated lies;
thy captive people are set free,
and endless life restored in thee.

All praise be thine, O risen Lord,
from death to endless life restored;
all praise to God the Father be
and Holy Ghost eternally.

Latin 7th–8th cent.; tr. John Mason Neale (1818–1866) and others

**203**

*Alleluia, alleluia! Alleluia, alleluia!*

O sons and daughters, let us sing!
The King of heaven, the glorious King,
o'er death and hell rose triumphing.
    Alleluia, alleluia!

That Easter morn, at break of day,
the faithful women went their way
to seek the tomb where Jesus lay.
    Alleluia, alleluia!

An angel clad in white they see,
who sat and spake unto the three,
"Your Lord doth go to Galilee."
    Alleluia, alleluia!

That night the apostles met in fear;
amidst them came their Lord most dear,
and said, "My peace be on all here."
    Alleluia, alleluia!

On this most holy day of days,
to God your hearts and voices raise,
in laud and jubilee and praise.
    Alleluia, alleluia!

*Alleluia, alleluia! Alleluia, alleluia!*

Jean Tisserand (15th cent.); tr. John Mason Neale (1818–1866)

## 204

Now the green blade riseth from the buried grain,
wheat that in dark earth many days has lain;
love lives again, that with the dead has been:

> *Love is come again*
> *like wheat that springeth green.*

In the grave they laid him, Love whom hate had slain,
thinking that never he would wake again,
laid in the earth like grain that sleeps unseen:

*Refrain*

Forth he came at Easter, like the risen grain,
he that for three days in the grave had lain,
quick from the dead my risen Lord is seen:

*Refrain*

When our hearts are wintry, grieving, or in pain,
thy touch can call us back to life again,
fields of our hearts that dead and bare have been:

*Refrain*

John Macleod Campbell Crum (1872–1958), alt.

## 205

Good Christians all, rejoice and sing!
Now is the triumph of our King!
To all the world glad news we bring:
 Alleluia, alleluia, alleluia!

The Lord of life is risen today!
Sing songs of praise along his way;
let all the earth rejoice and say:
   Alleluia, alleluia, alleluia!

Praise we in songs of victory
that love, that life which cannot die,
and sing with hearts uplifted high:
   Alleluia, alleluia, alleluia!

Your Name we bless, O risen Lord,
and sing today with one accord
the life laid down, the life restored:
   Alleluia, alleluia, alleluia!

To God the Father, God the Son,
to God the Spirit, always One,
we sing for life in us begun:
   Alleluia, alleluia, alleluia!

Cyril A. Alington (1872–1955), alt. St. 5, Norman Mealey (1923–1987)

## 206

*Alleluia, alleluia, alleluia!*

O sons and daughters, let us sing!
The King of heaven, the glorious King,
o'er death and hell rose triumphing.
   Alleluia!

That night the apostles met in fear;
amidst them came their Lord most dear,
and said, "My peace be on all here."
    Alleluia!

When Thomas first the tidings heard,
how they had seen the risen Lord,
he doubted the disciples' word.
    Alleluia!

"My piercèd side, O Thomas, see;
my hands, my feet, I show to thee;
not faithless, but believing be."
    Alleluia!

No longer Thomas then denied,
he saw the feet, the hands, the side;
"Thou art my Lord and God," he cried.
    Alleluia!

How blest are they who have not seen,
and yet whose faith has constant been,
for they eternal life shall win.
    Alleluia!

*Alleluia, alleluia, alleluia!*

Att. Jean Tisserand (15th cent.); tr. John Mason Neale (1818–1866)

## 207

Jesus Christ is risen today,
our triumphant holy day,
who did once upon the cross,
suffer to redeem our loss. Alleluia!

Hymns of praise then let us sing
unto Christ, our heavenly King,
who endured the cross and grave,
sinners to redeem and save. Alleluia!

But the pains which he endured,
our salvation have procured;
now above the sky he's King,
where the angels ever sing. Alleluia!

Sing we to our God above
praise eternal as his love;
praise him, all ye heavenly host, Alleluia!
Father, Son, and Holy Ghost. Alleluia!

Latin, 14th cent.; tr. *Lyra Davidica*, 1708, alt. St. 4, Charles Wesley (1707–1788)

## 208

*Alleluia, alleluia, alleluia!*

The strife is o'er, the battle done,
the victory of life is won;
the song of triumph has begun.
   Alleluia!

The powers of death have done their worst,
but Christ their legions hath dispersed:
let shout of holy joy outburst.
    Alleluia!

The three sad days are quickly sped,
he rises glorious from the dead:
all glory to our risen Head!
    Alleluia!

He closed the yawning gates of hell,
the bars from heaven's high portals fell;
let hymns of praise his triumphs tell!
    Alleluia!

Lord! by the stripes which wounded thee,
from death's dread sting thy servants free,
that we may live and sing to thee.
    Alleluia!

    *Alleluia, alleluia, alleluia!*

Latin, 1695; tr. Francis Pott (1832–1909), alt.

## 209

We walk by faith, and not by sight;
    no gracious words we hear
from him who spoke as none e'er spoke;
    but we believe him near.

We may not touch his hands and side,
    nor follow where he trod;

but in his promise we rejoice,
    and cry, "My Lord and God!"

Help then, O Lord, our unbelief;
    and may our faith abound,
to call on you when you are near,
    and seek where you are found:

that, when our life of faith is done,
    in realms of clearer light
we may behold you as you are,
    with full and endless sight.

Henry Alford (1810–1871), alt.

**210**

The day of resurrection!
    Earth, tell it out abroad;
the Passover of gladness,
    the Passover of God.
From death to life eternal,
    from earth unto the sky,
our Christ hath brought us over
    with hymns of victory.

Our hearts be pure from evil,
    that we may see aright
the Lord in rays eternal
    of resurrection light;
and, listening to his accents,
    may hear so calm and plain

his own "All hail!" and, hearing,
    may raise the victor strain.

Now let the heavens be joyful,
    let earth her song begin,
the round world keep high triumph,
    and all that is therein;
let all things seen and unseen
    their notes together blend,
for Christ the Lord is risen,
    our joy that hath no end.

John of Damascus (8th cent.); tr. John Mason Neale (1818–1866), alt.

# 211

The whole bright world rejoices now,
    *Hilariter, hilariter!*\*
The birds do sing on every bough,
    Alleluia, alleluia!

Then shout beneath the racing skies,
    *Hilariter, hilariter!*
To him who rose that we might rise,
    Alleluia, alleluia!

And all you living things make praise,
    *Hilariter, hilariter!*
He guideth you on all your ways,
    Alleluia, alleluia!

To Father, Son, and Holy Ghost—
> *Hilariter, hilariter!*
Our God most high, our joy and boast.
> Alleluia, alleluia!

Friedrich von Spee (1591–1635); tr. Percy Dearmer (1867–1936)

\* *"Hilariter" is Latin for "joyfully" and is pronounced "hi-lair-I-tair" in this hymn.*

## 212

Awake, arise, lift up your voice,
> let Easter music swell;
rejoice in Christ, again rejoice
> and on his praises dwell.

Oh, with what gladness and surprise
> the saints their Savior greet;
nor will they trust their ears and eyes
> but by his hands and feet,

those hands of liberal love indeed
> in infinite degree,
those feet still free to move and bleed
> for millions and for me.

His enemies had sealed the stone
> as Pilate gave them leave,
lest dead and friendless and alone
> he should their skill deceive.

O Dead arise! O Friendless stand
    by seraphim adored!
O Solitude again command
    your host from heaven restored!

Christopher Smart (1722–1771), alt.

## 213

Come away to the skies,
my beloved, arise
    and rejoice in the day thou wast born;
on this festival day,
come exulting away,
    and with singing to Zion return.

Now with singing and praise,
let us spend all the days,
    by our heavenly Father bestowed,
while his grace we receive
from his bounty, and live
    to the honor and glory of God.

For the glory we were
first created to share,
    both the nature and kingdom divine!
Now created again
that our lives may remain,
    throughout time and eternity thine.

We with thanks do approve
the design of that love
   which hath joined us to Jesus' Name;
so united in heart,
let us nevermore part,
   till we meet at the feast of the Lamb.

Hallelujah we sing,
to our Father and King,
   and his rapturous praises, repeat:
to the Lamb that was slain,
hallelujah again,
   sing, all heaven, and fall at his feet.

Charles Wesley (1707–1788)

## 214

Hail the day that sees him rise
glorious to his native skies;
Christ, awhile to mortals given,
enters now the highest heaven! Alleluia!

There the glorious triumph waits;
lift your heads, eternal gates!
Wide unfold the radiant scene;
take the King of glory in! Alleluia!

See! he lifts his hands above;
See! he shows the prints of love:
Hark! his gracious lips bestow,
blessings on his Church below. Alleluia!

Lord beyond our mortal sight,
raise our hearts to reach thy height,
there thy face unclouded see,
find our heaven of heavens in thee.  Alleluia!

Charles Wesley (1707–1788), alt.

## 215

See the Conqueror mounts in triumph;
    see the King in royal state,
riding on the clouds, his chariot,
    to his heavenly palace gate!
Hark! the choirs of angel voices
    joyful alleluias sing,
and the portals high are lifted
    to receive their heavenly King.

He who on the cross did suffer,
    he who from the grave arose,
he has vanquished sin and Satan;
    he by death has spoiled his foes.
While he lifts his hands in blessing,
    he is parted from his friends;
while their eager eyes behold him,
    he upon the clouds ascends.

Thou hast raised our human nature
    on the clouds to God's right hand:
there we sit in heavenly places,
    there with thee in glory stand.

Jesus reigns, adored by angels;
>   Man with God is on the throne;
> mighty Lord, in thine ascension,
>   we by faith behold our own.

Christopher Wordsworth (1807–1885), alt.

## 216

> *Hail thee, festival day!*
> > *blest day that art hallowed for ever,*
> *day when the Christ ascends,*
> > *high in the heavens to reign.*

He who was nailed to the cross is Lord
>    and ruler of nature;
all things created on earth sing to the glory of God:

*Refrain*

Daily the loveliness grows, adorned
>    with the glory of blossom;
heaven her gates unbars, flinging her increase
>    of light:

*Refrain*

God the Creator, the Lord who rulest
>    the earth and the heavens,
guard us from harm without, cleanse us
>    from evil within:

*Refrain*

Jesus the health of the world, enlighten
>our minds, thou Redeemer,
Son of the Father supreme, only-begotten of God:

*Refrain*

Spirit of life and of power, now flow in us,
>fount of our being,
light that dost lighten all, life that in all
>dost abide:

*Refrain*

Praise to the Giver of good! Thou Love
>who art author of concord,
pour out thy balm on our souls, order our ways
>in thy peace:

*Refrain*

Venantius Honorius Fortunatus (540?–600?); tr. *The English Hymnal*, 1906, alt.

## 217, 218

A hymn of glory let us sing,
new hymns throughout the world shall ring;
by a new way none ever trod
Christ takes his place—the throne of God!

You are a present joy, O Lord;
you will be ever our reward;
and great the light in you we see
to guide us to eternity.

O risen Christ, ascended Lord,
all praise to you let earth accord,
who are, while endless ages run,
with Father and with Spirit, One.

The Venerable Bede (673–735); sts. 1–2, tr. Elizabeth Rundle
Charles (1828–1896), alt.; st. 3, tr. Benjamin Webb (1819–1885), alt.

## 219

The Lord ascendeth up on high,
the Lord hath triumphed gloriously,
   in power and might excelling;
the grave and hell are captive led.
Lo! he returns, our glorious Head,
   to his eternal dwelling.

The heavens with joy receive their Lord,
by saints, by angel hosts adored;
   O day of exultation!
O earth, adore thy glorious King!
His rising, his ascension sing
   with grateful adoration!

Our great High Priest hath gone before,
upon his Church his grace to pour;
   and still his love he giveth.
O may our hearts to him ascend;
may all within us upward tend
   to him who ever liveth!

Arthur T. Russell (1806–1874), alt.

## 220, 221

O Lord Most High, eternal King,
by thee redeemed thy praise we sing.
The bonds of death are burst by thee,
and grace has won the victory.

Ascending to the Father's throne
thou claim'st the kingdom as thine own;
and angels wonder when they see
how changed is our humanity.

Be thou our joy, O Mighty Lord,
as thou wilt be our great reward;
let all our glory be in thee
both now and through eternity.

O risen Christ, ascended Lord,
all praise to thee let earth accord,
who art, while endless ages run,
with Father and with Spirit, One.

Medieval Latin; sts. 1–3, tr. F. Bland Tucker (1895–1984); st. 4, tr. Benjamin Webb (1819–1885)

## 222

Rejoice, the Lord of life ascends
    in triumph from earth's battlefield:
his strife with human hatred ends,
    as sin and death their conquests yield.

No more his mortal form we see;
    he reigns invisible but near:
for in the midst of two or three
    he makes his gracious presence clear.

He reigns, but with a love that shares
    the troubles of our earthly life;
he takes upon his heart the cares,
    the pain, and shame of human strife.

He reigns in heaven until the hour
    when he, who once was crucified,
shall come in all love's glorious power
    to rule the world for which he died.

Albert F. Bayly (1901–1984), alt.

**223, 224**

Hail this joyful day's return,
hail the Pentecostal morn,
morn when our ascended Lord
on his Church his Spirit poured!

Like to cloven tongues of flame
on the twelve the Spirit came
tongues, that earth may hear their call,
fire, that love may burn in all.

Lord, to you your people bend;
unto us your Spirit send;

blessings of this sacred day
grant us, dearest Lord, we pray.

You who did our forebears guide,
with their children still abide;
grant us pardon, grant us peace,
till our earthly wanderings cease.

Att. Hilary of Poitiers (4th cent.); tr. Robert Campbell (1814–1868), alt.

## 225

> *Hail thee, festival day!*
> *blest day that art hallowed for ever,*
> *day when the Holy Ghost*
> *shone in the world with God's grace.*

Lo, in the likeness of fire, on those
                who await his appearing,
he whom the Lord foretold
                suddenly, swiftly, descends:

*Refrain*

Forth from the Father he comes with
                sevenfold mystical offering,
pouring on all human souls infinite riches
                of God:

*Refrain*

Hark! for in myriad tongues Christ's own,
             his chosen apostles,
preach to the ends of the earth Christ
             and his wonderful works:

*Refrain*

Praise to the Spirit of Life, all praise
             to the fount of our being,
light that dost lighten all, life that in all dost abide:

*Refrain*

Venantius Honorius Fortunatus (540?–600?); tr. *English Hymnal*, 1906, alt.

## 226, 227

Come, thou Holy Spirit bright;
come with thy celestial light;
   pour on us thy love divine.
Come, protector of the poor;
come, thou source of blessings sure;
   come within our hearts to shine.

Thou, of comforters the best,
thou, the soul's most welcome guest,
   of our peace thou art the sign.
In our labor, be our aid;
in our summer, cooling shade.
   Every bitter tear refine.

Brighter than the noonday sun,
fill our lives which Christ hath won;
    fill our hearts and make them thine.
Where thou art not, we have nought:
all our word and deed and thought
    twisted from thy true design.

Bend the stubborn heart and will;
melt the frozen, warm the chill;
    rule us by thy judgment's line.
Cleanse us with thy healing power;
what is barren bring to flower;
    to thy love our sins consign.

To thy people who adore
and confess thee evermore,
    thy blest sevenfold gift assign.
Grant us thy salvation, Lord,
boundless mercy our reward,
    joys which earth and heaven entwine.

Latin, 12th cent.; tr. Charles P. Price (b. 1920)

## 228

Holy Spirit, font of light,
focus of God's glory bright,
    shed on us a shining ray.
Father of the fatherless,
giver of gifts limitless,
    come and touch our hearts today.

Source of strength and sure relief,
comforter in time of grief,
    enter in and be our guest.
On our journey grant us aid,
freshening breeze and cooling shade,
    in our labor inward rest.

Enter each aspiring heart,
occupy its inmost part
    with your dazzling purity.
All that gives to us our worth,
all that benefits the earth,
    you bring to maturity.

With your soft, refreshing rains
break our drought, remove our stains;
    bind up all our injuries.
Shake with rushing wind our will;
melt with fire our icy chill;
    bring to light our perjuries.

As your promise we believe,
make us ready to receive
    gifts from your unbounded store.
Grant enabling energy,
courage in adversity,
    joys that last for evermore.

Latin, 12th cent.; tr. John Webster Grant (b. 1919), alt.

## 229

Spirit of mercy, truth, and love,
O shed thine influence from above;
and still from age to age convey
the wonders of this sacred day.

In every clime, by every tongue,
be God's amazing glory sung:
let all the listening earth be taught
the deeds our great Redeemer wrought.

Unfailing Comfort, heavenly Guide,
still o'er thy holy Church preside;
O shed thine influence from above,
Spirit of mercy, truth, and love.

Anon., *Psalms, Hymns, and Anthems*, 1774, alt.

## 230

A mighty sound from heaven
   at Pentecost there came,
and filled the place of meeting
   with rushing wind and flame:
what Christ had promised now occurred
as each Apostle spoke the word
   beneath the Spirit's thunder,
and to the ears of all who heard
   proclaimed salvation's wonder.

In Salem's street was gathered
 a crowd from many a land,
and all in their own tongues did
 the Gospel understand:
for by the triumph of the Son
the curse of Babel was undone
 when God did send the Spirit;
so to the blessed Three in One
 be honor, praise, and merit.

Then come, all Christian people,
 keep festival today,
for God the Holy Spirit
 dwells with the Church alway:
and grieve him not, O Christian soul,
his grace within shall make you whole
 in body, mind, and spirit,
until you reach the promised goal,
 a kingdom to inherit.

George B. Timms (b. 1910), alt.

## 231, 232

By all your saints still striving,
    for all your saints at rest,
your holy Name, O Jesus,
    for evermore be blessed.
You rose, our King victorious,
    that they might wear the crown
and ever shine in splendor
    reflected from your throne.

*(Insert the stanza appropriate to the day)*

*Saint Andrew    November 30*

All praise, O Lord, for Andrew,
    the first to follow you;
he witnessed to his brother,
    "This is Messiah true."
You called him from his fishing
    upon Lake Galilee;
he rose to meet your challenge,
    "Leave all and follow me."

*Saint Thomas    December 21*

All praise, O Lord, for Thomas
    whose short-lived doubtings prove
your perfect two-fold nature,
    the depth of your true love.
To all who live with questions
    a steadfast faith afford;
and grant us grace to know you,
    made flesh, yet God and Lord.

*Saint Stephen    December 26*
>All praise, O Lord, for Stephen
>>who, martyred, saw you stand
>to help in time of torment,
>>to plead at God's right hand.
>Like you, our suffering Savior,
>>his enemies he blessed,
>with "Lord, receive my spirit,"
>>his faith, in death, confessed.

*Saint John    December 27*
>For John, your loved disciple,
>>exiled to Patmos' shore,
>and for his faithful record,
>>we praise you evermore;
>praise for the mystic vision
>>his words to us unfold.
>Instill in us his longing,
>>your glory to behold.

*The Holy Innocents    December 28*
>Praise for your infant martyrs,
>>whom your mysterious love
>called early from life's conflicts
>>to share your peace above.
>O Rachel, cease your weeping;
>>they're free from pain and cares.
>Lord, grant us crowns as brilliant
>>and lives as pure as theirs.

*Confession of Saint Peter     January 18*
　　We praise you, Lord, for Peter,
　　　　so eager and so bold:
　　thrice falling, yet repentant,
　　　　thrice charged to feed your fold.
　　Lord, make your pastors faithful
　　　　to guard your flock from harm
　　and hold them when they waver
　　　　with your almighty arm.

*Conversion of Saint Paul     January 25*
　　Praise for the light from heaven
　　　　and for the voice of awe:
　　praise for the glorious vision
　　　　the persecutor saw.
　　O Lord, for Paul's conversion,
　　　　we bless your Name today.
　　Come shine within our darkness
　　　　and guide us in the Way.

*Saint Matthias     February 24*
　　For one in place of Judas,
　　　　the apostles sought God's choice:
　　the lot fell to Matthias
　　　　for whom we now rejoice.
　　May we like true apostles
　　　　your holy Church defend,
　　and not betray our calling
　　　　but serve you to the end.

*Saint Joseph     March 19*
    All praise, O God, for Joseph,
        the guardian of your Son,
    who saved him from King Herod
        when safety there was none.
    He taught the trade of builder,
        when they to Nazareth came,
    and Joseph's love made "Father"
        to be, for Christ, God's Name.

*Saint Mark     April 25*
    For Mark, O Lord, we praise you,
        the weak by grace made strong:
    his witness in his Gospel
        becomes victorious song.
    May we, in all our weakness,
        receive your power divine,
    and all, as faithful branches,
        grow strong in you, the Vine.

*Saint Philip and Saint James     May 1*
    We praise you, Lord, for Philip,
        blest guide to Greek and Jew,
    and for young James the faithful,
        who heard and followed you,
    O grant us grace to know you,
        the victor in the strife,
    that we with all your servants
        may wear the crown of life.

*Saint Barnabas    June 11*
    For Barnabas we praise you,
        who kept your law of love
    and, leaving earthly treasures,
        sought riches from above.
    O Christ, our Lord and Savior,
        let gifts of grace descend,
    that your true consolation
        may through the world extend.

*The Nativity of Saint John the Baptist    June 24*
    All praise for John the Baptist,
        forerunner of the Word,
    our true Elijah, making
        a highway for the Lord.
    The last and greatest prophet,
        he saw the dawning ray
    of light that grows in splendor
        until the perfect day.

*Saint Peter and Saint Paul    June 29*
    We praise you for Saint Peter;
        we praise you for Saint Paul.
    They taught both Jew and Gentile
        that Christ is all in all.
    To cross and sword they yielded
        and saw the kingdom come:
    O God, your two apostles
        won life through martyrdom.

*Saint Mary Magdalene   July 22*
>All praise for Mary Magdalene,
>>whose wholeness was restored
>by you, her faithful Master,
>>her Savior and her Lord.
>On Easter morning early,
>>a word from you sufficed:
>her faith was first to see you,
>>her Lord, the risen Christ.

*Saint James   July 25*
>O Lord, for James, we praise you,
>>who fell to Herod's sword.
>He drank the cup of suffering
>>and thus fulfilled your word.
>Lord, curb our vain impatience
>>for glory and for fame,
>equip us for such sufferings
>>as glorify your Name.

*Saint Mary the Virgin   August 15*
>We sing with joy of Mary
>>whose heart with awe was stirred
>when, youthful and unready,
>>she heard the angel's word;
>yet she her voice upraises,
>>God's glory to proclaim,
>as once for our salvation
>>your mother she became.

*Saint Bartholomew     August 24*
>Praise for your blest apostle
>>surnamed Bartholomew;
>
>we know not his achievements
>>but know that he was true,
>
>for he at the ascension
>>was an apostle still.
>
>May we discern your presence
>>and seek, like him, your will.

*Saint Matthew     September 21*
>We praise you, Lord, for Matthew,
>>whose gospel words declare
>
>that, worldly gain forsaking,
>>your path of life we share.
>
>From all unrighteous mammon,
>>O raise our eyes anew,
>
>that we, whate'er our station
>>may rise and follow you.

*Saint Luke     October 18*
>For Luke, beloved physician,
>>all praise, whose Gospel shows
>
>the healer of the nations,
>>the one who shares our woes.
>
>Your wine and oil, O Savior,
>>upon our spirits pour,
>
>and with true balm of Gilead
>>anoint us evermore.

*Saint James of Jerusalem     October 23*
>Praise for the Lord's own brother,
>>James of Jerusalem;
>he saw the risen Savior
>>and placed his faith in him.
>Presiding at the council
>>that set the Gentiles free,
>he welcomed them as kindred
>>on equal terms to be.

*Saint Simon and Saint Jude     October 28*
>Praise, Lord, for your apostles,
>>Saint Simon and Saint Jude.
>One love, one hope, impelled them
>>to tread the way, renewed.
>May we with zeal as earnest
>>the faith of Christ maintain,
>be bound in love together,
>>and life eternal gain.

*All Saints' Day     November 1*
>Apostles, prophets, martyrs,
>>and all the noble throng
>who wear the spotless raiment
>>and raise the ceaseless song:
>for them and those whose witness
>>is only known to you—
>by walking in their footsteps
>>we give you praise anew.

Then let us praise the Father
    and worship God the Son
and sing to God the Spirit,
    eternal Three in One,
till all the ransomed number
    who stand before the throne
ascribe all power and glory
    and praise to God alone.

Horatio Bolton Nelson (1823–1913); ver. *Hymnal 1982*

## 233, 234

The eternal gifts of Christ the King,
the apostles' glorious deeds we sing,
and all, with hearts of gladness, raise
due hymns of thankful love and praise.

The princes of the Church are they,
triumphant leaders in the fray,
in heaven's hall a victor band,
true lights that lighten every land.

Theirs is the steadfast faith of saints,
the hope that never yields nor faints;
the perfect love of Christ they know:
these lay the prince of this world low.

In them the Father's glory shone,
in them the Spirit's will was done,
the Son himself exults in them;
joy fills the new Jerusalem.

Ambrose of Milan (340–397); ver. *Hymnal 1940*, alt.

**235**

Come sing, ye choirs exultant,
    those messengers of God,
through whom the living Gospels
    came sounding all abroad!
Whose voice proclaimed salvation
    that poured upon the night,
and drove away the shadows,
    and filled the world with light.

In one harmonious witness
    the chosen four combine,
while each his own commission
    fulfills in every line;
as, in the prophet's vision
    from out the amber flame
in mystic form and image
    four living creatures came.

Foursquare on this foundation
    the Church of Christ remains,
a house to stand unshaken
    by floods or winds or rains.
How blest this habitation
    of gospel liberty,
where with a holy people
    God dwells in Unity.

Latin, 12th cent.; tr. Jackson Mason (1833–1889), alt.

## 236

King of the martyrs' noble band,
crown of the true of every land,
strength of the pilgrim on the way,
beacon by night and cloud by day:

hear us as now we celebrate
faith undeterred by cruel hate;
hear and forgive us, sinners who
are burdened by the wrong we do.

Dying, through thee they overcame;
living, were faithful to thy Name.
Turn our rebellious hearts, and thus
win a like victory in us.

Glory to God the Father be;
glory to Christ, who set us free;
and to the Spirit, living flame,
glory unceasing we proclaim.

Latin; tr. John Webster Grant (b. 1919), alt.

## 237

Let us now our voices raise,
    wake the day with gladness;
God himself to joy and praise
    turns our human sadness;

joy that martyrs won their crown,
    opened heaven's portal,
when they laid the mortal down
    for the life immortal.

Never flinched they from the flame,
    from the torment never;
vain the tyrant's sharpest aim,
    vain each fierce endeavor:
for by faith they saw the land
    decked in all its glory,
where triumphant now they stand
    with the victor's story.

Up and follow, Christians all:
    press through toil and sorrow;
turn from fear, and heed the call
    to a glorious morrow!
Who will venture on the strife;
    who will first begin it?
Who will grasp the land of Life?
    Christians, up and win it!

Joseph the Hymnographer (9th cent.); tr. John Mason Neale (1818–1866), alt.

## 238, 239

Blessèd feasts of blessèd martyrs,
    holy women, holy men,
with affection's recollections
    greet we your return again.
Worthy deeds they wrought, and wonders,
    worthy of the Name they bore;
we, with meetest praise and sweetest,
    honor them for evermore.

Faith prevailing, hope unfailing,
    loving Christ with single heart,
thus they, glorious and victorious,
    bravely bore the martyr's part,
by contempt of every anguish,
    by unyielding battle done;
victors at the last, they triumph,
    with the host of angels one.

Therefore, ye that reign in glory,
    fellow-heirs with Christ on high,
join to ours your supplication
    when before him we draw nigh,
praying that, this life completed,
    all its fleeting moments past,
by his grace we may be worthy
    of eternal bliss at last.

Latin, 12th cent.; tr. John Mason Neale (1818–1866), alt.

## 240, 241

Hearken to the anthem glorious
   of the martyrs robed in white;
they, like Christ, in death victorious
   dwell forever in the light.

Living, they proclaimed salvation,
   heaven-endowed with grace and power;
and they died in imitation
   of their Savior's final hour.

Christ, for cruel traitors pleading,
   triumphed in his parting breath
o'er all miracles preceding
   his inestimable death.

Take from him what ye will give him,
   of his fullness grace for grace;
strive to think him, speak him, live him,
   till you find him face to face.

Christopher Smart (1722–1771), alt.

## 242

How oft, O Lord, thy face hath shone
   on doubting souls whose wills were true!
Thou Christ of Peter and of John,
   thou art the Christ of Thomas too.

He loved thee well, and firmly said,
   "Come, let us go, and die with him";
yet when thine Easter-news was spread,
   mid all its light his faith was dim.

His brethren's word he would not take,
   but craved to touch those hands of thine;
when thou didst thine appearance make,
   he saw, and hailed his Lord Divine.

He saw thee risen; at once he rose
   to full belief's unclouded height;
and still through his confession flows
   to Christian souls thy life and light.

O Savior, make thy presence known
   to all who doubt thy Word and thee;
and teach us in that Word alone
   to find the truth that sets us free.

William Bright (1824–1901), alt.

## 243

When Stephen, full of power and grace,
   went forth throughout the land,
he bore no shield before his face,
   no weapon in his hand;
but only in his heart a flame
   and on his lips a sword
wherewith he smote and overcame
   the foemen of the Lord.

When Stephen preached against the laws
    and by those laws was tried,
he had no friend to plead his cause,
    no spokesman at his side;
but only in his heart a flame
    and on his eyes a light
wherewith God's daybreak to proclaim
    and rend the veils of night.

When Stephen, young and doomed to die,
    fell crushed beneath the stones,
he had no curse nor vengeful cry
    for those who broke his bones;
but only in his heart a flame
    and on his lips a prayer
that God, in sweet forgiveness' name,
    should understand and spare.

Let me, O Lord, thy cause defend,
    a knight without a sword;
no shield I ask, no faithful friend,
    no vengeance, no reward;
but only in my heart a flame
    and in my soul a dream,
so that the stones of earthly shame
    a jeweled crown may seem.

Jan Struther (1901–1953), alt.

## 244

Come, pure hearts, in joyful measure
sing of those who spread the treasure
   in the holy Gospels shrined;
blessed tidings of salvation,
peace on earth their proclamation,
   love from God to lost mankind.

See the rivers four that gladden,
with their streams, the better Eden
   planted by our Lord most dear;
Christ the fountain, these the waters;
drink, O Zion's sons and daughters,
   drink, and find salvation here.

O that we, thy truth confessing,
and thy holy word possessing,
   Jesus may thy love adore;
unto thee our voices raising,
thee with all thy ransomed praising,
   ever and for evermore.

Latin, 12th cent.; tr. *Hymns Ancient and Modern*, 1861, after Robert Campbell (1814–1868), alt.

# 245

Praise God for John, evangelist,
  who bore the Spirit's sword,
whose words reflect, like eagles' wings,
  the glory of our Lord.
Your brightness, O eternal Word,
  Apostle John unfurled,
the fullness of your grace and truth
  for us and all the world.

Your great I AM's Saint John records,
  signs of your grace divine:
"I am the way, the truth, the life;
  the light; the living vine;
your soul's true bread; thirst-quenching stream.
  All these I am, and more:
the faithful shepherd of the flock,
  the sheepfold's only door."

O Word made flesh, your deeds and words
  refresh our hearts like dew.
Our thanks we raise that all John wrote
  bears witness, Lord, to you.
We praise you that John's voice still lives
  your glory to proclaim
whereby your Spirit gives us life,
  the faith to bear your Name.

F. Samuel Janzow (b. 1913)

## 246

In Bethlehem a newborn boy
was hailed with songs of praise and joy.
Then warning came of danger near:
King Herod's troops would soon appear.

The soldiers sought the child in vain:
not yet was he to share our pain.
But down the ages rings the cry
of those who saw their children die.

Still rage the fires of hate today,
and innocents the price must pay,
while aching hearts in every land
cry out "We cannot understand!"

Lord Jesus, through our night of loss
shines out the wonder of your cross,
the love that cannot cease to bear
our human anguish everywhere.

May that great love our lives control
and conquer hate in every soul,
till, pledged to build and not destroy,
we share your pain and find your joy.

Rosamond E. Herklots (1905–1987)

## 247

> *Lully, lullay, thou little tiny child,*
> *bye-bye, lully lullay.*

O sisters, too,
how may we do
   for to preserve this day
this poor youngling
for whom we sing
   bye-bye, lully lullay?

Herod the King,
in his raging
   charged he hath this day
his men of might,
in his own sight,
   all young children to slay.

That woe is me,
poor child for thee!
   And every morn and day,
for thy parting
nor say nor sing
   bye-bye, lully lullay?

> *Lully, lullay, thou little tiny child,*
> *bye-bye, lully lullay.*

Coventry carol, 15th cent.

## 248, 249

To the Name of our salvation
 laud and honor let us pay,
which for many a generation
 hid in God's foreknowledge lay;
but with holy exultation
 we may sing aloud today.

Jesus is the Name we treasure;
 Name beyond what words can tell;
Name of gladness, Name of pleasure,
 ear and heart delighting well;
Name of sweetness, passing measure,
 saving us from sin and hell.

'Tis the Name that whoso preacheth
 speaks like music to the ear;
who in prayer this Name beseecheth
 sweetest comfort findeth near;
who its perfect wisdom reacheth,
 heavenly joy possesseth here.

Therefore we, in love adoring,
 this most blessèd Name revere,
holy Jesus, thee imploring
 so to write it in us here
that hereafter, heavenward soaring,
 we may sing with angels there.

Latin, 15th cent.; tr. *Hymns Ancient and Modern*, 1861

## 250

Now greet the swiftly changing year
  with joy and penitence sincere;
rejoice, rejoice, with thanks embrace
  another year of grace.

For Jesus came to wage sin's war;
  this Name of names for us he bore;
rejoice, rejoice, with thanks embrace
  another year of grace.

His love abundant far exceeds
  the volume of a whole year's needs;
rejoice, rejoice, with thanks embrace
  another year of grace.

With such a Lord to lead our way
  in hazard and prosperity,
what need we fear in earth or space
  in this new year of grace?

"All glory be to God on high
  and peace on earth," the angels cry;
rejoice, rejoice, with thanks embrace
  another year of grace.

Slovak, 17th cent.; tr. Jaroslav J. Vajda (b. 1919), alt.

## 251

O God, whom neither time nor space
    can limit, hold, or bind,
look down from heaven, thy dwelling-place,
    with love for humankind.

Another year its course has run;
    thy loving care renew:
forgive the ill that we have done,
    the good we failed to do.

In doubt or danger, all our days,
    be near to guard us still;
let all our thoughts and all our ways
    be governed by thy will.

O help us here on earth to live
    from selfish passions free;
to us at last in mercy give
    eternal life with thee.

Horace Smith (1836–1922) and others

## 252

Jesus! Name of wondrous love!
Name all other names above!
Unto which must every knee
bow in deep humility.

Jesus! Name decreed of old,
to the maiden mother told,
kneeling in her lowly cell,
by the angel Gabriel.

Jesus! Name of priceless worth
to the fallen of the earth,
for the promise that it gave,
"Jesus shall his people save."

Jesus! Name of mercy mild,
given to the holy child
when the cup of human woe
first he tasted here below.

Jesus! only Name that's given
under all the mighty heaven,
whereby those to sin enslaved,
burst their fetters and are saved.

Jesus! Name of wondrous love!
Human Name of God above;
pleading only this we flee,
helpless, O our God, to thee.

William Walsham How (1823–1897), alt.

## 253

Give us the wings of faith to rise
    within the veil, and see
the saints above, how great their joys,
    how bright their glories be.

We ask them whence their victory came;
    they, with united breath,
ascribe their conquest to the Lamb,
    their triumph to his death.

They marked the footsteps that he trod,
    his zeal inspired their quest,
and following their incarnate God,
    they reached the promised rest.

Our glorious Leader claims our praise
    for his own pattern given;
while the long cloud of witnesses
    show the same path to heaven.

Isaac Watts (1674–1748); alt.

## 254

You are the Christ, O Lord,
 the Son of God most high!
For ever be adored
 that Name in earth and sky,
in which, though mortal strength may fail,
 the saints of God at last prevail!

Oh! Peter was most blest
 with blessedness unpriced,
who, taught of God, confessed
 the Godhead in the Christ!
For of your Church, Lord, you made known
 this saint a true foundation-stone.

William Walsham How (1823–1897), alt.

## 255

We sing the glorious conquest
 before Damascus' gate,
when Saul, the church's spoiler
 came spreading fear and hate.
God's light shone down from heaven
 and broke across the path.
His presence pierced and blinded
 the zealot in his wrath.

O Voice that spoke within him;
 O strong, reproving Word;
O Love that sought and held him
 a prisoner of his Lord;
help us to know your kingship
 that we, in every hour,
in all that may confront us,
 will trust your hidden power.

Your grace, by ways mysterious,
 our sinful wrath can bind,
and in those least expected
 true servants you can find.
In us you seek disciples
 to share your cross and crown
and give you final service
 in glory at your throne.

John Ellerton (1826–1893), alt.

## 256

A light from heaven shone around,
 and in that light a voice was heard.
Then Saul fell blinded to the ground
 and cried aloud, "Who are you, Lord?"

It was the blessed Son come down
 to save him from his fearful ways
and free him from the bonds of sin,
 a sinner saved by Jesus' grace.

Saint Paul was changed by God's free love.
    The scales fell from his eyes, he saw
the love of God, the cosmos move
    in time with grace, beyond the law.

Renew us with your love, O Lord.
    Your new creation let us be;
redeemed for ever and restored,
    with Paul's new vision, let us see.

Gracia Grindal (b. 1943), alt.

**257**

O Zion, open wide thy gates,
    let symbols disappear;
a priest and victim, both in one,
    the Truth himself, is here.

Aware of hidden deity,
    the lowly virgin brings
her newborn babe, with two young doves,
    her humble offerings.

The aged Simeon sees at last
    his Lord, so long desired,
and Anna welcomes Israel's hope,
    with holy rapture fired.

But silent knelt the mother blest
    of the yet silent Word,

and pondering all things in her heart,
  with speechless praise adored.

All glory to the Father be,
  all glory to the Son,
all glory, Holy Ghost, to thee,
  while endless ages run.

Jean Baptiste de Santeüil (1630–1697); tr. Edward Caswall (1814–1878), alt.

## 258

Virgin-born, we bow before thee:
blessèd was the womb that bore thee;
Mary, Mother meek and mild,
blessèd was she in her child.
Blessèd was the breast that fed thee;
Blessèd was the hand that led thee;
blessèd was the parent's eye
that watched thy slumbering infancy.

Blessèd she by all creation,
who brought forth the world's salvation,
and blessèd they, for ever blest,
who love thee most and serve thee best.
Virgin-born, we bow before thee;
blessèd was the womb that bore thee;
Mary, Mother meek and mild,
blessèd was she in her Child.

Reginald Heber (1783–1826)

**259**

Hail to the Lord who comes,
    comes to his temple gate;
not with his angel host,
    not in his kingly state;
no shouts proclaim him nigh,
    no crowds his coming wait;

but, borne upon the throne
    of Mary's gentle breast,
watched by her duteous love,
    in her fond arms at rest,
thus to his Father's house
    he comes, the heavenly guest.

There Joseph at her side
    in reverent wonder stands;
and, filled with holy joy,
    old Simeon in his hands
takes up the promised child,
    the glory of all lands.

O Light of all the earth,
    thy children wait for thee!
Come to thy temples here,
    that we, from sin set free,
before thy Father's face
    may all presented be!

John Ellerton (1826–1893), alt.

## 260

Come now, and praise the humble saint
    of David's house and line,
the carpenter whose life fulfilled
    our gracious God's design.

The Architect's high miracles
    he saw, and what was done,
the Virgin's spouse, the guardian of
    great David's greater Son.

For him there was no glory here,
    no crown or martyr's fame;
for him there was the patient life
    of faith and humble name.

But now within the Father's grace
    where saints and angels throng,
beside his spouse, before the Son,
    he joins the heavenly song.

George W. Williams (b. 1922)

## 261, 262

By the Creator, Joseph was appointed
spouse of the Virgin, guardian of the Incarnate;
he by his caring ministered to Jesus,
    source of salvation.

Christ in whose presence hosts of hell must tremble,
Ruler of all things, Lord of earth and heaven,
Monarch of monarchs, to his earthly father
    freely was subject.

To God eternal be all praise and glory,
who to Saint Joseph gave supernal honor;
grant that we also may like him be faithful
  in our obedience.

Hieronimo Casanate (d. 1700); tr. *Hymnal 1982*

## 263, 264

The Word whom earth and sea and sky
adore and laud and magnify,
whose might they show, whose praise they tell,
in Mary's body deigned to dwell.

To Mary the Archangel came
and God's new message did proclaim,
"Hail, Mary, you shall bear a son
who shall be called the Holy One."

Blest in the message Gabriel brought,
blest in the work the Spirit wrought,
most blest to bring to human birth
the long-desired of all the earth.

Lord Jesus, Virgin-born, to thee
eternal praise and glory be,
whom with the Father we adore
and Holy Spirit evermore.

Latin, 7th–8th cent.; sts. 1 and 3–4, tr. *Hymns Ancient and Modern*, 1861, after John Mason Neale (1818–1866); st. 2, tr. Anne K. LeCroy (b. 1930)

## 265

The angel Gabriel from heaven came,
his wings as drifted snow, his eyes as flame;
    "All hail," said he, "thou lowly maiden Mary,
    most highly favored lady," Gloria!

"For know a blessèd Mother thou shalt be,
all generations laud and honor thee,
    thy Son shall be Emmanuel, by seers foretold,
    most highly favored lady," Gloria!

Then gentle Mary meekly bowed her head,
"To me be as it pleaseth God," she said,
    "my soul shall laud and magnify his holy Name."
    Most highly favored lady, Gloria!

Of her, Emmanuel, the Christ, was born
in Bethlehem, all on a Christmas morn,
    and Christian folk throughout the world
        will ever say–
    "Most highly favored lady," Gloria!

Basque carol; para. Sabine Baring-Gould (1834–1924)

# 266

*Burden: Nova, nova.*
*Ave fit ex Eva.*

Gabriel of high degree,
he was sent from the Trinity,
to Nazareth in Galilee.
Nova, nova.

*Burden*

He met a maiden in that place;
there he knelt down before her face
and said, "Hail, Mary, full of grace."
Nova, nova.

*Burden*

When the maiden heard his song,
she was filled with confusion strong
and feared that she had done a wrong.
Nova, nova.

*Burden*

Said the angel, "Have no fear;
by conception without compare
the Savior Jesus shall you bear."
Nova, nova.

*Burden*

"There are yet but six months gone
since Elizabeth conceivèd John,
to be the herald of God's Son."
Nova, nova.

*Burden*

Said the maiden, "Verily,
I am your servant right truly,
the handmaid of the Lord now see."
Nova, nova.

*Burden*

Hunterian MS. 83, 15th cent.; adapt. Carl P. Daw, Jr. (b. 1944)

*The following burden and final line may be used with each stanza:
"Tidings! Tidings! Promise of salvation!" and "Tidings! Tidings!"*

## 267

Praise we the Lord this day,
    this day so long foretold,
whose promise shone with cheering ray
    on waiting saints of old.

The prophet gave the sign
    for faithful folk to read:
a virgin born of David's line
    shall bear the promised seed.

Ask not how this should be,
    but worship and adore,
like her whom heaven's Majesty
    came down to shadow o'er.

She meekly bowed her head
 to hear the gracious word,
Mary, the pure and lowly maid,
 the favored of the Lord.
Most blest shall be her name
 in all the Church on earth,
through whom that wondrous mercy came,
 the incarnate Savior's birth.

Anon., *Hymns for Festivals and Saints' Days of the Church of England*, 1846, alt.

## 268, 269

Ye who claim the faith of Jesus,
 sing the wonders that were done
when the love of God the Father
 over sin the victory won,
when he made the Virgin Mary
 mother of his only Son.

*Hail Mary, full of grace.* \*

Blessèd were the chosen people
 out of whom the Lord did come;
blessèd was the land of promise
 fashioned for his earthly home;
but more blessed far the mother,
 she who bore him in her womb.

*Refrain*

Therefore let all faithful people
    sing the honor of her name;
let the Church, in her foreshadowed,
    part in her thanksgiving claim;
what Christ's mother sang in gladness
    let Christ's people sing the same:

*Refrain*

"Magnify, my soul, God's greatness;
    in my Savior I rejoice;
all the ages call me blessed,
    in his praise I lift my voice;
he has cast down all the mighty,
    and the lowly are his choice."

*Refrain*

\*Refrain used in Hymn 269.

Sts. 1–3, Vincent Stucky Stratton Coles (1845–1929), alt.; st. 4, F. Bland Tucker (1895–1984) metrical *Magnificat*

## 270

Gabriel's message does away
Satan's curse and Satan's sway,
out of darkness brings our Day:

> *so, behold,*
> *all the gates of heaven unfold.*

He that comes despised shall reign;
he that cannot die, be slain;
death by death its death shall gain:

*Refrain*

Weakness shall the strong confound;
by the hands, in grave clothes wound,
Adam's chains shall be unbound:

*Refrain*

Art by art shall be assailed;
to the cross shall Life be nailed;
from the grave shall hope be hailed:

*Refrain*

*Piae Cantiones*, 1582; tr. John Mason Neale (1818–1866)

## 271, 272

The great forerunner of the morn,
the herald of the Word, is born;
and faithful hearts shall never fail
with thanks and praise his light to hail.

With heavenly message Gabriel came,
that John should be that herald's name,
and with prophetic utterance told
his actions great and manifold.

John, still unborn, yet gave aright
his witness to the coming light;
and Christ, the Sun of all the earth,
fulfilled that witness at his birth.

His mighty deeds exalt his fame
to greater than a prophet's name;

of woman born shall never be
a greater prophet than was he.

To God the Father, God the Son,
and God the Spirit, Three in One,
praise, honor, might, and glory be
from age to age eternally.

The Venerable Bede (673–735); tr. John Mason Neale (1818–1866), alt.

## 273, 274

Two stalwart trees both rooted
in faith and holy love,
by hope of God united
they reach to heaven above.

One on a cross is martyred,
one by the sword is slain;
both triumph in their dying,
both glorious sainthood gain.

The words of Paul assure us
of Christ's redeeming word;
the works of Peter show us
how we may serve the Lord.

All glory to the Father,
all glory to the Son,
who with the Holy Spirit,
now reign, blest Three in One.

Latin; tr. Anne K. LeCroy (b. 1930)

## 275

Hark! the sound of holy voices,
    chanting at the crystal sea,
Alleluia, alleluia,
    alleluia! Lord, to thee!
Multitude which none can number
    like the stars in glory stands,
clothed in white apparel, holding
    palms of victory in their hands.

Patriarch, and holy prophet,
    who prepared the way for Christ,
king, apostle, saint, confessor,
    martyr and evangelist,
saintly maiden, godly matron,
    widows who have watched to prayer,
joined in holy concert, singing
    to the Lord of all, are there.

Marching with thy cross, their banner,
    they have triumphed following
thee, the Captain of salvation,
    thee, their Savior and their King.
Gladly, Lord, with thee they suffered;
    gladly, Lord, with thee they died;
and by death to life immortal
    they were born and glorified.

Now they reign in heavenly glory,
    now they walk in golden light,
now they drink, as from a river,
    holy bliss and infinite;
love and peace they taste for ever,
    and all truth and knowledge see
in the beatific vision
    of the blessèd Trinity.

Christopher Wordsworth (1807–1885)

## 276

For thy blest saints, a noble throng,
    who fell by fire and sword,
or early died or flourished long,
    we praise thy Name, O Lord.

For James who left his father's side,
    not lingering by the sea:
he heard what could not be denied,
    thy summons, "Follow me";

he stood with thee beside the dead;
    he climbed the mount with thee,
and saw the glory round thy head,
    one of thy chosen three;

he knelt beneath the olive shade;
    he drank thy cup of pain;
and slain by Herod's flashing blade,
    he saw thy face again.

Lord, may we learn to drink thy cup,
    and meek and firm be found,
when thou shalt come to take us up
    where thine elect are crowned.

Cecil Frances Alexander (1823–1895), alt.

**277**

Sing of Mary, pure and lowly,
    virgin-mother undefiled;
sing of God's own Son most holy,
    who became her little child.
Fairest child of fairest mother,
    God the Lord who came to earth,
Word made flesh, our very brother,
    takes our nature by his birth.

Sing of Jesus, son of Mary,
    in the home at Nazareth,
toil and labor cannot weary
    love enduring unto death.
Constant was the love he gave her,
    though he went forth from her side,
forth to preach, and heal, and suffer,
    till on Calvary he died.

Glory be to God the Father;
    glory be to God the Son;
glory be to God the Spirit;
    glory to the Three in One.

From the heart of blessed Mary,
    from all saints the song ascends,
and the Church the strain re-echoes
    unto earth's remotest ends.

Roland Ford Palmer (b. 1891)

## 278

Sing we of the blessèd Mother
    who received the angel's word,
and obedient to the summons
    bore in love the infant Lord;
sing we of the joys of Mary
    at whose breast the child was fed
who is Son of God eternal
    and the everlasting Bread.

Sing we, too, of Mary's sorrows,
    of the sword that pierced her through,
when beneath the cross of Jesus
    she his weight of suffering knew,
looked upon her Son and Savior
    reigning from the awful tree,
saw the price of our redemption
    paid to set the sinner free.

Sing again the joys of Mary
    when she saw the risen Lord,
and in prayer with Christ's apostles,
    waited on his promised word;

from on high the blazing glory
   of the Spirit's presence came,
heavenly breath of God's own being,
   manifest in wind and flame.

Sing the chiefest joy of Mary
   when on earth her work was done,
and the Lord of all creation
   brought her to his heavenly home;
where, raised high with saints and angels,
   in Jerusalem above,
she beholds her son and Savior
   reigning as the Lord of love.

George B. Tims (b. 1910), alt.

**279**

For thy dear saints, O Lord,
   who strove in thee to live,
who followed thee, obeyed, adored,
   our grateful hymn receive.

They all in life and death,
   with thee their Lord in view,
learned from thy Holy Spirit's breath
   to suffer and to do.

Thine earthly members fit
   to join thy saints above,
in one communion ever knit,
   one fellowship of love.

Jesus, thy Name we bless,
    and humbly pray that we
may follow them in holiness,
    who lived and died for thee.

Richard Mant (1776–1848), alt.

## 280

God of saints, to whom the number
    of the starry host is known:
many saints by earth forgotten
    live for ever round your throne.

In the roll of your apostles
    stands the name Bartholomew,
for this faithful saint we offer,
    year by year, our thanks to you.

All his faith and prayer and patience,
    all his toiling and his strife,
all are veiled from us, but written
    in the Lamb's great book of life.

There are named the blessèd faithful
    of the new Jerusalem.
When Christ comes again in glory,
    number us, we pray, with them.

John Ellerton (1826–1893), alt.

## 281

He sat to watch o'er customs paid,
a man of scorned and hardening trade,
alike the symbol and the tool
of foreign master's hated rule.

But grace within his heart had stirred,
there needed but the timely word;
it came, true Lord of souls, from thee,
that royal summons, "Follow me."

Enough, when thou wast passing by,
to hear thy voice, to meet thine eye;
he rose, responsive to the call,
and left his task, his gains, his all.

O wise exchange! with these to part,
and lay up treasures in the heart;
let them of Matthew's wealth partake,
who yield up all for Jesus' sake.

William Bright (1824–1901), alt.

## 282, 283

> Christ, the fair glory of the holy angels,
> maker of all things, ruler of all nations,
> grant of thy mercy unto us thy servants
> >  steps up to heaven.
>
> Send thine archangel Michael to our succor;
> peacemaker blessèd, may he banish from us
> striving and hatred, so that for the peaceful
> > all things may prosper.
>
> Send thine archangel Gabriel, the mighty;
> herald of heaven, may he, from us mortals,
> drive every evil, watching o'er the temples
> > where thou art worshiped.
>
> Send from the heavens Raphael thine archangel,
> health-bringer blessèd, aiding every sufferer,
> that, in thy service, he may wisely guide us,
> > healing and blessing.
>
> May the blest mother of our God and Savior,
> may the celestial company of angels,
> may the assembly of the saints in heaven
> > help us to praise thee.
>
> Father Almighty, Son, and Holy Spirit,
> God ever blessèd, hear our thankful praises;
> thine is the glory which from all creation
> > ever ascendeth.

Rabanus Maurus (776–856); ver. *Hymnal 1940*, alt.

## 284

O ye immortal throng
   of angels round the throne,
join with our earthbound song
    to make the Savior known.
    On earth ye knew
      his wondrous grace,
      his beauteous face
    in heaven ye view.

Ye saw the heaven-born child
   in human flesh arrayed,
so innocent and mild
    while in the manger laid.
    "Glory to God
      and peace on earth,"
      for such a birth
    ye sang aloud.

Ye in the wilderness
   beheld the Tempter spoiled,
unmasked in every dress,
    in every combat foiled.
    With great delight
      ye crowned his head
      when Satan fled
    the Savior's might.

In dark Gethsemane
    the night before he died,
ye saw his agony,
    ye heard the plaint he cried.
    When hope was dim,
        and pain and grief
        beyond belief,
    ye tended him.

Ye thronged to Calvary
    and pressed with sad desire
that aweful sight to see—
    the Lord of life expire.
    E'en angel eyes
        slow tears did shed:
        ye mourned the dead
    in sad surprise.

Around his sacred tomb
    a willing watch ye kept;
till out from death's vast room,
    up from the grave, he leapt.
    Ye rolled the stone,
        and all adored
        your rising Lord
    with joy unknown.

When all arrayed in light
	the shining conqueror rode,
ye hailed his wondrous flight
	up to the throne of God.
	And waved around
		your golden wings,
		and struck your strings
	of sweetest sound.

The joyous notes pursue
	and louder anthems raise;
while mortals sing with you
	their own Redeemer's praise.
	With equal flame
		and equal art,
		do thou my heart
	extol his name.

Sts. 1–3 and 5–8, Philip Doddridge (1702–1751), alt.; st. 4, Charles P. Price (b. 1920)

## 285

What thanks and praise to thee we owe,
	eternal God and Word divine,
for Luke, thy saint, through whom we know
	so many gracious words of thine.

O happy saint! his sacred page,
	so rich in words of truth and love,
pours on the Church from age to age
	the healing unction from above.

Historian of the Savior's life,
 the great apostle's chosen friend,
through weary years of toil and strife
 was still found faithful to the end.

So grant us, Lord, like him to live,
 beloved on earth, approved by thee,
till thou at last the summons give,
 and we, with him, thy face shall see.

William Dalrymple Maclagan (1826–1910), alt.

## 286

Who are these like stars appearing,
 these, before God's throne who stand?
Each a golden crown is wearing;
 who are all this glorious band?
  Alleluia! hark, they sing,
   praising loud their heavenly King.

Who are these of dazzling brightness,
 these in God's own truth arrayed,
clad in robes of purest whiteness,
 robes whose luster ne'er shall fade,
  ne'er be touched by time's rude hand?
   Whence comes all this glorious band?

These are they who have contended
 for their Savior's honor long,
wrestling on till life was ended,
 following not the sinful throng;

> these, who well the fight sustained,
> triumph by the Lamb have gained.

These are they whose hearts were riven,
   sore with woe and anguish tried,
who in prayer full oft have striven
   with the God they glorified;
> now, their painful conflict o'er,
> God has bid them weep no more.

These, like priests, have watched and waited,
   offering up to Christ their will,
soul and body consecrated,
   day and night they serve him still.
> Now in God's most holy place,
> blest they stand before his face.

Theobald Heinrich Schenck (1656–1727); tr. Frances Elizabeth Cox (1812–1897), alt.

## 287

For all the saints, who from their labors rest,
who thee by faith before the world confessed,
thy Name, O Jesus, be for ever blessed.
   Alleluia, alleluia!

Thou wast their rock, their fortress, and their might:
thou, Lord, their Captain in the well-fought fight;
thou, in the darkness drear, the one true Light.
   Alleluia, alleluia!

O may thy soldiers, faithful, true, and bold,
fight as the saints who nobly fought of old,
and win, with them, the victor's crown of gold.
   Alleluia, alleluia!

O blest communion, fellowship divine!
We feebly struggle, they in glory shine;
yet all are one in thee, for all are thine.
   Alleluia, alleluia!

And when the strife is fierce, the warfare long,
steals on the ear the distant triumph song,
and hearts are brave again, and arms are strong.
   Alleluia, alleluia!

The golden evening brightens in the west;
soon, soon to faithful warriors cometh rest;
sweet is the calm of paradise the blest.
   Alleluia, alleluia!

But lo! there breaks a yet more glorious day;
the saints triumphant rise in bright array;
the King of glory passes on his way.
   Alleluia, alleluia!

From earth's wide bounds, from ocean's farthest coast,
through gates of pearl streams in the countless host
singing to Father, Son, and Holy Ghost,
   Alleluia, alleluia!

William Walsham How (1823–1897)

**288**

Praise to God, immortal praise,
for the love that crowns our days;
bounteous source of every joy,
let thy praise our tongues employ:
all to thee, our God, we owe,
source whence all our blessings flow.

All the plenty summer pours;
autumn's rich o'erflowing stores;
flocks that whiten all the plain;
yellow sheaves of ripened grain:
Lord, for these our souls shall raise
grateful vows and solemn praise.

As thy prospering hand hath blessed,
may we give thee of our best;
and by deeds of kindly love
for thy mercies grateful prove;
singing thus through all our days
praise to God, immortal praise.

Anna Laetitia Barbauld (1743–1825)

## 289

Our Father, by whose servants
 our house was built of old,
whose hand hath crowned her children
 with blessings manifold,
for thine unfailing mercies
 far-strewn along our way,
with all who passed before us,
 we praise thy Name today.

The changeful years unresting
 their silent course have sped,
new comrades ever bringing
 in comrades' steps to tread:
and some are long forgotten,
 long spent their hopes and fears;
safe rest they in thy keeping,
 who changest not with years.

They reap not where they labored;
 we reap what they have sown:
our harvest may be garnered
 by ages yet unknown.
The days of old have dowered us
 with gifts beyond all praise:
our Father, make us faithful
 to serve the coming days.

George Wallace Briggs (1875–1959)

## 290

Come, ye thankful people, come,
raise the song of harvest-home:
all is safely gathered in,
ere the winter storms begin;
God, our Maker, doth provide
for our wants to be supplied;
come to God's own temple, come,
raise the song of harvest-home.

All the world is God's own field,
fruit unto his praise to yield;
wheat and tares together sown,
unto joy or sorrow grown:
first the blade, and then the ear,
then the full corn shall appear:
grant, O harvest Lord, that we
wholesome grain and pure may be.

For the Lord our God shall come,
and shall take his harvest home;
from his field shall in that day
all offenses purge away;
give his angels charge at last
in the fire the tares to cast,
but the fruitful ears to store
in his garner evermore.

Even so, Lord, quickly come
to thy final harvest-home;
gather thou thy people in,
free from sorrow, free from sin;
there, for ever purified,
in thy presence to abide;
come, with all thine angels, come,
raise the glorious harvest-home.

Henry Alford (1810–1871), alt.

## 291

We plow the fields, and scatter
    the good seed on the land,
but it is fed and watered
    by God's almighty hand;
he sends the snow in winter,
    the warmth to swell the grain,
the breezes and the sunshine,
    and soft refreshing rain.

*All good gifts around us*
    *are sent from heaven above;*
*then thank the Lord, O thank the Lord*
    *for all his love.*

He only is the Maker
    of all things near and far;
he paints the wayside flower,
    he lights the evening star;

the winds and waves obey him,
    by him the birds are fed;
much more to us, his children,
    he gives our daily bread.

*Refrain*

We thank thee, then, O Father,
    for all things bright and good,
the seedtime and the harvest,
    our life, our health, our food:
the gifts we have to offer
    are what thy love imparts,
but chiefly thou desirest
    our humble thankful hearts.

*Refrain*

Matthias Claudius (1740–1815); tr. Jane Montgomery Campbell (1817–1878), alt.

## 292

O Jesus, crowned with all renown,
    since thou the earth hast trod,
thou reignest and by thee come down
    henceforth the gifts of God.
Thine is the health and thine the wealth
    that in our halls abound,
and thine the beauty and the joy
    with which the years are crowned.

Lord, in their change, let frost and heat,
  and winds and dews be given;
all fostering power, all influence sweet,
  breathe from the bounteous heaven.
Attemper fair with gentle air
  the sunshine and the rain,
that kindly earth with timely birth
  may yield her fruits again:

that we may feed the poor aright,
  and, gathering round thy throne,
here, in the holy angels' sight,
  repay thee of thine own:
That we may praise thee all our days,
  and with the Father's Name,
and with the Holy Spirit's gifts,
  the Savior's love proclaim.

Edward White Benson (1829–1896), alt.

## 293

I sing a song of the saints of God,
patient and brave and true,
who toiled and fought and lived and died
for the Lord they loved and knew.
And one was a doctor, and one was a queen,
and one was a shepherdess on the green:
they were all of them saints of God and I mean,
God helping, to be one too.

They loved their Lord so dear, so dear,
and his love made them strong;
and they followed the right, for Jesus' sake,
the whole of their good lives long.
And one was a soldier, and one was a priest,
and one was slain by a fierce wild beast;
and there's not any reason no, not the least,
why I shouldn't be one too.

They lived not only in ages past,
there are hundreds of thousands still,
the world is bright with the joyous saints
who love to do Jesus' will.
You can meet them in school, or in lanes, or at sea,
in church, or in trains, or in shops, or at tea,
for the saints of God are just folk like me,
and I mean to be one too.

Lesbia Scott (b. 1898), alt.

**294**

Baptized in water,
sealed by the Spirit,
cleansed by the blood of Christ our King:
heirs of salvation,
trusting his promise,
faithfully now God's praise we sing.

Baptized in water,
sealed by the Spirit,

dead in the tomb with Christ our King:
one with his rising,
freed and forgiven,
thankfully now God's praise we sing.

Baptized in water,
sealed by the Spirit,
marked with the sign of Christ our King:
born of one Father,
we are his children,
joyfully now God's praise we sing.

Michael Saward (b. 1932), alt.

## 295

Sing praise to our Creator,
 O you of Adam's race–
God's children by adoption,
 baptized into his grace.

To Jesus Christ give glory,
 God's co-eternal Son;
as members of his Body
 we live in him as one.

And praise the Holy Spirit
 poured forth upon the earth;
who sanctifies and guides us,
 made strong in our rebirth.

Mark Evans (b. 1916), alt.

## 296

We know that Christ is raised and dies no more.
Embraced by death he broke its fearful hold;
and our despair he turned to blazing joy.
    Alleluia!

We share by water in his saving death.
Reborn we share with him an Easter life
as living members of a living Christ.
    Alleluia!

The Father's splendor clothes the Son with life.
The Spirit's power shakes the Church of God.
Baptized we live with God the Three in One.
    Alleluia!

A new creation comes to life and grows
as Christ's new body takes on flesh and blood.
The universe restored and whole will sing:
    Alleluia! Amen.

John Brownlow Geyer (b. 1932), alt.

## 297

Descend, O Spirit, purging flame,
brand us this day with Jesus' Name!
Confirm our faith, consume our doubt;
sign us as Christ's, within, without.

Forbid us not this second birth;
grant unto us the greater worth!
Enlist us in your service, Lord;
baptize all nations with your Word.

Scott Francis Brenner (b. 1903), alt.

## 298

All who believe and are baptized
    shall see the Lord's salvation;
baptized into the death of Christ,
    each is a new creation.
Through Christ's redemption we shall stand
among the glorious heavenly band
    of every tribe and nation.

With one accord, O God, we pray:
    grant us thy Holy Spirit;
help us in our infirmity
    through Jesus' blood and merit.
Grant us to grow in grace each day
that as is promised here we may
    eternal life inherit.

Thomas Hansen Kingo (1634–1703); tr. George Alfred Taylor Rygh (1860–1942), alt.

## 299

Spirit of God, unleashed on earth
with rush of wind and roar of flame!
With tongues of fire saints spread good news;
earth, kindling, blazed her loud acclaim.

You came in power; the Church was born;
O Holy Spirit, come again!
From living waters raise new saints;
let new tongues hail the risen Lord.

With burning words of victory won
inspire our hearts grown cold with fear,
revive in us baptismal grace,
and fan our smoldering lives to flame.

John W. Arthur (1922–1980), alt.

## 300

Glory, love, and praise, and honor
   for our food
   now bestowed
   render we the Donor.
Bounteous God, we now confess thee:
   God, who thus
   blessest us,
   right it is to bless thee.

Thankful for our every blessing,
    let us sing
    Christ the Spring,
    never, never ceasing.
Source of all our gifts and graces,
    Christ we own;
    Christ alone
    calls for all our praises.

He dispels our sin and sadness,
    life imparts,
    cheers our hearts,
    fills with food and gladness.
Who himself for all hath given,
    us he feeds,
    us he leads
    to a feast in heaven.

Charles Wesley (1707–1788), alt.

## 301

Bread of the world, in mercy broken,
    Wine of the soul, in mercy shed,
by whom the words of life were spoken,
    and in whose death our sins are dead:
look on the heart by sorrow broken,
    look on the tears by sinners shed;
and be thy feast to us the token
    that by thy grace our souls are fed.

Reginald Heber (1783–1826)

## 302, 303

Father, we thank thee who hast planted
  thy holy Name within our hearts.
Knowledge and faith and life immortal
  Jesus thy Son to us imparts.
Thou, Lord, didst make all for thy pleasure,
  didst give us food for all our days,
giving in Christ the Bread eternal;
  thine is the power, be thine the praise.

Watch o'er thy Church, O Lord, in mercy,
  save it from evil, guard it still,
perfect it in thy love, unite it,
  cleansed and conformed unto thy will.
As grain, once scattered on the hillsides,
  was in this broken bread made one,
so from all lands thy Church be gathered
  into thy kingdom by thy Son.

Greek, ca. 110; tr. F. Bland Tucker (1895–1984), rev.

## 304

I come with joy to meet my Lord,
forgiven, loved, and free,
in awe and wonder to recall
his life laid down for me.

I come with Christians far and near
to find, as all are fed,

> the new community of love
> in Christ's communion bread.
>
> As Christ breaks bread and bids us share,
> each proud division ends.
> That love that made us makes us one,
> and strangers now are friends.
>
> And thus with joy we meet our Lord.
> His presence, always near,
> is in such friendship better known:
> we see, and praise him here.
>
> Together met, together bound,
> we'll go our different ways,
> and as his people in the world,
> we'll live and speak his praise.

Brian A. Wren (b. 1936), alt.

## 305, 306

> Come, risen Lord, and deign to be our guest;
>     nay, let us be thy guests; the feast is thine;
> thyself at thine own board make manifest
>     in thine own Sacrament of Bread and Wine.
>
> We meet, as in that upper room they met;
>     thou at the table, blessing, yet dost stand:
> "This is my Body"; so thou givest yet:
>     faith still receives the cup as from thy hand.

One body we, one Body who partake,
    one Church united in communion blest;
one Name we bear, one Bread of life we break,
    with all thy saints on earth and saints at rest.

One with each other, Lord, for one in thee,
    who art one Savior and one living Head;
then open thou our eyes, that we may see;
    be known to us in breaking of the Bread.

George Wallace Briggs (1875–1959), alt.

**307**

Lord, enthroned in heavenly splendor,
    first-begotten from the dead.
Thou alone, our strong defender,
    liftest up thy people's head.
        Alleluia! Alleluia! Alleluia!
    Jesus, true and living bread!

Here our humblest homage pay we,
    here in loving reverence bow;
here for faith's discernment pray we,
    lest we fail to know thee now.
        Alleluia! Alleluia! Alleluia!
    Thou art here, we ask not how.

Though the lowliest form doth veil thee
    as of old in Bethlehem,

here as there thine angels hail thee,
   branch and flower of Jesse's stem.
      Alleluia! Alleluia! Alleluia!
   We in worship join with them.

Paschal Lamb, thine offering, finished
   once for all when thou wast slain,
in its fullness undiminished
   shall for evermore remain.
      Alleluia! Alleluia! Alleluia!
   Cleansing us from every stain.

Life-imparting heavenly Manna,
   smitten Rock with streaming side,
heaven and earth with loud hosanna
   worship thee, the Lamb who died.
      Alleluia! Alleluia! Alleluia!
   Risen, ascended, glorified!

George Hugh Bourne (1840–1925), alt.

## 308, 309

O Food to pilgrims given,
O Bread of life from heaven,
   O Manna from on high!
We hunger; Lord, supply us,
nor thy delights deny us,
   whose hearts to thee draw nigh.

O stream of love past telling,
O purest fountain, welling
   from out the Savior's side!
We faint with thirst; revive us,
of thine abundance give us,
   and all we need provide.

O Jesus, by thee bidden,
   we here adore thee, hidden
in forms of bread and wine.
Grant when the veil is riven,
we may behold, in heaven,
   thy countenance divine.

Latin, 1661; tr. John Athelstan Laurie Riley (1858–1945), alt.

## 310, 311

O saving Victim, opening wide
   the gate of heaven to us below,
our foes press on from every side,
   thine aid supply, thy strength bestow.

All praise and thanks to thee ascend
   for evermore, blest One in Three;
O grant us life that shall not end
   in our true native land with thee.

St. Thomas Aquinas (1225?–1274); tr. Edward Caswall (1814–1878)

## 312

Strengthen for service, Lord, the hands
    that holy things have taken;
let ears that now have heard thy songs
    to clamor never waken.

Lord, may the tongues which "Holy" sang,
    keep free from all deceiving;
the eyes which saw thy love be bright,
    thy blessed hope perceiving.

The feet that tread thy hallowed courts
    from light do thou not banish;
the bodies by thy Body fed
    with thy new life replenish.

Syriac Liturgy of Malabar; tr. Charles William Humphreys (1840–1921); alt. Percy Dearmer (1867–1936)

## 313

Let thy Blood in mercy poured,
    let thy gracious Body broken,
be to me, O gracious Lord,
    of thy boundless love the token.

> *Thou didst give thyself for me,*
> *now I give myself to thee.*

Thou didst die that I might live;
   blessèd Lord, thou cam'st to save me;
all that love of God could give
   Jesus by his sorrows gave me.

*Refrain*

By the thorns that crowned thy brow,
   by the spear-wound and the nailing,
by the pain and death, I now
   claim, O Christ, thy love unfailing.

*Refrain*

Wilt thou own the gift I bring?
   All my penitence I give thee;
thou art my exalted King,
   of thy matchless love forgive me.

*Refrain*

Greek; tr. John Brownlie (1859–1925)

# 314

Humbly I adore thee, Verity unseen,
who thy glory hidest 'neath these shadows mean;
lo, to thee surrendered, my whole heart is bowed,
tranced as it beholds thee, shrined within the cloud.

Taste and touch and vision to discern thee fail;
faith, that comes by hearing, pierces through the veil.

I believe whate'er the Son of God hath told;
what the Truth hath spoken, that for truth I hold.

O memorial wondrous of the Lord's own death;
living Bread that givest all thy creatures breath,
grant my spirit ever by thy life may live,
to my taste thy sweetness never-failing give.

Jesus, whom now hidden, I by faith behold,
what my soul doth long for, that thy word foretold:
face to face thy splendor, I at last shall see,
in the glorious vision, blessed Lord, of thee.

Att. Thomas Aquinas (1225?–1274); sts. 1–3, tr. *Hymnal 1940*;
st. 4, tr. *Hymnal 1982*

## 315

Thou, who at thy first Eucharist didst pray
    that all thy Church might be for ever one,
grant us at every Eucharist to say
    with longing heart and soul, "Thy will be done."
O may we all one bread, one body be,
through this blest sacrament of unity.

For all thy Church, O Lord, we intercede;
    make thou our sad divisions soon to cease;
draw us the nearer each to each, we plead,
    by drawing all to thee, O Prince of Peace;
thus may we all one bread, one body be,
through this blest sacrament of unity.

So, Lord, at length when sacraments shall cease,
   may we be one with all thy Church above,
one with thy saints in one unbroken peace,
   one with thy saints in one unbounded love;
more blessèd still, in peace and love to be
one with the Trinity in Unity.

William Harry Turton (1856–1938)

## 316, 317

This is the hour of banquet and of song;
   this is the heavenly table spread for me;
here let me feast, and feasting, still prolong
   the brief, bright hour of fellowship with thee.

Too soon we rise; we go our several ways;
the feast, though not the love, is past and gone,
   the Bread and Wine consumed: yet all our days
thou still art here with us—our Shield and Sun.

Feast after feast thus comes and passes by,
   yet, passing, points to the glad feast above,
giving us foretaste of the festal joy,
   the Lamb's great marriage feast of bliss and love.

Horatius Bonar (1808–1889), alt.

## 318

Here, O my Lord, I see thee face to face;
  here would I touch and handle things unseen;
here grasp with firmer hand eternal grace,
  and all my weariness upon thee lean.

Here would I feed upon the Bread of God;
  here drink with thee the royal Wine of heaven;
here would I lay aside each earthly load,
  here taste afresh the calm of sin forgiven.

I have no help but thine; nor do I need
  another arm save thine to lean upon;
it is enough, my Lord, enough indeed;
  my strength is in thy might, thy might alone.

Mine is the sin, but thine the righteousness;
  mine is the guilt, but thine the cleansing Blood.
Here is my robe, my refuge, and my peace;
  thy Blood, thy righteousness, O Lord, my God.

Horatius Bonar (1808–1889)

# 319

You, Lord, we praise in songs of celebration
for this feast of our salvation.
Here at your table every life you nourish;
by your grace we all may flourish.
> *Kyrie eleison.*

In the light of your Incarnation
> all creation
>> knows the love of God,

and in you finds release
that we all might live in peace.
> *Kyrie eleison.*

You, Lord, in our stead to the grave descended
when by sin our life was ended.
No greater love than this to you could bind us;
daily still your mercies find us.
> *Kyrie eleison.*

Bind our hearts as one we implore you,
> who adore you
>> and confess your Name.

Thus may we ever be
yours in peace and unity.
> *Kyrie eleison.*

Russell Schulz-Widmar (b. 1944); based on German folk hymn
and Martin Luther (1483–1546)

## 320

Zion, praise thy Savior, singing
hymns with exultation ringing,
    praise thy King and Shepherd true.
Honor Christ, thy voice upraising,
who surpasseth all thy praising;
    never canst thou reach his due.

Let the Bread, life-giving, living,
be our theme of glad thanksgiving,
    now in truth before thee set;
as of old the Lord provided
when the twelve, divinely guided,
    at the holy table met.

What he did, at supper seated,
Christ ordained to be repeated,
    his memorial ne'er to cease;
his command for guidance taking,
bread and wine we hallow, making
    thus our sacrifice of peace.

Full and clear sing out thy praising,
gracious hymns of joy upraising
    in thy heart and soul today;
for today the new oblation
of the new King's revelation
    bids us feast in glad array.

Very Bread, good Shepherd, tend us,
Jesus, of thy love befriend us,
Lord, refresh us and defend us,
thine eternal goodness send us
   in the land of life to see:

thou, who all things canst and knowest,
who on earth such food bestowest,
grant us, with thy saints, though lowest,
where the heavenly feast thou showest,
   fellow-heirs and guests to be.

Att. St. Thomas Aquinas (1225?–1274); tr. *Hymnal 1940*; rev. *Hymnal 1982*

**321**

My God, thy table now is spread,
   thy cup with love doth overflow;
be all thy children thither led,
   and let them thy sweet mercies know.

O let thy table honored be,
   and furnished well with joyful guests;
and may each soul salvation see,
   that here its sacred pledges tastes.

Drawn by thy quickening grace, O Lord,
   in countless number let them come
and gather from their Father's board
   the Bread that lives beyond the tomb.

Nor let thy spreading Gospel rest
> till through the world thy truth has run,
till with this Bread shall all be blessed
> who see the light or feel the sun.

Sts. 1–3, Philip Doddridge (1702–1751), alt.; st. 4, Isaac Watts (1674–1748), alt.

## 322

When Jesus died to save us,
a word, an act he gave us;
and still that word is spoken,
and still the bread is broken.

He was the Word that spake it,
he took the bread and brake it,
and what that Word did make it,
I do believe and take it.

St. 1, F. Bland Tucker (1895–1984); st. 2 att. to John Donne (1573–1631)

## 323

Bread of heaven, on thee we feed,
for thy Flesh is meat indeed;
ever may our souls be fed
with this true and living Bread;
day by day with strength supplied,
through the life of him who died.

Vine of heaven, thy Blood supplies
this blest cup of sacrifice;
Lord, thy wounds our healing give,
to thy cross we look and live:
Jesus, may we ever be
grafted, rooted, built in thee.

Josiah Conder (1789–1855), alt.

**324**

Let all mortal flesh keep silence,
    and with fear and trembling stand;
ponder nothing earthly-minded,
    for with blessing in his hand
Christ our God to earth descendeth,
    our full homage to demand.

King of kings, yet born of Mary,
    as of old on earth he stood,
Lord of lords in human vesture,
    in the Body and the Blood
he will give to all the faithful
    his own self for heavenly food.

Rank on rank the host of heaven
    spreads its vanguard on the way,
as the Light of Light descendeth
    from the realms of endless day,
that the powers of hell may vanish
    as the darkness clears away.

At his feet the six-winged seraph;
    cherubim with sleepless eye
veil their faces to the Presence,
    as with ceaseless voice they cry,
"Alleluia, alleluia!
    Alleluia, Lord Most High!"

Liturgy of St. James; para. Gerard Moultrie (1829–1885)

## 325

Let us break bread together on our knees;

> *when I fall on my knees,*
> *with my face to the rising sun,*
> *O Lord, have mercy on me.*

Let us drink wine together on our knees;

> *when I fall on my knees,*
> *with my face to the rising sun,*
> *O Lord, have mercy on me.*

Let us praise God together on our knees;

> *when I fall on my knees,*
> *with my face to the rising sun,*
> *O Lord, have mercy on me.*

African-American spiritual

## 326

From glory to glory advancing, we praise thee,
>O Lord;
thy Name with the Father and Spirit
>be ever adored.
From strength unto strength we go forward
>on Zion's highway,
to appear before God in the city of infinite day.

Thanksgiving, and glory and worship,
>and blessing and love,
one heart and one song have the saints
>upon earth and above.
O Lord, evermore to thy servants
>thy presence be nigh;
ever fit us by service on earth for thy service on high.

Liturgy of St. James; tr. Charles William Humphreys (1840–1921)

## 327, 328

Draw nigh and take the Body of the Lord,
and drink the holy Blood for you outpoured.

Saved by that Body and that holy Blood,
with souls refreshed, we render thanks to God.

Salvation's giver, Christ, the only Son,
by his dear cross and blood the victory won.

Offered was he for greatest and for least,
himself the Victim, and himself the Priest.

Approach ye then with faithful hearts sincere,
and take the pledges of salvation here.

He that his saints in this world rules and shields
to all believers life eternal yields;

with heavenly bread he makes the hungry whole,
gives living waters to the thirsting soul.

Alpha-Omega, unto whom shall bow
all nations at the doom, is with us now.

*Bangor Antiphoner*, ca. 690; tr. John Mason Neale (1818–1866), alt.

## 329, 330, 331

Now, my tongue, the mystery telling
 of the glorious Body sing,
and the Blood, all price excelling,
 which the Gentiles' Lord and King,
once on earth among us dwelling,
 shed for this world's ransoming.

Given for us, and condescending
 to be born for us below,
he with us in converse blending
 dwelt, the seed of truth to sow,
till he closed with wondrous ending
 his most patient life of woe.

That last night at supper lying
    mid the twelve, his chosen band,
Jesus, with the Law complying,
    keeps the feast its rites demand;
then, more precious food supplying,
    gives himself with his own hand.

Word made flesh, the bread he taketh,
    by his word his Flesh to be;
wine his sacred Blood he maketh,
    though the senses fail to see;
faith alone the true heart waketh
    to behold the mystery.

Therefore we, before him bending,
    this great Sacrament revere;
types and shadows have their ending,
    for the newer rite is here;
faith, our outward sense befriending,
    makes our inward vision clear.

Glory let us give and blessing
    to the Father and the Son,
honor, thanks, and praise addressing,
    while eternal ages run;
ever too his love confessing
    who from both with both is One.

Att. St. Thomas Aquinas (1225?–1274); ver. *Hymnal 1940*, rev.

## 332

O God, unseen yet ever near,
 thy presence may we feel;
and thus inspired with holy fear,
 before thine altar kneel.

Here may thy faithful people know
 the blessings of thy love,
the streams that through the desert flow,
 the manna from above.

We come, obedient to thy word,
 to feast on heavenly food:
our meat the Body of the Lord,
 our drink his precious Blood.

Thus may we all thy word obey,
 for we, O God, are thine;
and go rejoicing on our way,
 renewed with strength divine.

Edward Osler (1798–1863)

## 333

Now the silence
Now the peace
Now the empty hands uplifted
Now the kneeling
Now the plea

Now the Father's arms in welcome
Now the hearing
Now the power
Now the vessel brimmed for pouring
Now the Body
Now the Blood
Now the joyful celebration
Now the wedding
Now the songs
Now the heart forgiven leaping
Now the Spirit's visitation
Now the Son's epiphany
Now the Father's blessing
Now Now Now

Jaroslav J. Vajda (b. 1919)

**334**

Praise the Lord, rise up rejoicing,
worship, thanks, devotion voicing;
  glory be to God on high!
Christ, your cross and passion sharing,
by this Eucharist declaring
  yours the final victory.

Scattered flock, one shepherd sharing,
lost and lonely, one voice hearing,
  ears attentive to your word;

by your Blood new life receiving,
in your Body, firm believing,
    we are yours, and you the Lord.

Sins forgiven, wrongs forgiving, we
go forth alert and living
    in your Spirit, strong and free.
Partners in your new creation,
seeking peace in every nation,
    may we faithful followers be.

Howard Charles Adie Gaunt (1902–1983), alt.

## 335

I am the bread of life;
they who come to me shall not hunger;
they who believe in me shall not thirst.
No one can come to me
unless the Father draw them.

> *And I will raise them up,*
> *and I will raise them up on the*
> *last day.*

The Bread that I will give
is my Flesh for the life of the world,
and they who eat of this bread,
they shall live for ever.

*Refrain*

Unless you eat
of the Flesh of the Son of Man
and drink of his Blood,
you shall not have life within you.

*Refrain*

I am the resurrection,
I am the life.
They who believe in me,
even if they die,
they shall live for ever.

*Refrain*

Yes, Lord, we believe
that you are the Christ,
the Son of God
who has come into the world.

*Refrain*

Suzanne Toolan (b. 1927), adapt. of John 6

## 336

Come with us, O blessèd Jesus,
    with us evermore to be;
and though leaving now thine altar,
    let us nevermore leave thee.
Be thou one with us for ever,
    in our life thy love divine
our own flesh and blood has taken,
    and to us thou givest thine.

Come with us, O mighty Savior,
    God from God, and Light from Light;
thou art God, thy glory veiling,
    so that we may bear the sight.
Now we go to seek and serve thee,
    through our work as through our prayer;
grant us light to see and know thee,
    in thy people everywhere.

Come with us, O King of glory,
    by angelic voices praised;
in our hearts as in thy heaven,
    be enraptured anthems raised.
Let the mighty chorus ever
    sing its glad exultant songs;
let its hymn be heard for ever—
    peace for which creation longs.

John Henry Hopkins, Jr. (1861–1945) and Charles P. Price (b. 1920)

## 337

And now, O Father, mindful of the love
  that bought us, once for all, on Calvary's tree,
and having with us him that pleads above,
  we here present, we here spread forth to thee,
that only offering perfect in thine eyes,
the one true, pure, immortal sacrifice.

Look Father, look on his anointed face,
  and only look on us as found in him;
look not on our misusings of thy grace,
  our prayer so languid, and our faith so dim:
for lo! between our sins and their reward,
we set the passion of thy Son our Lord.

And then for those, our dearest and our best,
  by this prevailing presence we appeal;
O fold them closer to thy mercy's breast!
  O do thine utmost for their soul's true weal!
From tainting mischief keep them pure and clear,
and crown thy gifts with strength to persevere.

And so we come; O draw us to thy feet,
  most patient Savior, who canst love us still!
And by this food, so awesome and so sweet,
  deliver us from every touch of ill:
in thine own service make us glad and free,
and grant us nevermore to part from thee.

William Bright (1824–1901), alt.

## 338

Wherefore, O Father, we thy humble servants
here bring before thee Christ thy well belovèd.
All perfect Offering, sacrifice immortal,
spotless oblation.

See now thy children, making intercession
through him our Savior, Son of God incarnate,
for all thy people, living and departed,
pleading before thee.

William Henry Hammond Jervois (1852–1905)

## 339

Deck thyself, my soul, with gladness,
leave the gloomy haunts of sadness,
come into the daylight's splendor,
there with joy thy praises render
unto him whose grace unbounded
hath this wondrous banquet founded–
high o'er all the heavens he reigneth,
yet to dwell with thee he deigneth.

Sun, who all my life dost brighten;
Light, who dost my soul enlighten;
Joy, the best that any knoweth;
Fount, whence all my being floweth:
at thy feet I cry, my Maker,
let me be a fit partaker

of this blessèd food from heaven,
for our good, thy glory, given.

Jesus, Bread of Life, I pray thee,
let me gladly here obey thee;
never to my hurt invited,
be thy love with love requited;
from this banquet let me measure,
Lord, how vast and deep its treasure;
through the gifts thou here dost give me,
as thy guest in heaven receive me.

Johann Franck (1618–1677); tr. Catherine Winkworth (1827–1878), alt.

## 340, 341

For the bread which you have broken,
    for the wine which you have poured,
for the words which you have spoken,
    now we give you thanks, O Lord.

By this pledge, Lord, that you love us,
    by your gift of peace restored,
by your call to heaven above us,
    hallow all our lives, O Lord.

As our blessèd ones adore you,
    seated at our Father's board,
may the Church still waiting for you
    keep love's tie unbroken, Lord.

In your service, Lord, defend us;
> in our hearts keep watch and ward,
in the world to which you send us
> let your kingdom come, O Lord.

Louis F. Benson (1855–1930), alt.

## 342

O Bread of life, for sinners broken,
of God's own love his dearest token,
we hear the words so gently spoken,
> "Do this for me in my remembrance."

For all we seek your grace sustaining;
your love shines though your strength is waning,
thus by your death our life obtaining.
> "Come unto me, you heavy laden."

Now may your life to us descending
enter our lives, all veils thus rending;
Emmanuel, our joy unending.
> "I am with you, this day and ever."

Timothy T'ing Fang Lew (1892–1947); tr. Frank W. Price (1895–1974), alt.

## 343

Shepherd of souls, refresh and bless
    thy chosen pilgrim flock
with manna in the wilderness,
    with water from the rock.

We would not live by bread alone,
    but by thy word of grace,
in strength of which we travel on
    to our abiding-place.

Be known to us in breaking bread,
    and do not then depart;
Savior, abide with us, and spread
    thy table in our heart.

Lord, sup with us in love divine,
    thy Body and thy Blood,
that living bread, that heavenly wine,
    be our immortal food.

James Montgomery (1771–1845), alt.

## 344

Lord, dismiss us with thy blessing;
    fill our hearts with joy and peace;
let us each, thy love possessing,
triumph in redeeming grace:
    O refresh us, O refresh us

traveling through this wilderness.

Thanks we give and adoration
    for thy Gospel's joyful sound:
may the fruits of thy salvation
in our hearts and lives abound:
    ever faithful, ever faithful
to thy truth may we be found;

so that when thy love shall call us,
    Savior, from the world away,
fear of death shall not appall us,
glad thy summons to obey.
    May we ever, may we ever
reign with thee in endless day.

Att. to John Fawcett (1739/40–1817)

## 345

Savior, again to thy dear Name we raise
with one accord our parting hymn of praise;
guard thou the lips from sin, the hearts from shame,
that in this house have called upon thy Name.

Grant us thy peace upon our homeward way;
with thee began, with thee shall end the day:
from harm and danger keep thy children free,
for dark and light are both alike to thee.

Grant us thy peace throughout our earthly life;

peace to thy Church from error and from strife;
peace to our land, the fruit of truth and love;
peace in each heart, thy Spirit from above:

thy peace in life, the balm of every pain;
thy peace in death, the hope to rise again;
then, when thy voice shall bid our conflict cease,
call us, O Lord, to thine eternal peace.

John Ellerton (1825–1893), alt.

## 346

Completed, Lord, the Holy Mysteries,
    as far as lies within our mortal power!
Thy death remembered, feeding thus on thee,
    we here have known the resurrection hour.

Here we have tasted infinite delights,
    beheld afar that life which soon shall be;
oh, count us worthy, Christ, thy joys to share
    for ever in eternity with thee.

Through God's good grace these Mysteries are ours,
    ordained by thee, the everlasting Son;
blest by the Spirit, breath and flame of life,
    to whom be praise while endless ages run.

Liturgy of St. Basil; tr. Cyril E. Pocknee (1906–1980)

## 347

Go forth for God; go to the world in peace;
    be of good courage, armed with heavenly grace,
in God's good Spirit daily to increase,
    till in his kingdom we behold his face.

Go forth for God; go to the world in love;
    strengthen the faint, give courage to the weak;
help the afflicted; richly from above
    his love supplies the grace and power we seek.

Go forth for God; go to the world in strength;
    hold fast the good, be urgent for the right;
render to no one evil; Christ at length
    shall overcome all darkness with his light.

Go forth for God; go to the world in joy,
    to serve God's people every day and hour,
and serving Christ, our every gift employ,
    rejoicing in the Holy Spirit's power.

John Raphael Peacey (1896–1971) and *English Praise*, 1975, alt.

## 348

Lord, we have come at your own invitation,
    chosen by you, to be counted as friends:
yours is the strength that sustains our vocation,
    ours a commitment we know never ends.

Here, at your table, confirm our intention
    ever to cherish the gifts you provide;
teach us to serve without pride or pretension,
    led by your Spirit, defender and guide.

When, at your table, each time of returning,
    vows are renewed, and our courage restored:
may we increasingly glory in learning
    all that it means to accept you as Lord.

So, in the world where each duty assigned us
    gives us the chance to create or destroy,
help us to make those decisions that bind us,
    Lord, to yourself, in obedience and joy.

F. Pratt Green (b. 1903), rev.

## 349

Holy Spirit, Lord of love,
who descended from above,
gifts of blessing to bestow
on your waiting Church below,
once again in love draw near
to your servants gathered here;
from their bright baptismal day
you have led them on their way.

When the sacred vow is made,
when the hands are on them laid,
come in this most solemn hour

with your strengthening gift of power.
Give them light, your truth to see;
give them life, your own to be;
daily power to conquer sin;
patient faith, the crown to win.

William Dalrymple Maclagan (1826–1910), alt.

# 350

O God of love, to thee we bow,
and pray for these before thee now,
that closely knit in holy vow,
they may in thee be one.

Whatever comes to be their share
of quickening joy or burdening care,
in power to do and grace to bear,
may they in thee be one.

Eternal love, with them abide;
through change and chance be thou their guide,
let nothing in this life divide
those whom thou makest one.

William Vaughan Jenkins (1868–1920), alt.

## 351

May the grace of Christ our Savior,
    and the Father's boundless love,
with the Holy Spirit's favor,
    rest upon them from above.

Thus may they abide in union
    with each other and the Lord,
and possess, in sweet communion,
    joys which earth cannot afford.

John Newton (1725–1807), alt.

## 352

O God, to those who here profess
    their vows of lifelong love,
grant joy and peace; their marriage bless
    with gladness from above.

Christ, grant that neither grief nor place
    nor life nor death may part
those who, enjoying your sweet grace,
    in you are one in heart.

Spirit of God, whom we adore:
    preserve, protect, defend,
increase, rekindle, and restore
    their love till life shall end.

Sts. 1 and 3, Charles P. Price (b. 1920); st. 2, Charles Wesley (1707–1788), alt.

## 353

Your love, O God, has called us here,
    for all love finds its source in you,
the perfect love that casts out fear,
    the love that Christ makes ever new.

O gracious God, you consecrate
    all that is lovely, good, and true.
Bless those who in your presence wait
    and every day their love renew.

O God of love, inspire our life,
    reveal your will in all we do;
join every husband, every wife
    in mutual love and love for you.

Russell Schulz-Widmar (b. 1944)

## 354

Into paradise may the angels lead you.
At your coming may the martyrs receive you,
and bring you into the holy city Jerusalem.

May the choirs of angels welcome you,
and with Lazarus who once was poor
may you have peace everlasting.

Latin; tr. The Book of Common Prayer, 1979, and Theodore Marier (b. 1912)

**355**

Give rest, O Christ, to your servant(s)
                  with your saints,
where sorrow and pain are no more,
neither sighing, but life everlasting.
You only are immortal,
the creator and maker of mankind;
and we are mortal, formed of the earth,
and to earth shall we return.
For so did you ordain,
when you created me, saying,
"You are dust, and to dust you shall return."
All of us go down to the dust;
yet even at the grave we make our song:
Alleluia, alleluia, alleluia.

Eastern Orthodox Memorial Service; tr. The Book of Common Prayer, 1979

**356**

May choirs of angels lead you
    to Paradise on high,
where dwell the white-robed martyrs
    who now no more can die.

And at your coming thither
    may you be brought by them
into the holy city,
    God's true Jerusalem.

As angels gave poor Lazarus
   from all his ills release,
so may they give you welcome
   to everlasting peace.

Latin; tr. F. Bland Tucker (1895–1984)

## 357

Jesus, Son of Mary,
   fount of life alone,
now we hail thee present
   on thine altar throne.
Humbly we adore thee,
   Lord of endless might,
in the mystic symbols
   veiled from earthly sight.

Think, O Lord, in mercy
   on the souls of those
who, in faith gone from us,
   now in death repose.
Here mid stress and conflict
   toils can never cease;
there, the warfare ended,
   bid them rest in peace.

Often were they wounded
   in the deadly strife;
heal them, Good Physician,
   with the balm of life.

Every taint of evil,
 frailty and decay,
good and gracious Savior,
 cleanse and purge away.

Rest eternal grant them,
 after weary fight;
shed on them the radiance
 of thy heavenly light.
Lead them onward, upward,
 to the holy place,
where thy saints made perfect
 gaze upon thy face.

Edmund Stuart Palmer (1856–1931)

## 358

Christ the Victorious, give to your servants
rest with your saints in the regions of light.
Grief and pain ended, and sighing no longer,
there may they find everlasting life.

Only Immortal One, Mighty Creator!
We are your creatures and children of earth.
From earth you formed us, both glorious and mortal,
and to the earth shall we all return.

God-spoken prophecy, word at creation:
"You came from dust and to dust shall return."
Yet at the grave shall we raise up our glad song,
"Alleluia, alleluia!"

Christ the Victorious, give to your servants
rest with your saints in the regions of light.
Grief and pain ended, and sighing no longer,
there may they find everlasting life.

Carl P. Daw, Jr. (b. 1944)

## 359

God of the prophets, bless the prophets' heirs!
   Elijah's mantle o'er Elisha cast:
each age for thine own solemn task prepares,
   make each one stronger, nobler than the last.

Anoint them prophets! Teach them thine intent:
   to human need their quickened hearts awake;
fill them with power, their lips make eloquent
   for righteousness that shall all evil break.

Anoint them priests! help them to intercede
   with all thy royal priesthood born of grace;
through them thy Church presents in word and deed
   Christ's one true sacrifice with thankful praise.

Anoint them kings! Yea, kingly kings, O Lord!
   Anoint them with the Spirit of thy Son:

theirs not a monarch's crown or tyrant's sword;
> theirs by the love of Christ a kingdom won.

Make them apostles, heralds of thy cross;
> forth may they go to tell all realms thy grace:
> inspired of thee, may they count all but loss,
> and stand at last with joy before thy face.

Sts. 1–2 and 4–5, Denis Wortman (1835–1922), alt.; st. 3, Carl P. Daw, Jr. (b. 1944)

## 360, 361

Only-begotten, Word of God eternal,
Lord of creation, merciful and mighty,
hear now thy servants when their joyful voices
> rise to thy presence.

This is thy temple; here thy presence-chamber;
here may thy servants, at the mystic banquet,
humbly adoring, take thy Body broken,
> drink of thy chalice.

Here in our sickness healing grace aboundeth,
light in our blindness, in our toil refreshment:
sin is forgiven, hope o'er fear prevaileth,
> joy over sorrow.

Hallowed this dwelling where the Lord abideth,
this is none other than the gate of heaven;
strangers and pilgrims, seeking homes eternal,
> pass through its portals.

Lord, we beseech thee, as we throng thy temple,
by thy past blessings, by thy present bounty,
favor thy children, and with tender mercy
   hear our petitions.

God in three Persons, Father everlasting,
Son co-eternal, ever-blessèd Spirit,
thine be the glory, praise, and adoration,
   now and for ever.

Latin, ca. 9th cent.; tr. Maxwell Julius Blacker (1822–1888)

## 362

Holy, holy, holy! Lord God Almighty!
   Early in the morning our song shall rise to thee:
Holy, holy, holy! Merciful and mighty,
   God in three Persons, blessèd Trinity.

Holy, holy, holy! All the saints adore thee,
   casting down their golden crowns
             around the glassy sea;
cherubim and seraphim falling down before thee,
   which wert, and art, and evermore shalt be.

Holy, holy, holy! Though the darkness hide thee,
   though the sinful human eye thy glory may
             not see,
only thou art holy; there is none beside thee,
   perfect in power, in love, and purity.

Holy, holy, holy! Lord God Almighty!
   All thy works shall praise thy Name, in earth,
               and sky, and sea;
Holy, holy, holy! Merciful and mighty,
   God in three Persons, blessèd Trinity.

Reginald Heber (1783–1826), alt.

## 363

Ancient of Days, who sittest throned in glory,
   to thee all knees are bent, all voices pray;
thy love has blessed the wide world's wondrous story
   with light and life since Eden's dawning day.

O holy Father, who hast led thy children
   in all the ages with the fire and cloud,
through seas dry-shod, through
               weary wastes bewildering
   to thee in reverent love our hearts are bowed.

O holy Jesus, Lord of our salvation,
   calling the least, the last, the lost to thee,
summoning all to share thy new creation,
   thou, Lord, by death hast won life's victory.

O Holy Ghost, the Lord and the Life-giver,
   thine is the quickening power that gives increase:
from thee have flowed, as from a mighty river,
   our faith and hope, our fellowship and peace.

O Triune God, with heart and voice adoring,
　　praise we the goodness that doth crown our days;
pray we that thou wilt hear us, still imploring
　　thy love and favor, kept to us always.

William Croswell Doane (1832–1913), alt.

## 364

*Part I*
　　O God, we praise thee, and confess
　　　　that thou the only Lord
　　and everlasting Father art,
　　　　by all the earth adored.

To thee all angels cry aloud;
　　to thee the powers on high,
both cherubim and seraphim,
　　continually do cry:

O holy, holy, holy Lord,
　　whom heavenly hosts obey,
the world is with the glory filled
　　of thy majestic sway!

The apostles' glorious company,
　　and prophets crowned with light,
with all the martyrs' noble host,
　　thy constant praise recite.

The holy Church in faith acclaims
　　thy Son who for us died,

also the Holy Comforter,
　　　　　our advocate and guide.

*Part II*
　　　Thou art the King of glory, Christ,
　　　　　the everlasting Son;
　　　humbly thou cam'st to set us free,
　　　　　nor Virgin womb didst shun.

　　　When thou hadst overcome death's sting
　　　　　and opened heaven's door,
　　　thou didst ascend to God's right hand
　　　　　in glory evermore.

　　　When thou shalt come to be our judge,
　　　　　bring us whom thou hast bought
　　　to dwell on high with all thy saints
　　　　　in joy surpassing thought.

Para. of the *Te Deum* Sts. 1–5, *A Supplement to the New Version of the Psalms of David,* 1698, alt.; sts. 6–8, ver. *Hymnal 1982*

## 365

　　　Come, thou almighty King,
　　　help us thy Name to sing,
　　　　　help us to praise.
　　　Father whose love unknown
　　　all things created own,
　　　build in our hearts thy throne,
　　　　　Ancient of Days.

Come, thou incarnate Word,
by heaven and earth adored;
   our prayer attend:
come, and thy people bless;
come, give thy word success;
stablish thy righteousness,
   Savior and friend.

Come, holy Comforter,
thy sacred witness bear
   in this glad hour:
thou, who almighty art,
now rule in every heart,
and ne'er from us depart,
   Spirit of power.

To Thee, great One in Three,
the highest praises be,
   hence evermore;
thy sovereign majesty
may we in glory see,
and to eternity
   love and adore.

Anonymous, ca. 1757, alt.

# 366

*Part I*

Holy God, we praise thy Name,
   Lord of all, we bow before thee;
all on earth thy scepter claim,
   all in heaven above adore thee;
infinite thy vast domain,
everlasting is thy reign.

Hark, the loud celestial hymn
   angel choirs above are raising;
cherubim and seraphim,
   in unceasing chorus praising,
fill the heavens with sweet accord:
holy, holy, holy Lord!

Lo, the apostolic train
   join, thy sacred Name to hallow;
prophets swell the loud refrain,
   and the white-robed martyrs follow;
and, from morn till set of sun,
through the Church the song goes on.

Holy Father, holy Son,
   Holy Spirit, Three we name thee,
while in essence only One,
   undivided God we claim thee;
then, adoring, bend the knee
and confess the mystery.

*Part II*

    Christ, thou art our glorious King,
        Son of God enthroned in splendor;
    but deliverance to bring
        thou all honors didst surrender,
    and wast of a virgin born
    humbly on that blessèd morn.

    Thou didst take the sting from death,
        Son of God, as Savior given;
    on the cross thy dying breath
        opened wide the realm of heaven.
    In the glory of that land
    thou art set at God's right hand.

    As our judge thou wilt appear.
        Savior, who hast died to win us,
    help thy servants, drawing near.
        Lord, renew our hearts within us.
    Grant that with thy saints we may
    dwell in everlasting day.

Para. the *Te Deum*, Sts. 1–4, Ignaz Franz (1719–1790), tr. Clarence Walworth (1820–1900). Sts. 5–7, F. Bland Tucker (1895–1984)

## 367

Round the Lord in glory seated
   cherubim and seraphim
filled his temple, and repeated
   each to each the alternate hymn;
"Lord, thy glory fills the heaven,
   earth is with thy fullness stored;
unto thee be glory given,
   holy, holy, holy Lord."

Heaven is still with glory ringing,
   earth takes up the angels' cry,
"Holy, holy, holy," singing,
   "Lord of hosts, the Lord Most High."
With his seraph train before him,
   with his holy Church below,
thus unite we to adore him,
   bid we thus our anthem flow:

"Lord, thy glory fills the heaven,
   earth is with thy fullness stored;
unto thee be glory given,
   holy, holy, holy Lord."
Thus thy glorious Name confessing,
   with thine angel hosts we cry
"Holy, holy, holy," blessing
   thee, the Lord of hosts Most High.

Richard Mant (1776–1848)

# 368

Holy Father, great Creator,
    source of mercy, love, and peace,
look upon the Mediator,
    clothe us with his righteousness;
        heavenly Father,
    through the Savior hear and bless.

Holy Jesus, Lord of glory,
    whom angelic hosts proclaim,
while we hear thy wondrous story,
    meet and worship in thy Name,
        dear Redeemer,
    in our hearts thy peace proclaim.

Holy Spirit, Sanctifier,
    Come with unction from above,
touch our hearts with sacred fire,
    fill them with the Savior's love.
        Source of comfort,
    cheer us with the Savior's love.

God the Lord, through every nation
    let thy wondrous mercies shine.
In the song of thy salvation
    every tongue and race combine.
        Great Jehovah,
    form our hearts and make them thine.

Alexander Viets Griswold (1766–1843), alt.

How wondrous great, how glorious bright
    must our Creator be,
who dwells amidst the dazzling light
    of vast eternity.

Our soaring spirits upward rise
    to reach the burning throne
and long to see the blessèd Three
    in the Almighty One.

Our reason stretches all its wings,
    and climbs above the skies;
but still how far beneath thy feet
    our groundling knowledge lies!

While all the heavenly powers conspire
    eternal praise to sing,
let faith in humble notes adore
    the great mysterious King.

Isaac Watts (1674–1748), alt.; st. 3, alt. Caryl Micklem (b. 1925)

# 370

I bind unto myself today
    the strong Name of the Trinity,
by invocation of the same,
    the Three in One, and One in Three.

I bind this day to me for ever,
    by power of faith, Christ's Incarnation;
his baptism in the Jordan river;
    his death on cross for my salvation;
his bursting from the spicèd tomb;
    his riding up the heavenly way;
his coming at the day of doom:
    I bind unto myself today.

I bind unto myself the power
    of the great love of cherubim;
the sweet "Well done" in judgment hour;
    the service of the seraphim;
confessors' faith, apostles' word,
    the patriarchs' prayers, the prophets' scrolls;
all good deeds done unto the Lord,
    and purity of virgin souls.

I bind unto myself today
    the virtues of the starlit heaven
the glorious sun's life-giving ray,
    the whiteness of the moon at even,
the flashing of the lightning free,
    the whirling wind's tempestuous shocks,

the stable earth, the deep salt sea,
  around the old eternal rocks.

I bind unto myself today
  the power of God to hold and lead,
his eye to watch, his might to stay,
  his ear to hearken, to my need;
the wisdom of my God to teach,
  his hand to guide, his shield to ward;
the word of God to give me speech,
  his heavenly host to be my guard.

Christ be with me, Christ within me,
  Christ behind me, Christ before me,
Christ beside me, Christ to win me,
  Christ to comfort and restore me,
Christ beneath me, Christ above me,
  Christ in quiet, Christ in danger,
Christ in hearts of all that love me,
  Christ in mouth of friend and stranger.

I bind unto myself the Name,
  the strong Name of the Trinity,
by invocation of the same,
  the Three in One, and One in Three.
Of whom all nature hath creation,
  eternal Father, Spirit, Word:
praise to the Lord of my salvation,
  salvation is of Christ the Lord.

Att. Patrick (372–466); tr. Cecil Frances Alexander (1818–1895)

## 371

Thou, whose almighty word
chaos and darkness heard,
    and took their flight;
hear us, we humbly pray,
and, where the Gospel day
sheds not its glorious ray,
    let there be light!

Thou who didst come to bring
on thy redeeming wing
    healing and sight,
health to the sick in mind,
sight to the inly blind,
now to all humankind,
    let there be light!

Spirit of truth and love,
life-giving, holy Dove,
    speed forth thy flight!
Move on the waters' face
bearing the gifts of grace,
and, in earth's darkest place,
    let there be light!

Holy and blessèd Three,
glorious Trinity,
    wisdom, love, might;

boundless as ocean's tide,
   rolling in fullest pride,
through the world, far and wide,
   let there be light!

John Marriott (1780–1825), alt.

**372**

Praise to the living God!
   All praisèd be his Name
who was, and is, and is to be
   for ay the same.
The one eternal God
   ere aught that now appears:
the first, the last, beyond all thought
   his timeless years!

Formless, all lovely forms
   declare his loveliness;
holy, no holiness of earth
   can his express.
Lo, he is Lord of all.
   Creation speaks his praise,
and everywhere above, below,
   his will obeys.

His Spirit floweth free,
   high surging where it will:
in prophet's word he spoke of old;
   he speaketh still.

Established is his law,
    and changeless it shall stand,
deep writ upon the human heart,
    on sea, on land.

Eternal life hath he
    implanted in the soul;
his love shall be our strength and stay
    while ages roll.
Praise to the living God!
    All praisèd be his Name
who was, and is, and is to be,
    for ay the same.

Medieval Jewish liturgy; tr. Max Landsberg (1845–1928) and Newton M. Mann (1836–1926)

## 373

Praise the Lord! ye heavens adore him;
    praise him angels, in the height;
sun and moon, rejoice before him;
    praise him, all ye stars of light.
Praise the Lord! for he hath spoken;
    worlds his mighty voice obeyed;
laws which never shall be broken
    for their guidance he hath made.

Praise the Lord! for he is glorious;
    never shall his promise fail;

God hath made his saints victorious;
   sin and death shall not prevail.
Praise the God of our salvation!
   Hosts on high, his power proclaim;
heaven and earth, and all creation,
   laud and magnify his Name.

Anon. *Foundling Hospital Psalms and Hymns,* 1796; para. of Psalm 148

## 374

Come, let us join our cheerful songs
   with angels round the throne;
ten thousand thousand are their tongues,
   but all their joys are one.

"Worthy the Lamb that died," they cry
   "to be exalted thus";
"Worthy the Lamb," our lips reply,
   "for he was slain for us."

Jesus is worthy to receive
   honor and power divine;
may blessings, more than we can give,
   be, Lord, for ever thine.

The whole creation joins in one
   to bless the sacred Name
of him that sits upon the throne,
   and to adore the Lamb.

Isaac Watts (1674–1748); para. of *A Song of the Lamb*

## 375

Give praise and glory unto God,
    the Father of all blessing;
his mighty wonders tell abroad,
    his graciousness confessing.
With balm my inmost heart he fills,
his comfort all my anguish stills.
    To God be praise and glory.

The host of heaven praiseth thee,
    O Lord of all dominions;
and mortals then, on land and sea,
    beneath thy shadowing pinions,
exult in thy creative might
that doeth all things well and right.
    To God be praise and glory.

What God hath wrought to show his power
    he evermore sustaineth;
he watches o'er us every hour,
    his mercy never waneth.
Through all his kingdom's wide domain,
his righteousness and justice reign.
    To God be praise and glory.

Johann Jacob Schütz (1640–1690); tr. Arthur William Farlander (1898–1952) and Charles Winfred Douglas (1867–1944), alt.

# 376

Joyful, joyful, we adore thee,
    God of glory, Lord of love;
hearts unfold like flowers before thee,
    praising thee, their sun above.
Melt the clouds of sin and sadness;
    drive the dark of doubt away;
giver of immortal gladness,
    fill us with the light of day.

All thy works with joy surround thee,
    earth and heaven reflect thy rays,
stars and angels sing around thee,
    center of unbroken praise.
Field and forest, vale and mountain,
    blooming meadow, flashing sea,
chanting bird and flowing fountain,
    call us to rejoice in thee.

Thou art giving and forgiving,
    ever blessing, ever blest,
well-spring of the joy of living,
    ocean-depth of happy rest!
Thou our Father, Christ our Brother:
    all who live in love are thine;
teach us how to love each other,
    lift us to the joy divine.

Henry Van Dyke (1852–1933)

## 377, 378

All people that on earth do dwell,
   sing to the Lord with cheerful voice:
him serve with mirth, his praise forth tell,
   come ye before him and rejoice.

Know that the Lord is God indeed;
   without our aid he did us make:
we are his folk, he doth us feed,
   and for his sheep he doth us take.

O enter then his gates with praise,
   approach with joy his courts unto;
praise, laud, and bless his Name always,
   for it is seemly so to do.

For why? the Lord our God is good,
   his mercy is for ever sure;
his truth at all times firmly stood,
   and shall from age to age endure.

To Father, Son, and Holy Ghost,
   the God whom heaven and earth adore,
from men and from the angel host
   be praise and glory evermore.

William Kethe (d. 1608?); para. of Psalm 100

**379**

God is Love, let heaven adore him;
 God is Love, let earth rejoice;
let creation sing before him
 and exalt him with one voice.
God who laid the earth's foundation,
 God who spread the heaven above,
God who breathes through all creation:
 God is Love, eternal Love.

God is Love; and Love enfolds us,
 all the world in one embrace:
with unfailing grasp God holds us,
 every child of every race.
And when human hearts are breaking
 under sorrow's iron rod,
then we find that selfsame aching
 deep within the heart of God.

God is Love; and though with blindness
 sin afflicts all human life,
God's eternal loving-kindness
 guides us through our earthly strife.
Sin and death and hell shall never
 o'er us final triumph gain;
God is Love, so Love for ever
 o'er the universe must reign.

Timothy Rees (1874–1939), alt.

## 380

From all that dwell below the skies
let the Creator's praise arise!
Let the Redeemer's Name be sung
through every land, by every tongue!

Eternal are thy mercies, Lord,
and truth eternal is thy word:
thy praise shall sound from shore to shore
till suns shall rise and set no more.

Praise God, from whom all blessings flow;
praise him, all creatures here below;
praise him above, ye heavenly host:
praise Father, Son, and Holy Ghost.

Isaac Watts (1674–1748), para. of Psalm 117. St. 3, Thomas Ken (1637–1711)

## 381

Thy strong word did cleave the darkness;
    at thy speaking it was done;
for created light we thank thee,
    while thine ordered seasons run:
Alleluia, alleluia!
    Praise to thee who light dost send!
Alleluia, alleluia!
    Alleluia without end!

Lo, on those who dwelt in darkness,
    dark as night and deep as death,
broke the light of thy salvation,
    breathed thine own life-giving breath:
Alleluia, alleluia!
    Praise to thee who light dost send!
Alleluia, alleluia!
    Alleluia without end!

Thy strong word bespeaks us righteous;
    bright with thine own holiness,
glorious now, we press toward glory,
    and our lives our hopes confess:
Alleluia, alleluia!
    Praise to thee who light dost send!
Alleluia, alleluia!
    Alleluia without end!

God the Father, Light-Creator,
    to thee laud and honor be;
to thee, Light of Light begotten,
    praise be sung eternally;
Holy Spirit, Light-Revealer,
    glory, glory be to thee;
mortals, angels, now and ever
    praise the Holy Trinity.

Martin H. Franzmann (1907–1976)

## 382

King of glory, King of peace,
    I will love thee;
and that love may never cease,
    I will move thee.
Thou hast granted my request,
    thou hast heard me;
thou didst note my working breast,
    thou hast spared me.

Wherefore with my utmost art,
    I will sing thee;
and the cream of all my heart,
    I will bring thee.
Though my sins against me cried,
    thou didst clear me;
and alone, when they replied,
    thou didst hear me.

Seven whole days, not one in seven,
    I will praise thee;
in my heart, though not in heaven,
    I can raise thee.
Small it is in this poor sort
    to enroll thee;
e'en eternity's too short
    to extol thee.

George Herbert (1593–1633)

## 383, 384

Fairest Lord Jesus,
Ruler of all nature,
O thou God of man the Son;
thee will I cherish,
thee will I honor,
thou, my soul's glory, joy, and crown.

Fair are the meadows,
fairer still the woodlands,
robed in the blooming garb of spring:
Jesus is fairer,
Jesus is purer,
who makes the woeful heart to sing.

Fair is the sunshine,
fairer still the moonlight,
and all the twinkling, starry host:
Jesus shines brighter,
Jesus shines purer,
than all the angels heaven can boast.

German composite; tr. pub. New York, 1850, alt.

## 385

Many and great, O God, are thy works,
maker of earth and sky;
thy hands have set the heavens with stars;
thy fingers spread the mountains and plains.

Lo, at thy word the waters were formed;
deep seas obey thy voice.

Grant unto us communion with thee,
thou star-abiding one;
come unto us and dwell with us;
with thee are found the gifts of life.
Bless us with life that has no end,
eternal life with thee.

American folk hymn; para. Philip Frazier (1892–1964), alt.

## 386, 387

We sing of God, the mighty source
of all things; the stupendous force
    on which all strength depends;
from whose right arm, beneath whose eyes,
all period, power, and enterprise
    commences, reigns, and ends.

Tell them I AM, the Lord God said,
to Moses while on earth in dread
    and smitten to the heart,
at once, above, beneath, around,
all nature without voice or sound
    replied, O Lord, thou art.

Glorious the sun in mid career;
glorious the assembled fires appear;
    glorious the comet's train:

glorious the trumpet and alarm;
glorious the almighty stretched-out arm;
   glorious the enraptured main:

Glorious, most glorious, is the crown
of him that brought salvation down
   by meekness, Mary's son;
seers that stupendous truth believed,
and now the matchless deed's achieved,
   determined, dared, and done.

Christopher Smart (1722–1771), alt.

## 388

O worship the King, all glorious above!
O gratefully sing his power and his love!
Our shield and defender, the Ancient of Days,
pavilioned in splendor, and girded with praise.

O tell of his might! O sing of his grace!
Whose robe is the light, whose canopy space.
His chariots of wrath the deep thunderclouds form,
and dark is his path on the wings of the storm.

The earth, with its store of wonders untold,
Almighty, thy power hath founded of old,
hath stablished it fast by a changeless decree,
and round it hath cast, like a mantle, the sea.

Thy bountiful care, what tongue can recite?
It breathes in the air; it shines in the light;

it streams from the hills, it descends to the plain,
and sweetly distills in the dew and the rain.

Frail children of dust, and feeble as frail,
in thee do we trust, nor find thee to fail;
thy mercies, how tender! how firm to the end!
Our Maker, Defender, Redeemer, and Friend!

Robert Grant (1779–1838)

## 389

Let us, with a gladsome mind,
praise the Lord, for he is kind:

> *for his mercies ay endure,*
> *ever faithful, ever sure.*

Let us blaze his Name abroad,
for of gods he is the God:

*Refrain*

He with all-commanding might
filled the new-made world with light:

*Refrain*

He the golden-tressèd sun
caused all day his course to run:

*Refrain*

The hornèd moon to shine by night,
mid her spangled sisters bright:

*Refrain*

All things living he doth feed,
his full hand supplies their need:

*Refrain*

Let us, with a gladsome mind,
praise the Lord, for he is kind:

*Refrain*

John Milton (1608–1674); para. Psalm 136

## 390

Praise to the Lord, the Almighty, the King of creation;
O my soul, praise him, for he is thy health
      and salvation:
 join the great throng,
 psaltery, organ, and song,
sounding in glad adoration.

Praise to the Lord; over all things
      he gloriously reigneth:
borne as on eagle-wings, safely his saints
      he sustaineth.
 Hast thou not seen
 how all thou needest hath been
granted in what he ordaineth?

Praise to the Lord, who doth prosper
                thy way and defend thee;
surely his goodness and mercy shall
                ever attend thee;
   ponder anew
   what the Almighty can do,
who with his love doth befriend thee.

Praise to the Lord! O let all that is
                in me adore him!
All that hath life and breath come now
                with praises before him!
   Let the amen
   sound from his people again;
gladly for ever adore him.

Joachim Neander (1650–1680); tr. *Hymnal 1940*, alt.

## 391

Before the Lord's eternal throne,
   ye nations, bow with sacred joy;
know that the Lord is God alone;
   he can create, and he destroy.

His sovereign Power without our aid
   formed us of clay and gave us breath;
and when like wandering sheep we strayed,
   he saved us from the power of death.

We are his people, we his care,
   our souls, and all our mortal frame:

what lasting honors shall we rear,
   almighty Maker, to thy Name?

We'll crowd thy gates with thankful songs,
   high as the heavens our voices raise;
and earth, with her ten thousand tongues,
   shall fill thy courts with sounding praise.

Wide as the world is thy command,
   vast as eternity thy love;
firm as a rock thy truth must stand,
   when rolling years shall cease to move.

Isaac Watts (1674–1748), alt.; para. of Psalm 100

**392**

Come, we that love the Lord,
   and let our joys be known;
join in a song with sweet accord
   and thus surround the throne.

> *Hosanna, hosanna!*
> *Rejoice, give thanks and sing.*

Let those refuse to sing
   that never knew our God;
but children of the heavenly King
   may speak their joys abroad.

*Refrain*

The heirs of grace have found
    glory begun below;
celestial fruits on earthly ground
    from faith and hope may grow.

*Refrain*

Then let our song abound
    and let our tears be dry;
we're marching through Emmanuel's ground
    to fairer worlds on high.

*Refrain*

Isaac Watts (1674–1748), alt.

## 393

Praise our great and gracious Lord,
    call upon his holy Name;
raising hymns in glad accord,
    all his mighty acts proclaim:
how he leads his chosen
    unto Canaan's promised land,
        how the word
        we have heard
firm and changeless still shall stand.

God has given the cloud by day,
    given the moving fire by night;
guides his Israel on their way
    from the darkness into light.

God it is who grants us
>   sure retreat and refuge nigh;
>>  light of dawn
>>  leads us on:
>   'tis the Dayspring from on high.

Harriet Auber (1773–1862), alt.

## 394, 395

Creating God, your fingers trace
the bold designs of farthest space;
let sun and moon and stars and light
and what lies hidden praise your might.

Sustaining God, your hands uphold
earth's mysteries known or yet untold;
let water's fragile blend with air,
enabling life, proclaim your care.

Redeeming God, your arms embrace
all now despised for creed or race;
let peace, descending like a dove,
make known on earth your healing love.

Indwelling God, your gospel claims
one family with a billion names;
let every life be touched by grace
until we praise you face to face.

Jeffery Rowthorn (b. 1934), alt.

## 396, 397

Now thank we all our God,
  with heart, and hands, and voices,
who wondrous things hath done,
  in whom his world rejoices;
who from our mother's arms
  hath blessed us on our way
with countless gifts of love,
  and still is ours today.

O may this bounteous God
  through all our life be near us!
With ever-joyful hearts
  and blessed peace to cheer us;
and keep us in his grace,
  and guide us when perplexed,
and free us from all ills
  in this world and the next.

All praise and thanks to God
  the Father now be given,
the Son, and him who reigns
  with them in highest heaven,
eternal, Triune God,
  whom earth and heaven adore;
for thus it was, is now,
  and shall be, evermore.

Martin Rinkart (1586–1649); tr. Catherine Winkworth (1827–1878), alt.

## 398

I sing the almighty power of God,
    that made the mountains rise,
that spread the flowing seas abroad
    and built the lofty skies.
I sing the wisdom that ordained
    the sun to rule the day;
the moon shines full at his command,
    and all the stars obey.

I sing the goodness of the Lord,
    that filled the earth with food;
he formed the creatures with his Word,
    and then pronounced them good.
Lord, how thy wonders are displayed,
    where'er I turn my eye,
if I survey the ground I tread,
    or gaze upon the sky!

There's not a plant or flower below,
    but makes thy glories known;
and clouds arise, and tempests blow,
    by order from thy throne;
while all that borrows life from thee
    is ever in thy care,
and everywhere that I could be,
    thou, God, art present there.

Isaac Watts (1674–1748), alt.

## 399

To God with gladness sing,
    your Rock and Savior bless;
into his temple bring
    your songs of thankfulness!
        O God of might,
            to you we sing,
        enthroned as King
        on heaven's height!

He cradles in his hand
    the heights and depths of earth;
he made the sea and land,
    he brought the world to birth!
        O God Most High,
            we are your sheep;
        on us you keep
        your shepherd's eye!

Your heavenly Father praise,
    acclaim his only Son,
your voice in homage raise
    to him who makes all one!
        O Dove of peace,
            on us descend
        that strife may end
        and joy increase!

James Quinn (b. 1919), alt.; para. of Psalm 95 (Venite)

# 400

All creatures of our God and King,
lift up your voices, let us sing:
   Alleluia, alleluia!
Bright burning sun with golden beams,
pale silver moon that gently gleams,

> *O praise him, O praise him,*
> *Alleluia, alleluia, alleluia!*

Great rushing winds and breezes soft,
you clouds that ride the heavens aloft,
   O praise him, Alleluia!
Fair rising morn, with praise rejoice,
stars nightly shining, find a voice,

*Refrain*

Swift flowing water, pure and clear,
make music for your Lord to hear,
   Alleluia, alleluia!
Fire, so intense and fiercely bright,
you give to us both warmth and light,

*Refrain*

Dear mother earth, you day by day
unfold your blessings on our way,
   O praise him, Alleluia!

All flowers and fruits that in you grow,
let them his glory also show:

*Refrain*

All you with mercy in your heart,
forgiving others, take your part,
   O sing now: Alleluia!
All you that pain and sorrow bear,
praise God, and cast on him your care:

*Refrain*

And even you, most gentle death,
waiting to hush our final breath,
   O praise him, Alleluia!
You lead back home the child of God,
for Christ our Lord that way has trod:

*Refrain*

Let all things their creator bless,
and worship him in humbleness,
   O praise him, Alleluia!
Praise God the Father, praise the Son,
and praise the Spirit, Three in One:

*Refrain*

St. Francis of Assisi (1882–1226); tr. William H. Draper (1855–1933), alt.

## 401

The God of Abraham praise,
   who reigns enthroned above;
Ancient of everlasting days,
   and God of love;
the Lord, the great I AM,
   by earth and heaven confessed:
we bow and bless the sacred Name
   for ever blest.

He by himself hath sworn:
   we on his oath depend;
we shall, on eagle-wings upborne,
   to heaven ascend:
we shall behold his face,
   we shall his power adore,
and sing the wonders of his grace
   for evermore.

There dwells the Lord, our King,
   the Lord, our Righteousness,
triumphant o'er the world and sin,
   the Prince of Peace;
on Zion's sacred height
   his kingdom he maintains,
and, glorious with his saints in light,
   for ever reigns.

The God who reigns on high
    the great archangels sing,
and "Holy, holy, holy," cry,
    "Almighty King!
Who was, and is, the same,
    and evermore shall be:
eternal Father, great I AM,
    we worship thee."

The whole triumphant host
    give thanks to God on high;
"Hail, Father, Son, and Holy Ghost!"
    they ever cry;
hail, Abraham's Lord divine!
    With heaven our songs we raise;
all might and majesty are thine,
    and endless praise.

Thomas Olivers (1725–1799), alt.

## 402, 403

*Antiphon: Let all the world in every corner sing,
          my God and King!*

The heavens are not too high,
his praise may thither fly;
the earth is not too low,
his praises there may grow.

*Antiphon*

The Church with psalms must shout,
no door can keep them out;
but, above all, the heart
must bear the longest part.

*Antiphon*

George Herbert (1593–1633)

## 404

We will extol you, ever-blessèd Lord;
   your holy Name for ever be adored;
each day we live our psalm to you we raise;
   you, God and King, are worthy of all praise,
   great and unsearchable in all your ways.

Age shall to age pass on the endless song,
   telling the wonders which to you belong,
your mighty acts with joy and fear relate;
   praise we your glory while on you we wait,
   glad in the knowledge of your love so great.

You, Lord, are gracious, merciful to all,
   close to your children when on you they call;
and slow to anger, merciful and kind,
   in your compassion we your blessings find.
   We love you with our heart and strength and mind.

J. Nichol Grieve, alt.; para. of Psalm 145

## 405

*All things bright and beautiful,*
  *all creatures great and small,*
*all things wise and wonderful,*
  *the Lord God made them all.*

Each little flower that opens,
  each little bird that sings,
he made their glowing colors,
  he made their tiny wings.

*Refrain*

The purple-headed mountain,
  the river running by,
the sunset, and the morning
  that brightens up the sky,

*Refrain*

The cold wind in the winter,
  the pleasant summer sun,
the ripe fruits in the garden,
  he made them every one.

*Refrain*

He gave us eyes to see them,
  and lips that we might tell
how great is God Almighty,
  who has made all things well.

*Refrain*

Cecil Frances Alexander (1818–1895)

## 406, 407

Most High, omnipotent, good Lord,
to thee be ceaseless praise outpoured,
    and blessing without measure.
From thee alone all creatures came;
no one is worthy thee to name.

My Lord be praised by brother sun
who through the skies his course doth run,
    and shines in brilliant splendor:
with brightness he doth fill the day,
and signifies thy boundless sway.

My Lord be praised by sister moon
and all the stars, that with her soon
    will point the glittering heavens.
Let wind and air and cloud and calm
and weathers all, repeat the psalm.

By sister water be thou blessed,
most humble, useful, precious, chaste;
    be praised by brother fire;
jocund is he, robust and bright,
and strong to lighten all the night.

By mother earth my Lord be praised;
governed by thee she hath upraised
    what for our life is needful.
Sustained by thee, through every hour,
she bringeth forth fruit, herb, and flower.

My Lord be praised by those who prove
in free forgivingness their love,
    nor shrink from tribulation.
Happy, who peaceably endure;
with thee, Lord, their reward is sure.

For death our sister, praisèd be,
from whom no one alive can flee.
    Woe to the unpreparèd!
But blest be they who do thy will
and follow thy commandments still.

Most High, omnipotent, good Lord,
to thee be ceaseless praise outpoured,
    and blessing without measure.
Let creatures all give thanks to thee,
and serve in great humility.

Francis of Assisi (1182–1226); tr. Howard Chandler Robbins
(1876–1952), alt.

## 408

Sing praise to God who reigns above,
    the God of all creation,
the God of power, the God of love,
    the God of our salvation;
with healing balm my soul he fills,
and every faithless murmur stills:
    to God all praise and glory.

What God's almighty power hath made,
   his gracious mercy keepeth;
by morning glow or evening shade
   his watchful eye ne'er sleepeth.
Within the kingdom of his might,
lo! all is just and all is right:
   to God all praise and glory.

Let all who name Christ's holy Name
   give God all praise and glory;
let all who know his power proclaim
   aloud the wondrous story!
Cast each false idol from its throne,
the Lord is God, and he alone:
   to God all praise and glory.

Johann Jakob Schütz (1640–1690); tr. Frances Elizabeth Cox (1812–1897), alt.

## 409

The spacious firmament on high,
with all the blue eternal sky,
and spangled heavens, a shining frame,
their great Original proclaim.
The unwearied sun from day to day
does his Creator's power display;
and publishes to every land
the work of an almighty hand.

Soon as the evening shades prevail,
the moon takes up the wondrous tale,
and nightly to the listening earth
repeats the story of her birth:
whilst all the stars that round her burn,
and all the planets in their turn,
confirm the tidings, as they roll
and spread the truth from pole to pole.

What though in solemn silence all
move round the dark terrestrial ball?
What though no real voice nor sound
amid their radiant orbs be found?
In reason's ear they all rejoice,
and utter forth a glorious voice;
for ever singing as they shine,
"The hand that made us is divine."

Joseph Addison (1672–1719); para. of Psalm 19: 1–6

# 410

Praise, my soul, the King of heaven;
    to his feet thy tribute bring;
ransomed, healed, restored, forgiven,
    evermore his praises sing:
        Alleluia, alleluia!
    Praise the everlasting King.

Praise him for his grace and favor
    to his people in distress;
praise him still the same as ever,
    slow to chide, and swift to bless:
        Alleluia, alleluia!
    Glorious in this faithfulness.

Father-like he tends and spares us;
    well our feeble frame he knows;
in his hand he gently bears us,
    rescues us from all our foes.
        Alleluia, alleluia!
    Widely yet his mercy flows.

Angels, help us to adore him;
    ye behold him face to face;
sun and moon, bow down before him,
    dwellers all in time and space.
        Alleluia, alleluia!
    Praise with us the God of grace.

Henry Francis Lyte (1793–1847)

## 411

O bless the Lord, my soul!
 His grace to thee proclaim!
And all that is within me join
 to bless his holy Name!

O bless the Lord, my soul!
 His mercies bear in mind!
Forget not all his benefits!
 The Lord to thee is kind.

He will not always chide;
 he will with patience wait;
his wrath is ever slow to rise
 and ready to abate.

He pardons all thy sins,
 prolongs thy feeble breath;
he healeth thine infirmities
 and ransoms thee from death.

He clothes thee with his love,
 upholds thee with his truth;
and like the eagle he renews
 the vigor of thy youth.

Then bless his holy Name,
 whose grace hath made thee whole,
whose loving-kindness crowns thy days:
 O bless the Lord, my soul!

James Montgomery (1771–1854); para. of Psalm 103

# 412

Earth and all stars,
   loud rushing planets,
sing to the Lord a new song!
   O victory,
   loud shouting army,
sing to the Lord a new song!

> *He hath done marvelous things.*
> *I, too, will praise him with a new song!*

Hail, wind, and rain,
   loud blowing snowstorms,
sing to the Lord a new song!
   Flowers and trees,
   loud rustling dry leaves,
sing to the Lord a new song!

*Refrain*

Trumpet and pipes,
   loud clashing cymbals,
sing to the Lord a new song!
   Harp, lute, and lyre,
   loud humming cellos,
sing to the Lord a new song!

*Refrain*

Engines and steel,
   loud pounding hammers,
sing to the Lord a new song!
   Limestone and beams,
   loud building workers,
sing to the Lord a new song!

*Refrain*

Classrooms and labs,
   loud boiling test-tubes,
sing to the Lord a new song!
   Athlete and band,
   loud cheering people,
sing to the Lord a new song!

*Refrain*

Knowledge and truth,
   loud sounding wisdom,
sing to the Lord a new song!
   Daughter and son,
   loud praying members,
sing to the Lord a new song!

*Refrain*

Herbert F. Brokering (b. 1926)

**413**

New songs of celebration render
    to him who has great wonders done;
awed by his love his foes surrender
    and fall before the Mighty One.
He has made known his great salvation
    which all his friends with joy confess;
he has revealed to every nation
    his everlasting righteousness.

Joyfully, heartily resounding,
    let every instrument and voice
peal out the praise of grace abounding,
    calling the whole world to rejoice.
Trumpets and organs set in motion
    such sounds as make the heavens ring:
all things that live in earth and ocean,
    make music for your mighty King.

Rivers and seas and torrents roaring,
    honor the Lord with wild acclaim;
mountains and stones look up adoring
    and find a voice to praise his Name.
Righteous, commanding, ever glorious,
    praises be his that never cease;
just is our God, whose truth victorious
    establishes the world in peace.

Erik Routley (1917–1982); para. of Psalm 98

# 414

God, my King, thy might confessing,
    ever will I bless thy Name;
day by day thy throne addressing,
    still will I thy praise proclaim.

Honor great our God befitteth;
    who his majesty can reach?
Age to age his works transmitteth,
    age to age his power shall teach.

They shall talk of all thy glory,
    on thy might and greatness dwell,
speak of thy dread acts the story,
    and thy deeds of wonder tell.

Nor shall fail from memory's treasure
    works by love and mercy wrought,
works of love surpassing measure,
    works of mercy passing thought.

Full of kindness and compassion,
    slow to anger, vast in love,
God is good to all creation;
    all his works his goodness prove.

All thy works, O Lord, shall bless thee;
    thee shall all thy saints adore:
King supreme shall they confess thee,
    and proclaim thy sovereign power.

Richard Mant (1776–1848); para. of Psalm 145

**415**

When all thy mercies, O my God,
    my rising soul surveys,
transported with the view, I'm lost
    in wonder, love, and praise.

O how shall words with equal warmth
    the gratitude declare,
that glows within my fervent heart?
    But thou canst read it there.

Ten thousand thousand precious gifts
    my daily thanks employ;
nor is the least a cheerful heart
    that tastes those gifts with joy.

When nature fails, and day and night
    divide thy works no more,
my ever grateful heart, O Lord,
    thy mercy shall adore.

Through all eternity, to thee
    a joyful song I'll raise;
but oh, eternity's too short
    to utter all thy praise!

Joseph Addison (1672–1719), alt.

## 416

For the beauty of the earth,
   for the beauty of the skies,
for the love which from our birth
   over and around us lies,

> *Christ our God, to thee we raise*
> *this our hymn of grateful praise.*

For the beauty of each hour
   of the day and of the night,
hill and vale, and tree and flower,
   sun and moon, and stars of light,

*Refrain*

For the joy of ear and eye,
   for the heart and mind's delight,
for the mystic harmony
   linking sense to sound and sight,

*Refrain*

For the joy of human love,
   brother, sister, parent, child,
friends on earth, and friends above,
   for all gentle thoughts and mild,

*Refrain*

For the Church which evermore
   lifteth holy hands above,

offering up on every shore
   thy pure sacrifice of love,

*Refrain*

For each perfect gift of thine
   to the world so freely given,
faith and hope and love divine,
   peace on earth and joy in heaven,

*Refrain*

Folliot Sandford Pierpoint (1835–1917), alt.

## 417, 418

*Antiphon: This is the feast of victory for our God.*
   *Alleluia, alleluia, alleluia!*

Worthy is Christ, the Lamb who was slain,
whose blood set us free to be people of God.

*Antiphon*

Power, riches, wisdom, and strength, and honor,
blessing, and glory are his.

*Antiphon*

Sing with all the people of God,
and join in the hymn of all creation.

*Antiphon*

Blessing, honor, glory, and might
be to God and the Lamb for ever. Amen.

   *Antiphon*

For the Lamb who was slain
has begun his reign.  Alleluia!

   *Antiphon*

Revelation 5:12-13; adapt. John W. Arthur (1922–1980)

## 419

Lord of all being, throned afar,
thy glory flames from sun and star;
center and soul of every sphere,
yet to each loving heart how near!

Sun of our life, thy quickening ray
sheds on our path the glow of day;
star of our hope, thy softened light
cheers the long watches of the night.

Lord of all life, below, above,
whose light is truth, whose warmth is love,
before thy ever-blazing throne
we ask no luster of our own.

Grant us thy truth to make us free,
and kindling hearts that burn for thee,
till all thy living altars claim
one holy light, one heavenly flame.

Oliver Wendell Holmes (1809–1894)

## 420

When in our music God is glorified,
and adoration leaves no room for pride,
it is as though the whole creation cried
   Alleluia!

How often, making music, we have found
a new dimension in the world of sound,
as worship moved us to a more profound
   Alleluia!

So has the Church, in liturgy and song,
in faith and love, through centuries of wrong,
borne witness to the truth in every tongue,
   Alleluia!

And did not Jesus sing a psalm that night
when utmost evil strove against the Light?
Then let us sing, for whom he won the fight,
   Alleluia!

Let every instrument be tuned for praise!
Let all rejoice who have a voice to raise!
And may God give us faith to sing always
   Alleluia!

F. Pratt Green (b. 1903)

# 421

All glory be to God on high,
    and peace on earth from heaven,
and God's good will unfailingly
    be to all people given.
We bless, we worship you, we raise
for your great glory thanks and praise,
    O God, Almighty Father.

O Lamb of God, Lord Jesus Christ,
    whom God the Father gave us,
who for the world was sacrificed
    upon the cross to save us;
and, as you sit at God's right hand
and we for judgment there must stand,
    have mercy, Lord, upon us.

You only are the Holy One,
    who came for our salvation,
and only you are God's true Son,
    who was before creation.
You only, Christ, as Lord we own and,
with the Spirit, you alone
    share in the Father's glory.

Nikolaus Decius (1490?–1541); tr. F. Bland Tucker (1895–1984), rev.; para. of *Gloria in excelsis*

## 422

Not far beyond the sea, nor high
above the heavens, but very high
    thy voice, O God, is heard.
For each new step of faith we take
thou hast more truth and light to break
    forth from thy Holy Word.

Rooted and grounded in thy love,
with saints on earth and saints above
    we join in full accord:
to know the breadth, length, depth, and height,
the crucified and risen might
    of Christ, the incarnate Word.

Help us to press on toward that mark,
and, though our vision now is dark,
    to live by what we see.
So, when we see thee face to face,
thy truth and light our dwelling-place
for evermore shall be.

George B. Caird (b. 1917), alt.

## 423

Immortal, invisible, God only wise,
in light inaccessible hid from our eyes,
most blessed, most glorious, the Ancient of Days,
almighty, victorious, thy great Name we praise.

Unresting, unhasting, and silent as light,
nor wanting, nor wasting, thou rulest in might;
thy justice like mountains high soaring above
thy clouds, which are fountains of goodness and love.

To all life thou givest, to both great and small;
in all life thou livest, the true life of all;
we blossom and flourish, like leaves on the tree,
then wither and perish; but nought changeth thee.

Thou reignest in glory, thou rulest in light,
thine angels adore thee, all veiling their sight;
all laud we would render: O help us to see
'tis only the splendor of light hideth thee.

Walter Chalmers Smith (1824–1908), alt.

## 424

For the fruit of all creation,
    thanks be to God.
For his gifts to every nation,
    thanks be to God.
For the plowing, sowing, reaping,
silent growth while we are sleeping,

future needs in earth's safe-keeping,
>  thanks be to God.

In the just reward of labor,
>  God's will be done.
In the help we give our neighbor,
>  God's will be done.
In our world-wide task of caring
for the hungry and despairing,
in the harvests we are sharing,
>  God's will be done.

For the harvests of the Spirit,
>  thanks be to God.
For the good we all inherit,
>  thanks be to God.
For the wonders that astound us,
for the truths that still confound us,
most of all that love has found us,
>  thanks be to God.

F. Pratt Green (b. 1903), alt.

## 425

Sing now with joy unto the Lord,
>  for he has triumphed gloriously!
The horse, the rider, and the sword
>  he cast into the raging sea.

God is our strength, he is our song,
>  he saved us from our enemy.

All praise and thanks to him belong
   who came to set his people free.

He only is the mighty Lord.
   He only can destroy the foe.
He only is to be adored
   for he alone can strength bestow.

Anon., ca. 1976; alt.; based on Exodus 15:1–2

## 426

Songs of praise the angels sang,
heaven with alleluias rang,
when creation was begun,
when God spoke and it was done.

Songs of praise awoke the morn
when the Prince of Peace was born;
songs of praise arose when he
captive led captivity.

Heaven and earth must pass away;
songs of praise shall crown that day;
God will make new heaven and earth;
songs of praise shall hail their birth.

And shall Christians fail to sing
till on earth Christ come as King?
No; the Church delights to raise
psalms and hymns and songs of praise.

Saints below, with heart and voice,
still in songs of praise rejoice,
learning here, by faith and love,
songs of praise to sing above.

Borne upon their latest breath,
songs of praise shall conquer death;
then, amidst eternal joy,
songs of praise their powers employ.

James Montgomery (1771–1854), alt.

**427**

When morning gilds the skies,
my heart, awaking, cries,
   may Jesus Christ be praised!
When evening shadows fall,
this rings my curfew call,
   may Jesus Christ be praised!

When mirth for music longs,
this is my song of songs:
   may Jesus Christ be praised!
God's holy house of prayer
hath none that can compare
   with: Jesus Christ be praised!

No lovelier antiphon
in all high heaven is known
   than, Jesus Christ be praised!

There to the eternal Word
the eternal psalm is heard:
   may Jesus Christ be praised!

Ye nations of mankind,
in this your concord find:
   may Jesus Christ be praised!
Let all the earth around
ring joyous with the sound:
   may Jesus Christ be praised!

Sing, suns and stars of space,
sing, ye that see his face,
   sing, Jesus Christ be praised!
God's whole creation o'er,
both now and evermore
   shall Jesus Christ be praised!

German, ca. 1800; tr. Robert Seymour Bridges (1844–1930), alt.

## 428

O all ye works of God, now come
   to thank him and adore;
O angels, sing and bless the Lord
   and praise him evermore.

O sun and moon and stars of heaven,
   your endless praise outpour;
O changing seasons, bless the Lord
   and praise him evermore.

O heat and cold, O night and day,
  O storms and thunder's roar,
O fields and forests, bless the Lord
  and praise him evermore.

O earth and sea, O all that live
  in water or on shore,
O men and women, bless the Lord
  and praise him evermore.

O let his people bless the Lord
  like righteous souls of yore;
let those of holy, humble heart
  come praise him evermore.

So let us glorify and bless
  the God we bow before,
the Father, Holy Spirit, Son,
  and praise him evermore.

F. Bland Tucker (1895–1984), rev.; para. of *A Song of Creation*

**429**

I'll praise my Maker while I've breath;
and when my voice is lost in death,
  praise shall employ my nobler powers.
My days of praise shall ne'er be past
while life and thought and being last,
  or immortality endures.

How happy they whose hopes rely
on Israel's God, who made the sky
    and earth and seas with all their train;
whose truth for ever stands secure,
who saves the oppressed, and feeds the poor.
    And none shall find his promise vain.

The Lord pours eyesight on the blind;
the Lord supports the fainting mind
    and sends the laboring conscience peace.
He helps the stranger in distress,
the widowed and the fatherless,
    and grants the prisoner sweet release.

I'll praise him while he lends me breath;
and when my voice is lost in death,
    praise shall employ my nobler powers.
My days of praise shall ne'er be past
while life and thought and being last,
    or immortality endures.

Isaac Watts (1674–1748); alt. by John Wesley (1703–1791), alt.; based on Psalm 146

## 430

Come, O come, our voices raise,
sounding God Almighty's praise;
hither bring in one consent
heart, and voice, and instrument.
Alleluia!

Sound the trumpet, touch the lute,
let no tongue nor string be mute,
nor a voiceless creature found,
that hath neither note nor sound.
Alleluia!

Come ye all before his face,
in this chorus take your place;
and amid the mortal throng,
be you masters of the song.

Let, in praise of God, the sound
run a never-ending round,
that our songs of praise may be
everlasting, as is he.
Alleluia!

So this huge wide orb we see
shall one choir, one temple be;
where in such a praiseful tone
we will sing what he hath done.
Alleluia!

Thus our song shall overclimb
all the bounds of space and time;
come, then, come, our voices raise,
sounding God Almighty's praise.
Alleluia!

George Wither (1588–1667), alt.

## 431

The stars declare his glory;
    the vault of heaven springs
mute witness of the Master's hand
    in all created things,
and through the silences of space
    their soundless music sings.

The dawn returns in splendor,
    the heavens burn and blaze,
the rising sun renews the race
    that measures all our days
and writes in fire across the skies
    God's majesty and praise.

So shine the Lord's commandments
    to make the simple wise;
more sweet than honey to the taste,
    more rich than any prize,
a law of love within our hearts,
    a light before our eyes.

So order too this life of mine,
    direct it all my days;
the meditations of my heart
    be innocence and praise,
my rock, and my redeeming Lord,
    in all my words and ways.

Timothy Dudley-Smith (b. 1926); para. of Psalm 19

## 432

O praise ye the Lord!
  Praise him in the height;
rejoice in his word,
  ye angels of light;
ye heavens, adore him
  by whom ye were made,
and worship before him,
  in brightness arrayed.

O praise ye the Lord!
  Praise him upon earth,
in tuneful accord,
  all ye of new birth;
praise him who hath brought you
  his grace from above,
praise him who hath taught you
  to sing of his love.

O praise ye the Lord!
  All things that give sound;
each jubilant chord
  re-echo around;
loud organs, his glory
  forth tell in deep tone,
and sweet harp, the story
  of what he hath done.

O praise ye the Lord!
   Thanksgiving and song
to him be outpoured
   all ages along!
For love in creation,
   for heaven restored,
for grace of salvation,
   O praise ye the Lord!

Henry Williams Baker (1821–1877), alt.; based on Psalms 148 and 150

## 433

We gather together to ask the Lord's blessing;
   he chastens and hastens his will to make known;
the wicked oppressing now cease from distressing:
   sing praises to his Name; he forgets not his own.

Beside us to guide us, our God with us joining,
   ordaining, maintaining his kingdom divine;
so from the beginning the fight we were winning:
   thou, Lord, wast at our side: all glory be thine!

We all do extol thee, thou leader triumphant,
   and pray that thou still our defender wilt be.
Let thy congregation escape tribulation:
   thy Name be ever praised! O Lord, make us free!

Anon., 1625; tr. Theodore Baker (1851–1934)

## 434

Nature with open volume stands
    to spread her Maker's praise abroad
and every labor of his hands
    shows something worthy of a God.

But in the grace that rescued man
    his brightest form of glory shines;
here, on the cross, 'tis fairest drawn
    in precious blood and crimson lines.

Here his whole Name appears complete;
    nor wit can guess, nor reason prove
which of the letters best is writ,
    the power, the wisdom, or the love.

Oh, the sweet wonders of that cross
    where Christ my Savior loved and died!
Her noblest life my spirit draws
    from his dear wounds and bleeding side.

I would for ever speak his Name
    in sounds to mortal ears unknown,
with angels join to praise the Lamb
    and worship at his Father's throne!

Isaac Watts (1674–1748), alt.

## 435

At the Name of Jesus
    every knee shall bow,
every tongue confess him
    King of glory now;
'tis the Father's pleasure
    we should call him Lord
who from the beginning
    was the mighty Word.

Humbled for a season,
    to receive a Name
from the lips of sinners,
    unto whom he came,
faithfully he bore it
    spotless to the last,
brought it back victorious,
    when from death he passed;

bore it up triumphant,
    with its human light,
through all ranks of creatures,
    to the central height,
to the throne of Godhead,
    to the Father's breast;
filled it with the glory
    of that perfect rest.

Name him, Christians, name him,
    with love strong as death,
name with awe and wonder
    and with bated breath;
he is God the Savior,
    he is Christ the Lord,
ever to be worshiped,
    trusted, and adored.

In your hearts enthrone him;
    there let him subdue
all that is not holy,
    all that is not true;
crown him as your Captain
    in temptation's hour;
let his will enfold you
    in its light and power.

Christians, this Lord Jesus
    shall return again,
with his Father's glory
    o'er the earth to reign;
for all wreaths of empire
    meet upon his brow,
and our hearts confess him
    King of glory now.

Caroline Maria Noel (1817–1877), alt.

## 436

Lift up your heads, ye mighty gates;
behold the King of glory waits!
The King of kings is drawing near;
the Savior of the world is here.

O blest the land, the city blest,
where Christ the ruler is confessed!
O happy hearts and happy homes
to whom this King of triumph comes!

Fling wide the portals of your heart;
make it a temple, set apart
from earthly use for heaven's employ,
adorned with prayer and love and joy.

Redeemer, come! I open wide
my heart to thee: here, Lord, abide!
Let me thy inner presence feel:
thy grace and love in me reveal.

So come, my Sovereign; enter in!
Let new and nobler life begin;
thy Holy Spirit guide us on,
until the glorious crown be won.

Georg Weissel (1590–1635); tr. Catherine Winkworth (1827–1878)

## 437, 438

Tell out, my soul, the greatness of the Lord!
   Unnumbered blessings give my spirit voice;
tender to me the promise of his word;
   in God my Savior shall my heart rejoice.

Tell out, my soul, the greatness of his Name!
   Make known his might, the deeds
               his arm has done;
his mercy sure, from age the same;
   his holy Name–the Lord, the Mighty One.

Tell out, my soul, the greatness of his might!
   Powers and dominions lay their glory by.
Proud hearts and stubborn wills are put to flight,
   the hungry fed, the humble lifted high.

Tell out, my soul, the glories of his word!
   Firm is his promise, and his mercy sure.
Tell out, my soul, the greatness of the Lord
   to children's children and for evermore!

Timothy Dudley-Smith (b. 1926); based on *The Song of Mary*

## 439

What wondrous love is this,
   O my soul, O my soul!
What wondrous love is this,
   O my soul!
What wondrous love is this
that caused the Lord of bliss
   to lay aside his crown
      for my soul, for my soul,
   to lay aside his crown
      for my soul.

To God and to the Lamb,
   I will sing, I will sing,
to God and to the Lamb,
   I will sing.
To God and to the Lamb
who is the great I AM,
   while millions join the theme,
      I will sing, I will sing,
   while millions join the theme
      I will sing.

And when from death I'm free,
   I'll sing on, I'll sing on,
and when from death I'm free,
   I'll sing on.

And when from death I'm free
I'll sing and joyful be,
  and through eternity
    I'll sing on, I'll sing on,
  and through eternity
    I'll sing on, I'll sing on.

American folk hymn, ca. 1835

## 440

Blessèd Jesus, at thy word
  we are gathered all to hear thee;
let our hearts and souls be stirred
  now to seek and love and fear thee;
by thy teachings pure and holy,
drawn from earth to love thee solely.

All our knowledge, sense, and sight
  lie in deepest darkness shrouded,
till thy Spirit breaks our night
  with the beams of truth unclouded;
thou alone to God canst win us;
thou must work all good within us.

Gracious Lord, thyself impart!
  Light of Light, from God proceeding,
open thou our ears and heart,
  help us by thy Spirit's pleading.
Hear the cry thy Church upraises;
hear, and bless our prayers and praises.

Tobias Clausnitzer (1619–1684); tr. Catherine Winkworth (1829–1878); alt.

## 441, 442

In the cross of Christ I glory,
  towering o'er the wrecks of time;
all the light of sacred story
  gathers round its head sublime.

When the woes of life o'ertake me,
  hopes deceive, and fears annoy,
never shall the cross forsake me:
  lo, it glows with peace and joy.

When the sun of bliss is beaming
  light and love upon my way,
from the cross the radiance streaming
  adds new luster to the day.

Bane and blessing, pain and pleasure,
  by the cross are sanctified;
peace is there that knows no measure,
  joys that through all time abide.

In the cross of Christ I glory,
  towering o'er the wrecks of time;
all the light of sacred story
  gathers round its head sublime.

John Bowring (1792–1872)

**443**

From God Christ's deity came forth,
his manhood from humanity;
his priesthood from Melchizedek,
his royalty from David's tree:
   praised be his Oneness.

He joined with guests at wedding feast,
yet in the wilderness did fast;
he taught within the temple's gates;
his people saw him die at last:
   praised be his teaching.

The dissolute he did not scorn,
nor turn from those who were in sin;
he for the righteous did rejoice
but bade the fallen to come in:
   praised be his mercy.

He did not disregard the sick;
to simple ones his word was given;
and he descended to the earth
and his work done, went up to heaven:
   praised be his coming.

Who then, my Lord, compares with you?
The Watcher slept, the Great was small,
the Pure baptized, the Life who died,
the King abased to honor all:
   praised be your glory.

Ephrem of Edessa (4th cent.); tr. by J. Howard W. Rhys (b. 1917); adapt. and alt. F. Bland Tucker (1895–1984)

## 444

Blessed be the God of Israel,
    who comes to set us free;
he visits and redeems us,
    he grants us liberty.
The prophets spoke of mercy,
    of freedom and release;
God shall fulfill his promise
    and bring his people peace.

He from the house of David
    a child of grace has given;
a Savior comes among us
    to raise us up to heaven.
Before him goes his herald,
    forerunner in the way,
the prophet of salvation,
    the harbinger of Day.

On prisoners of darkness
    the sun begins to rise,
the dawning of forgiveness
    upon the sinner's eyes.
He guides the feet of pilgrims
    along the paths of peace.
O bless our God and Savior,
    with songs that never cease.

Michael A. Perry (b. 1942), alt.; para. of *The Song of Zechariah*

**445, 446**

Praise to the Holiest in the height,
    and in the depth be praise;
in all his words most wonderful,
    most sure in all his ways!

O loving wisdom of our God!
    When all was sin and shame,
a second Adam to the fight
    and to the rescue came.

O wisest love! that flesh and blood,
    which did in Adam fail,
should strive afresh against the foe,
    should strive, and should prevail;

and that the highest gift of grace
    should flesh and blood refine:
God's presence and his very self,
    and essence all-divine.

Praise to the Holiest in the height,
    and in the depth be praise;
in all his words most wonderful,
    most sure in all his ways!

John Henry Newman (1801–1890), alt.

## 447

The Christ who died but rose again
    triumphant from the grave,
now pleads our cause at God's right hand
    all-powerful to save.

What now can separate us from
    the love of Christ our Lord?
Can persecution, nakedness,
    or peril, or the sword?

The troubles that are ours to bear
    are trials we cannot flee;
yet he who loved us from the first
    ensures our victory.

Thus nothing in the heights or depths,
    no power earth can afford,
will separate us from the love
    of Jesus Christ our Lord.

Granton Douglas Hay (b. 1943); alt.; based on *Paraphrases*, 1781; para. of Romans 8:34–39

**448, 449**

O love, how deep, how broad, how high,
how passing thought and fantasy,
that God, the Son of God, should take
our mortal form for mortals' sake.

For us baptized, for us he bore
his holy fast and hungered sore;
for us temptations sharp he knew;
for us the tempter overthrew.

For us he prayed; for us he taught;
for us his daily works he wrought:
by words and signs and actions, thus
still seeking not himself, but us.

For us to wicked men betrayed,
scourged, mocked, in purple robe arrayed,
he bore the shameful cross and death;
for us gave up his dying breath.

For us he rose from death again;
for us he went on high to reign;
for us he sent his Spirit here
to guide, to strengthen, and to cheer.

All glory to our Lord and God
for love so deep, so high, so broad;
the Trinity whom we adore
for ever and for evermore.

Latin, 15th cent.; tr. Benjamin Webb (1819–1885), alt.

## 450, 451

All hail the power of Jesus' Name!
   Let angels prostrate fall;
bring forth the royal diadem,
   and crown him Lord of all!

Crown him, ye martyrs of our God,
   who from his altar call:
praise him whose way of pain ye trod,
   and crown him Lord of all!

Hail him, the Heir of David's line,
   whom David Lord did call,
the God incarnate, Man divine,
   and crown him Lord of all!

Ye heirs of Israel's chosen race,
   ye ransomed of the fall,
hail him who saves you by his grace,
   and crown him Lord of all!

Sinners, whose love can ne'er forget
   the wormwood and the gall,
go, spread your trophies at his feet,
   and crown him Lord of all!

Let every kindred, every tribe,
   on this terrestrial ball,
to him all majesty ascribe,
   and crown him Lord of all!

Edward Perronet (1726–1792), alt.

## 452

Glorious the day when Christ was born
to wear the crown that Caesars scorn,
whose life and death that love reveal
which mortals need and need to feel.

*Alleluia!*

Glorious the day when Christ arose,
the surest friend of all his foes;
who for the sake of those he grieves
transcends the world he never leaves.

*Alleluia!*

Glorious the days of gospel grace
when Christ restores the fallen race,
when doubters kneel and waverers stand
and faith achieves what reason planned.

*Alleluia!*

Glorious the day when Christ fulfills
what self rejects yet feebly wills;
when that strong Light puts out the sun
and all is ended, all begun.

*Alleluia!*

F. Pratt Green (b. 1903), rev.

## 453

As Jacob with travel was weary one day,
at night on a stone for a pillow he lay;
he saw in a vision a ladder so high,
that its foot was on earth and its top in the sky:

> *Alleluia to Jesus, who died on the tree*
> *and has raised up a ladder of mercy for me.*

The ladder is long, it is strong and well-made,
has stood hundreds of years and is not yet decayed;
many millions have climbed it  and reached
                        Zion's hill,
many millions by faith now are climbing it still :

*Refrain*

Come, let us ascend!  All may climb it who will,
for the angels of Jacob are guarding it still;
and remember, each step that by faith we pass o'er,
many prophets and martyrs have trod it before:

*Refrain*

And when we arrive at the haven of rest,
we shall hear the glad words,  "Come to me
                        all the blest,
here are regions of light, here are mansions of bliss."
Who would not want to climb such a ladder as this:

*Refrain*

English carol, ca. 18th cent.

## 454

Jesus came, adored by angels,
    came with peace from realms on high;
Jesus came for our redemption,
    lowly came on earth to die:
Alleluia, alleluia!
    came in deep humility.

Jesus comes again in mercy,
    when our hearts are bowed with care:
Jesus comes again in answer
    to our earnest heart-felt prayer;
Alleluia, alleluia!
    comes to save us from despair.

Jesus comes to hearts rejoicing,
    bringing news of sins forgiven;
Jesus comes in sounds of gladness,
    leading souls redeemed to heaven;
Alleluia, alleluia!
    now the gate of death is riven.

Jesus comes on clouds triumphant,
    when the heavens shall pass away;
Jesus comes again in glory;
    let us then our homage pay:
Alleluia, alleluia!
    till the dawn of endless day.

Godfrey Thring (1823–1903), alt.

## 455, 456

O Love of God, how strong and true,
eternal and yet ever new;
uncomprehended and unbought,
beyond all knowledge and all thought.

O wide-embracing, wondrous Love,
we read thee in the sky above;
we read thee in the earth below,
in seas that swell and streams that flow.

We read thee best in him who came
to bear for us the cross of shame,
sent by the Father from on high,
our life to live, our death to die.

We read thy power to bless and save
e'en in the darkness of the grave;
still more in resurrection light
we read the fullness of thy might.

Horatius Bonar (1808–1889)

**457**

Thou art the Way, to thee alone
 from sin and death we flee;
and all who would the Father seek,
 must seek him, Lord, by thee.

Thou art the Truth, thy word alone
 true wisdom can impart;
thou only canst inform the mind
 and purify the heart.

Thou art the Life, the rending tomb
 proclaims thy conquering arm;
and those who put their trust in thee
 nor death nor hell shall harm.

Thou art the Way, the Truth, the Life:
 grant us that way to know,
that truth to keep, that life to win,
 whose joys eternal flow.

George Washington Doane (1799–1859), alt.

## 458

My song is love unknown,
   my Savior's love to me,
love to the loveless shown
   that they might lovely be.
     O who am I
       that for my sake
       my Lord should take
     frail flesh, and die?

He came from his blest throne
   salvation to bestow,
but men made strange, and none
   the longed-for Christ would know.
     But O my friend,
       my friend indeed,
       who at my need
     his life did spend.

Sometimes they strew his way,
   and his strong praises sing,
resounding all the day
   hosannas to their King.
     Then "Crucify!"
       is all their breath,
       and for his death
     they thirst and cry.

Why, what hath my Lord done?
   What makes this rage and spite?
He made the lame to run,
   he gave the blind their sight.
     Sweet injuries!
       Yet they at these
       themselves displease,
     and 'gainst him rise.

They rise, and needs will have
   my dear Lord made away;
a murderer they save,
   the Prince of Life they slay.
     Yet steadfast he
       to suffering goes,
       that he his foes
     from thence might free.

In life no house, no home
   my Lord on earth might have;
in death no friendly tomb
   but what a stranger gave.
     What may I say?
       Heaven was his home;
       but mine the tomb
     wherein he lay.

Here might I stay and sing,
   no story so divine:
never was love, dear King,
   never was grief like thine,
     This is my friend,
       in whose sweet praise
      I all my days
     could gladly spend.

Samuel Crossman (1624–1683), alt.

## 459

And have the bright immensities
   received our risen Lord,
where light-years frame the Pleiades
   and point Orion's sword?
Do flaming suns his footsteps trace
   through corridors sublime,
the Lord of interstellar space
   and Conqueror of time?

The heaven that hides him from our sight
   knows neither near nor far;
an altar candle sheds its light
   as surely as a star:
and where his loving people meet
   to share the gift divine,
there stands he with unhurrying feet;
   there heavenly splendors shine.

Howard Chandler Robbins (1876–1952)

## 460, 461

Alleluia! sing to Jesus!
   his the scepter, his the throne;
Alleluia! his the triumph,
   his the victory alone;
Hark! the songs of peaceful Zion
   thunder like a mighty flood;
Jesus out of every nation
   hath redeemed us by his blood.

Alleluia! not as orphans
   are we left in sorrow now;
Alleluia! he is near us,
   faith believes, nor questions how:
though the cloud from sight received him,
   when the forty days were o'er,
shall our hearts forget his promise,
   "I am with you evermore"?

Alleluia! bread of Heaven,
   Thou on earth our food, our stay!
Alleluia! here the sinful
   flee to thee from day to day:
Intercessor, friend of sinners,
   earth's Redeemer, plead for me,
where the songs of all the sinless
   sweep across the crystal sea.

Alleluia! King eternal,
  thee the Lord of lords we own:
Alleluia! born of Mary,
  earth thy footstool, heaven thy throne:
thou within the veil hast entered,
  robed in flesh, our great High Priest:
thou on earth both Priest and Victim
  in the eucharistic feast.

Alleluia! sing to Jesus!
  his the scepter, his the throne;
Alleluia! his the triumph,
  his the victory alone;
Hark! the songs of holy Zion
  thunder like a mighty flood;
Jesus out of every nation
  hath redeemed us by his blood.

William Chatterton Dix (1837–1898)

# 462

The Lord will come and not be slow,
  his footsteps cannot err;
before him righteousness shall go,
  his royal harbinger.

Truth from the earth, like to a flower,
  shall bud and blossom show;
and justice, from her heavenly bower,
  look down on us below.

Rise, God, judge thou the earth in might,
    this wicked earth redress;
for thou art he who shalt by right
    the nations all possess.

The nations all whom thou hast made
    shall come, and all shall frame
to bow them low before thee, Lord,
    and glorify thy Name.

For great thou art, and wonders great
    by thy strong hand are done:
thou in thy everlasting seat
    remainest God alone.

John Milton (1608–1674), alt.

## 463, 464

He is the Way.
Follow him through the Land of Unlikeness;
you will see rare beasts and have unique adventures.

He is the Truth.
Seek him in the Kingdom of Anxiety:
you will come to a great city that has expected
                your return for years.

He is the Life.
Love him in the World of the Flesh:
and at your marriage all its occasions
                shall dance for joy.

W. H. Auden (1907–1973)

## 465, 466

Eternal light, shine in my heart;
    eternal hope, lift up my eyes;
eternal power, be my support;
    eternal wisdom, make me wise.

Eternal life, raise me from death;
    eternal brightness, help me see;
eternal Spirit, give me breath;
    eternal Savior come to me:

until by your most costly grace,
    invited by your holy word,
at last I come before your face
    to know you, my eternal God.

Christopher Idle (b. 1938), from a prayer of Alcuin (735?–804)

## 467

Sing, my soul, his wondrous love,
who, from yon bright throne above,
ever watchful o'er our race,
still to us extends his grace.

Heaven and earth by him were made;
all is by his scepter swayed;
what are we that he should show
so much love to us below?

God, the merciful and good,
bought us with the Savior's blood,
and, to make salvation sure,
guides us by his Spirit pure.

Sing, my soul, adore his Name!
Let his glory be thy theme:
praise him till he calls thee home;
trust his love for all to come.

Anon., 1800, alt.

**468**

It was poor little Jesus,
   yes, yes;
he was born on Christmas,
   yes, yes;
and laid in a manger,
   yes, yes;

> *wasn't that a pity and a shame,*
>    *Lord, Lord,*
> *wasn't that a pity and a shame?*

It was poor little Jesus,
   yes, yes;
child of Mary,
   yes, yes;
didn't have a cradle,
   yes, yes;

*Refrain*

It was poor little Jesus,
   yes, yes;
they nailed him to the cross, Lord
   yes, yes;
they hung him with a robber,
   yes, yes;

*Refrain*

It was poor little Jesus
   yes, yes;
he's risen from darkness,
   yes, yes;
he's 'scended into glory
   yes, yes;

> *no more a pity, and a shame*
> *Lord, Lord,*
> *no more pity and a shame.*

African-American Spiritual

## 469, 470

There's a wideness in God's mercy
   like the wideness of the sea;
there's a kindness in his justice,
   which is more than liberty.
There is welcome for the sinner,
   and more graces for the good;
there is mercy with the Savior;
   there is healing in his blood.

There is no place where earth's sorrows
    are more felt than up in heaven;
there is no place where earth's failings
    have such kindly judgment given.
There is plentiful redemption
    in the blood that has been shed;
there is joy for all the members
    in the sorrows of the Head.

For the love of God is broader
    than the measure of the mind;
and the heart of the Eternal
    is most wonderfully kind.
If our love were but more faithful,
    we should take him at his word;
and our life would be thanksgiving
    for the goodness of the Lord.

Frederick William Faber (1814–1863), alt.

**471**

We sing the praise of him who died,
    of him who died upon the cross;
the sinner's hope let sin deride:
    for this we count the world but loss.

Inscribed upon the cross we see
    in shining letters, God is love:
he bears our sins upon the tree:
    he brings us mercy from above.

The cross: it takes our guilt away,
    and holds the fainting spirit up;
it cheers with hope the gloomy day,
    and sweetens every bitter cup.

It makes the coward spirit brave,
    and nerves the feeble arm for fight;
it takes its terror from the grave,
    and gilds the bed of death with light.

The balm of life, the cure of woe,
    the measure and the pledge of love,
the sinner's refuge here below,
    the angels' theme in heaven above.

Thomas Kelly (1769–1855), alt.

## 472

Hope of the world, thou Christ of great compassion,
    speak to our fearful hearts by conflict rent.
Save us, thy people, from consuming passion,
    who by our own false hopes and aims are spent.

Hope of the world, God's gift from highest heaven,
    bringing to hungry souls the bread of life,
still let thy Spirit unto us be given
    to heal earth's wounds and end her bitter strife.

Hope of the world, afoot on dusty highways,
    showing to wandering souls the path of light,

walk thou beside us lest the tempting byways
  lure us away from thee to endless night.

Hope of the world, who by thy cross didst save us
  from death and dark despair, from sin and guilt,
we render back the love thy mercy gave us;
  take thou our lives, and use them as thou wilt.

Hope of the world, O Christ, o'er death victorious,
  who by this sign didst conquer grief and pain,
we would be faithful to thy gospel glorious;
  thou art our Lord! Thou dost for ever reign!

Georgia Harkness (1891–1974)

**473**

> *Lift high the cross,*
>   *the love of Christ proclaim*
> *till all the world adore*
>   *his sacred Name.*

Led on their way by this triumphant sign,
the hosts of God in conquering ranks combine.

*Refrain*

Each new-born servant of the Crucified
bears on the brow the seal of him who died.

*Refrain*

O Lord, once lifted on the glorious tree,
as thou hast promised, draw the world to thee.

*Refrain*

So shall our song of triumph ever be:
praise to the Crucified for victory.

*Refrain*

George William Kitchin (1827–1912) and Michael Robert Newbolt (1874–1956)

## 474

When I survey the wondrous cross
    where the young Prince of Glory died,
my richest gain I count but loss,
    and pour contempt on all my pride.

Forbid it, Lord, that I should boast,
    save in the cross of Christ, my God:
all the vain things that charm me most,
    I sacrifice them to his blood.

See, from his head, his hands, his feet
    sorrow and love flow mingled down!
Did e'er such love and sorrow meet,
    or thorns compose so rich a crown?

Were the whole realm of nature mine,
    that were an offering far too small;
love so amazing, so divine,
    demands my soul, my life, my all.

Isaac Watts (1674–1748)

## 475

God himself is with us;
let us all adore him,
and with awe appear before him.

God is here within us;
souls in silence fear him,
humbly, fervently draw near him.

Now his own who have known
God, in worship lowly,
yield their spirits wholly.

Gladly, Lord, we offer
thine to be for ever,
soul and life and each endeavor.

Help us to surrender
earth's deceitful treasures,
pride of life, and sinful pleasures:

thou alone shalt be known
Lord of all our being,
life's true way decreeing.

Thou pervadest all things:
let thy radiant beauty
light mine eyes to see my duty.

As the tender flowers
eagerly unfold them,
to the sunlight calmly hold them,

so let me quietly

in thy rays imbue me;
let thy light shine through me.

Come, abide within me;
let my soul, like Mary,
be thine earthly sanctuary.
Come, indwelling Spirit,
with transfiguring splendor;
love and honor will I render.
Where I go here below,
let me bow before thee,
know thee, and adore thee.

Gerhardt Tersteegen (1697–1769); tr. *Hymnal 1940*, alt.; st. 3, tr. Henry Sloane Coffin (1877–1954)

## 476

Can we by searching find out God
  or formulate his ways?
Can numbers measure what he is
  or words contain his praise?

Although his being is too bright
  for human eyes to scan,
his meaning lights our shadowed world
  through Christ, the Son of Man.

Our boastfulness is turned to shame,
  our profit counts as loss,
when earthly values stand beside
  the manger and the cross.

There God breaks in upon our search,
    makes birth and death his own;
he speaks to us in human terms
    to make his glory known.

Elizabeth Cosnett (b. 1936), alt.

## 477

All praise to thee, for thou, O King divine,
didst yield the glory that of right was thine,
that in our darkened hearts thy grace might shine.
    Alleluia!

Thou cam'st to us in lowliness of thought;
by thee the outcast and the poor were sought;
and by thy death was God's salvation wrought.
    Alleluia!

Let this mind be in us which was in thee,
who wast a servant that we might be free,
humbling thyself to death on Calvary.
    Alleluia!

Wherefore, by God's eternal purpose, thou
art high exalted o'er all creatures now,
and given the Name to which all knees shall bow.
    Alleluia!

Let every tongue confess with one accord
in heaven and earth that Jesus Christ is Lord;
and God the Father be by all adored.
    Alleluia! Amen.

F. Bland Tucker (1895–1984)

## 478

Jesus, our mighty Lord,
    our strength in sadness,
the Father's conquering Word,
    true source of gladness;
your Name we glorify,
O Jesus, throned on high;
you gave yourself to die
    for our salvation.

Good shepherd of your sheep,
    your own defending,
in love your children keep
    to life unending.
You are yourself the Way:
lead us then day by day
in your own steps, we pray,
    O Lord most holy.

Glorious their life who sing,
    with glad thanksgiving,
true hymns to Christ the King
    in all their living:
all who confess his Name,
come then with hearts aflame;
the God of peace acclaim
    as Lord and Savior.

St. Clement of Alexandria (ca. 170–ca. 220); para. F. Bland Tucker (1895–1984), rev.

**479**

Glory be to Jesus,
   who in bitter pains
poured for me the lifeblood
   from his veins!

Grace and life eternal
   in that blood I find,
blest be his compassion
   infinitely kind!

Blest through endless ages
   be the precious stream
which from sin and sorrow
   doth the world redeem!

Oft as earth exulting
   wafts its praise on high,
angel hosts, rejoicing,
   make their glad reply.

Lift ye then your voices;
   swell the mighty flood;
louder still and louder
   praise the precious blood.

Italian, 18th cent.; tr. Edward Caswall (1814–1878), alt.

## 480

When Jesus left his Father's throne,
    he chose an humble birth;
like us, unhonored and unknown,
    he came to dwell on earth.
Like him may we be found below,
    in wisdom's path of peace;
like him in grace and knowledge grow
    as years and strength increase.

Sweet were his words and kind his look,
    when mothers round him pressed;
their infants in his arms he took,
    and on his bosom blessed.
Safe from the world's alluring harms,
    beneath his watchful eye,
thus in the circle of his arms
    may we for ever lie.

When Jesus into Zion rode,
    the children sang around;
for joy they plucked the palms and strowed
    their garments on the ground.
Hosanna our glad voices raise,
    hosanna to our King!
Should we forget our Savior's praise,
    the stones themselves would sing.

James Montgomery (1771–1854)

# 481

Rejoice, the Lord is King!
   Your Lord and King adore!
Mortals, give thanks and sing,
   and triumph evermore.

> *Lift up your heart! lift up your voice!*
> *Rejoice! again I say, rejoice!*

The Lord the Savior reigns,
   the God of truth and love:
when he had purged our stains,
   he took his seat above.

*Refrain*

His kingdom cannot fail;
   he rules o'er earth and heaven;
the keys of death and hell
   to Christ the Lord are given.

*Refrain*

Rejoice in glorious hope!
   Our Lord the Judge shall come,
and take his servants up
   to their eternal home.

*Refrain*

Charles Wesley (1707–1788), alt.

## 482

Lord of all hopefulness, Lord of all joy,
whose trust, ever child-like, no cares could destroy,
be there at our waking, and give us, we pray,
your bliss in our hearts, Lord, at the break of the day.

Lord of all eagerness, Lord of all faith,
whose strong hands were skilled at the plane
                and the lathe,
be there at our labors, and give us, we pray,
your strength in our hearts, Lord, at the noon
                of the day.

Lord of all kindliness, Lord of all grace,
your hands swift to welcome, your arms to embrace,
be there at our homing, and give us, we pray,
your love in our hearts, Lord, at the eve of the day.

Lord of all gentleness, Lord of all calm,
whose voice is contentment, whose presence is balm,
be there at our sleeping, and give us, we pray,
your peace in our hearts, Lord, at the end of the day.

Jan Struther (1901–1953)

## 483

The head that once was crowned with thorns
    is crowned with glory now;
a royal diadem adorns
    the mighty victor's brow.

The highest place that heaven affords
    is his, is his by right,
the King of kings, and Lord of lords,
    and heaven's eternal Light;

the joy of all who dwell above,
    the joy of all below,
to whom he manifests his love
    and grants his name to know.

To them the cross with all its shame,
    with all its grace is given;
their name, an everlasting name;
    their joy, the joy of heaven.

They suffer with their Lord below,
    they reign with him above,
their profit and their joy to know
    the mystery of his love.

The cross he bore is life and health,
    though shame and death to him:
his people's hope, his people's wealth,
    their everlasting theme.

Thomas Kelly (1769–1855)

## 484, 485

Praise the Lord through every nation;
his holy arm hath wrought salvation;
   exalt him on his Father's throne.
Praise your King, ye Christian legions,
who now prepares in heavenly regions
   unfailing mansions for his own:
      with voice and minstrelsy
      extol his majesty:
         Alleluia!
His praise shall sound all nature round,
and hymns on every tongue abound.

Jesus, Lord, our Captain glorious,
o'er sin, and death, and hell victorious,
   wisdom and might to thee belong:
we confess, proclaim, adore thee;
we bow the knee, we fall before thee;
   thy love henceforth shall be our song.
      The cross meanwhile we bear,
      the crown erelong to wear:
         Alleluia!
Thy reign extend world without end;
let praise from all to thee ascend.

Rhijnvis Feith (1753–1824); para. James Montgomery (1771–1854), alt.

# 486

Hosanna to the living Lord!
Hosanna to the incarnate Word!
To Christ, Creator, Savior, King,
let earth, let heaven, hosanna sing!

*Hosanna, Lord! Hosanna in the highest!*

Hosanna, Lord! thine angels cry;
Hosanna, Lord! thy saints reply;
above, beneath us, and around,
both dead and living swell the sound:

*Refrain*

O Savior, with protecting care
abide in this thy house of prayer,
where we assembled in thy Name,
in faith, thy parting promise claim.

*Refrain*

But, chiefest, in our cleansèd breast,
Eternal! bid thy Spirit rest;
and make our secret soul to be
a temple pure and worthy thee.

*Refrain*

So in the last and dreadful day,
when earth and heaven shall melt away,
thy flock, redeemed from sinful stain,
shall swell the sound of praise again.

*Refrain*

Reginald Heber (1783–1826), alt.

# 487

Come, my Way, my Truth, my Life:
  such a way as gives us breath;
 such a truth as ends all strife;
  such a life as killeth death.

Come, my Light, my Feast, my Strength:
  such a light as shows a feast;
 such a feast as mends in length;
  such a strength as makes his guest.

Come, my Joy, my Love, my Heart:
  such a joy as none can move;
 such a love as none can part;
  such a heart as joys in love.

George Herbert (1593–1633)

## 488

Be thou my vision, O Lord of my heart;
all else be nought to me, save that thou art–
thou my best thought, by day or by night,
waking or sleeping, thy presence my light.

Be thou my wisdom, and thou my true word;
I ever with thee and thou with me, Lord;
thou my great Father; thine own may I be;
thou in me dwelling, and I one with thee.

High King of heaven, when victory is won,
may I reach heaven's joys, bright heaven's Sun!
Heart of my heart, whatever befall,
still be my vision, O Ruler of all.

Irish, ca. 700; versified Mary Elizabeth Byrne (1880–1931); tr. Eleanor H. Hull (1860–1935), alt.

## 489

The great Creator of the worlds,
    the sovereign God of heaven,
his holy and immortal truth
    to all on earth hath given.

He sent no angel of his host
    to bear this mighty word,
but him through whom the worlds were made,
    the everlasting Lord.

He sent him not in wrath and power,
  but grace and peace to bring;
in kindness, as a king might send
  his son, himself a king.

He sent him down as sending God;
  in flesh to us he came;
as one with us he dwelt with us,
  and bore a human name.

He came as Savior to his own,
  the way of love he trod;
he came to win us by good will,
  for force is not of God.

Not to oppress, but summon all
  their truest life to find,
in love God sent his Son to save,
  not to condemn mankind.

*Epistle to Diognetus,* ca. 150; tr. F. Bland Tucker (1895–1984), rev.

## 490

I want to walk as a child of the light.
  I want to follow Jesus.
God set the stars to give light to the world.
  The star of my life is Jesus.

> *In him there is no darkness at all.*
> *The night and the day are both alike.*
> *The Lamb is the light of the city of God.*
> *Shine in my heart, Lord Jesus.*

I want to see the brightness of God.
> I want to look at Jesus.
Clear sun of righteousness, shine on my path,
> and show me the way to the Father.

*Refrain*

I'm looking for the coming of Christ.
> I want to be with Jesus.
When we have run with patience the race,
> we shall know the joy of Jesus.

*Refrain*

Kathleen Thomerson (b. 1934)

**491**

Where is this stupendous stranger?
> Prophets, shepherds, kings, advise.
Lead me to my Master's manger,
> show me where my Savior lies.

O Most Mighty! O Most Holy!
> Far beyond the seraph's thought:
art thou then so mean and lowly
> as unheeded prophets taught?

O the magnitude of meekness!
> Worth from worth immortal sprung;
O the strength of infant weakness,
> if eternal is so young!

God all-bounteous, all-creative,
> whom no ills from good dissuade,
is incarnate, and a native
> of the very world he made.

Christopher Smart (1722–1771), alt.

## 492

Sing, ye faithful, sing with gladness,
> wake your noblest, sweetest strain,
with the praises of your Savior
> let his house resound again;
him let all your music honor,
> and your songs exalt his reign.

Sing how he came forth from heaven,
> bowed himself to Bethlehem's cave,
stooped to wear the servant's vesture,
> bore the pain, the cross, the grave,
passed within the gates of darkness,
> thence his banished ones to save.

So, he tasted death for mortals,
> he, of humankind the head,
sinless one, among the sinful,
> Prince of life, among the dead;
thus he wrought the full redemption,
> and the captor captive led.

Now on high, yet ever with us,
>from his Father's throne the Son
rules and guides the world he ransomed,
>till the appointed work be done,
till he see, renewed and perfect,
>all things gathered into one.

John Ellerton (1826–1893), alt.

**493**

O for a thousand tongues to sing
>my dear Redeemer's praise,
the glories of my God and King,
>the triumphs of his grace!

My gracious Master and my God,
>assist me to proclaim
and spread through all the earth
>abroad the honors of thy Name.

Jesus! the Name that charms our fears
>and bids our sorrows cease;
'tis music in the sinner's ears,
>'tis life and health and peace.

He speaks; and, listening to his voice,
>new life the dead receive,
the mournful broken hearts rejoice,
>the humble poor believe.

Hear him, ye deaf; ye voiceless ones,
    your loosened tongues employ;
ye blind, behold, your Savior comes;
    and leap, ye lame, for joy!

Glory to God and praise and love
    be now and ever given
by saints below and saints above,
    the Church in earth and heaven.

Charles Wesley (1707–1788), alt.

## 494

Crown him with many crowns,
    the Lamb upon his throne;
Hark! how the heavenly anthem drowns
    all music but its own;
awake, my soul, and sing
    of him who died for thee,
and hail him as thy matchless King
    through all eternity.

Crown him the Son of God
    before the worlds began,
and ye, who tread where he hath trod,
    crown him the Son of man;
who every grief hath known
    that wrings the human breast,
and takes and bears them for his own,
    that all in him may rest.

Crown him the Lord of life,
   who triumphed o'er the grave,
and rose victorious in the strife
   for those he came to save;
his glories now we sing
   who died, and rose on high,
who died, eternal life to bring,
   and lives that death may die.

Crown him of lords the Lord,
   who over all doth reign,
who once on earth, the incarnate Word,
   for ransomed sinners slain,
now lives in realms of light,
   where saints with angels sing
their songs before him day and night,
   their God, Redeemer, King.

Crown him the Lord of heaven,
   enthroned in worlds above;
Crown him the King, to whom is given
   the wondrous name of Love.
Crown him with many crowns,
   as thrones before him fall,
crown him, ye kings, with many crowns,
   for he is King of all.

Matthew Bridges (1800–1894)

## 495

Hail, thou once despisèd Jesus!
 Hail, thou Galilean King!
Thou didst suffer to release us;
 thou didst free salvation bring.
Hail, thou universal Savior,
 bearer of our sin and shame!
By thy merit we find favor:
 life is given through thy Name

Paschal Lamb, by God appointed,
 all our sins on thee were laid:
by almighty love anointed,
 thou hast full atonement made.
All thy people are forgiven
 through the virtue of thy blood:
opened is the gate of heaven,
 reconciled are we with God.

Jesus, hail! enthroned in glory,
 there for ever to abide;
all the heavenly hosts adore thee,
 seated at thy Father's side.
There for sinners thou art pleading:
 there thou dost our place prepare;
ever for us interceding,
 till in glory we appear.

Worship, honor, power, and blessing
 thou art worthy to receive;

highest praises, without ceasing,
   right it is for us to give.
Help, ye bright angelic spirits,
   all your noblest anthems raise;
help to sing our Savior's merits,
   help to chant Emmanuel's praise!

John Bakewell (1721–1819) and Martin Madan (1726–1790), alt.

## 496, 497

How bright appears the Morning Star,
with mercy beaming from afar;
   the host of heaven rejoices;
O righteous Branch, O Jesse's Rod!
Thou Son of Man and Son of God!
   We, too, will lift our voices:
      Jesus, Jesus!
   Holy, holy, yet most lowly,
      draw thou near us;
   great Emmanuel, come and hear us.

Though circled by the hosts on high,
he deigned to cast a pitying eye
   upon his helpless creature;
the whole creation's Head and Lord,
by highest seraphim adored,
   assumed our very nature;
      Jesus, grant us,
   through thy merit, to inherit
      thy salvation;
   hear, O hear our supplication.

Rejoice, ye heavens; thou earth, reply;
with praise, ye sinners, fill the sky,
   for this his Incarnation.
Incarnate God, put forth thy power,
ride on, ride on, great Conqueror,
   till all know thy salvation.
      Amen, amen!
   Alleluia, alleluia!
     Praise be given
evermore, by earth and heaven.

William Mercer (1811–1873); after Philip Nicolai (1556–1608)

## 498

Beneath the cross of Jesus
   I fain would take my stand,
the shadow of a mighty rock
   within a weary land,
a home within the wilderness,
   a rest upon the way,
from the burning of the noontide heat,
   and the burden of the day.

Upon the cross of Jesus
   mine eyes at times can see
the very dying form of one
   who suffered there for me;

and from my smitten heart with tears
    two wonders I confess:
the wonders of redeeming love,
    and my unworthiness.

I take, O cross, thy shadow
    for my abiding place;
I ask no other sunshine than
    the sunshine of his face;
content to let my pride go by,
    to know no gain nor loss,
my sinful self my only shame,
    my glory all the cross.

Elizabeth Cecilia Clephane (1830–1869), alt.

## 499

Lord God, you now have set your servant free
to go in peace as promised in your word;
my eyes have seen the Savior, Christ the Lord,
prepared by you for all the world to see,
to shine on nations trapped in darkest night,
the glory of your people, and their light.

Rae E. Whitney (b. 1927); para. of *The Song of Simeon*

## 500

Creator Spirit, by whose aid
the world's foundations first were laid,
come, visit every humble mind;
come, pour thy joys on human kind;
from sin and sorrow set us free,
and make thy temples worthy thee.

O Source of uncreated light,
the Father's promised Paraclete,
thrice holy Fount, thrice holy Fire,
our hearts with heavenly love inspire;
come, and thy sacred unction bring
to sanctify us while we sing.

Plenteous of grace, come from on high,
rich in thy sevenfold energy;
make us eternal truth receive,
and practice all that we believe;
give us thyself, that we may see
the Father and the Son by thee.

John Dryden (1631–1700); tr. of *Veni Creator Spiritus*

## 501, 502

O Holy Spirit, by whose breath
life rises vibrant out of death;
come to create, renew, inspire;
come, kindle in our hearts your fire.

You are the seeker's sure resource,
of burning love the living source,
protector in the midst of strife,
the giver and the Lord of life.

In you God's energy is shown,
to us your varied gifts make known.
Teach us to speak, teach us to hear;
yours is the tongue and yours the ear.

Flood our dull senses with your light;
in mutual love our hearts unite.
Your power the whole creation fills;
confirm our weak, uncertain wills.

From inner strife grant us release;
turn nations to the ways of peace.
To fuller life your people bring
that as one body we may sing:

Praise to the Father, Christ, his Word,
and to the Spirit: God the Lord,
to whom all honor, glory be
both now and for eternity.

Att. Rabanus Maurus (776–856); tr. John Webster Grant (b. 1919), alt.; para. of *Veni Creator Spiritus*

## 503, 504

Come, Holy Ghost, our souls inspire,
and lighten with celestial fire.

Thou the anointing Spirit art,
who dost thy sevenfold gifts impart.

Thy blessèd unction from above
is comfort, life, and fire of love.

Enable with perpetual light
the dullness of our blinded sight.

Anoint and cheer our soiled face
with the abundance of thy grace.

Keep far our foes, give peace at home:
where thou art guide, no ill can come.

Teach us to know the Father, Son,
and thee, of both, to be but One,

that through the ages all along,
this may be our endless song:

praise to thy eternal merit,
Father, Son, and Holy Spirit.

Latin, 9th cent.; tr. John Cosin (1594–1672); para. of *Veni Creator Spiritus*

**505**

O Spirit of Life, O Spirit of God,
in every need thou bringest aid;
thou comest forth from God's great throne,
from God, the Father and the Son;
O Spirit of Life, O Spirit of God.

O Spirit of Life, O Spirit of God,
increase our faith in our dear Lord;
unless thy grace the power should give,
none can believe in Christ and live;
O Spirit of Life, O Spirit of God.

O Spirit of Life, O Spirit of God,
make us to love thy sacred word;
the holy flame of love impart,
that charity may warm each heart;
O Spirit of Life, O Spirit of God.

O Spirit of Life, O Spirit of God,
enlighten us by that same word;
teach us to know the Father's love,
and his dear Son, who reigns above;
O Spirit of Life, O Spirit of God.

Johann Niedling (1602–1668); tr. John Caspar Mattes (1876–1948), alt.

## 506, 507

Praise the Spirit in creation,
   breath of God, life's origin:
Spirit, moving on the waters,
   quickening worlds to life within,
source of breath to all things breathing,
   life in whom all lives begin.

Praise the Spirit, close companion
   of our inmost thoughts and ways;
who, in showing us God's wonders,
   is himself the power to gaze;
and God's will, to those who listen
   by a still small voice conveys.

Praise the Spirit, who enlightened
   priests and prophets with the word;
his the truth behind the wisdoms
   which as yet know not our Lord;
by whose love and power, in Jesus
   God himself was seen and heard.

Tell of how the ascended Jesus
   armed a people for his own;
how a hundred men and women
   turned the known world upside down,
to its dark and furthest corners
   by the wind of heaven blown.

Pray we then, O Lord the Spirit,
    on our lives descend in might;
let your flame break out within us,
    fire our hearts and clear our sight,
till, white-hot in your possession,
    we, too, set the world alight.

Praise, O praise the Holy Spirit,
    praise the Father, praise the Word,
Source, and Truth, and Inspiration,
    Trinity in deep accord:
through your voice which speaks within us
    we, your creatures, call you Lord.

Michael Hewlett (b. 1916), alt.

**508**

Breathe on me, Breath of God,
    fill me with life anew,
that I may love what thou dost love,
    and do what thou wouldst do.

Breathe on me, Breath of God,
    until my heart is pure,
until with thee I will one will,
    to do or to endure.

Breathe on me, Breath of God,
    till I am wholly thine,
till all this earthly part of me
    glows with thy fire divine.

Breathe on me, Breath of God,
    so shall I never die;
but live with thee the perfect life
    of thine eternity.

Edwin Hatch (1835–1889), alt.

## 509

Spirit divine, attend our prayers,
    and make this house thy home;
descend with all thy gracious powers,
    O come, great Spirit, come!

Come as the light; to us reveal
    our emptiness and woe,
and lead us in those paths of life
    whereon the righteous go.

Come as the fire, and purge our hearts
    like sacrificial flame;
let our whole soul an offering be
    to our Redeemer's Name.

Come as the dove, and spread thy wings,
    the wings of peaceful love;
and let thy Church on earth become
    blest as the Church above.

Spirit divine, attend our prayers;
   make a lost world thy home;
descend with all thy gracious powers;
   O come, great Spirit, come!

Andrew Reed (1787–1862)

**510**

Come, Holy Spirit, heavenly Dove,
   with all thy quickening powers;
kindle a flame of sacred love
   in these cold hearts of ours.

See how we trifle here below,
   fond of these earthly toys;
our souls, how heavily they go,
   to reach eternal joys.

In vain we tune our formal songs,
   in vain we strive to rise:
hosannas languish on our tongues,
   and our devotion dies.

Come, Holy Spirit, heavenly Dove,
   with all thy quickening powers;
come, shed abroad a Savior's love,
   and that shall kindle ours.

Isaac Watts (1674–1748), alt.

## 511

Holy Spirit, ever living
  as the Church's very life;
Holy Spirit, ever striving
  through her in a ceaseless strife;
Holy Spirit, ever forming
  in the Church the mind of Christ;
thee we praise with endless worship
  for thy fruits and gifts unpriced.

Holy Spirit, ever working
  through the Church's ministry;
quickening, strengthening, and absolving,
  setting captive sinners free;
Holy Spirit, ever binding
  age to age, and soul to soul,
in a fellowship unending
  thee we worship and extol.

Timothy Rees (1874–1939), alt.

## 512

Come, gracious Spirit, heavenly Dove,
with light and comfort from above;
be thou our guardian, thou our guide;
o'er every thought and step preside.

The light of truth to us display,
and make us know and choose thy way;
plant holy fear in every heart,
that we from thee may ne'er depart.

Lead us to Christ, the living Way,
nor let us from his precepts stray;
lead us to holiness, the road
that we must take to dwell with God.

Lead us to heaven, that we may share
fullness of joy for ever there;
lead us to God, our final rest,
to be with him for ever blest.

Simon Browne (1680–1732), alt.

**513**

Like the murmur of the dove's song,
like the challenge of her flight,
like the vigor of the wind's rush,
like the new flame's eager might:
come, Holy Spirit, come.

To the members of Christ's Body,
to the branches of the Vine,
to the Church in faith assembled,
to her midst as gift and sign:
come, Holy Spirit, come.

With the healing of division,
with the ceaseless voice of prayer,
with the power to love and witness,
with the peace beyond compare:
come, Holy Spirit, come.

Carl P. Daw, Jr. (b. 1944)

## 514

To thee, O Comforter divine,
for all thy grace and power benign,
   sing we alleluia!

To thee, whose faithful love had place
in God's great covenant of grace,
   sing we alleluia!

To thee, whose faithful power doth heal,
enlighten, sanctify, and seal,
   sing we alleluia!

To thee, by Jesus Christ sent down,
of all his gifts the sum and crown,
   sing we alleluia!

Frances Ridely Havergal (1836–1879)

## 515

Holy Ghost, dispel our sadness;
   pierce the clouds of nature's night;
come, thou source of joy and gladness,
   breathe thy life, and spread thy light.
From the height which knows no measure,
   as a gracious shower descend,
bringing down the richest treasure
   we can wish, or God can send.

Author of the new creation,
   come with unction and with power.

Make our hearts thy habitation;
> with thy grace our spirits shower.
Hear, oh, hear our supplication,
> blessèd Spirit, God of peace!
Rest upon this congregation,
> with the fullness of thy grace.

Paul Gerhardt (1607–1676); tr. John Christian Jacobi (1670–1750), alt.

## 516

> Come down, O Love divine,
> seek thou this soul of mine,
> and visit it with thine own ardor glowing;
> > O Comforter, draw near,
> > within my heart appear,
> and kindle it, thy holy flame bestowing.

> O let it freely burn,
> till earthly passions turn
> to dust and ashes in its heat consuming;
> > and let thy glorious light
> > shine ever on my sight,
> and clothe me round, the while my path illuming.

> And so the yearning strong,
> with which the soul will long,
> shall far outpass the power of human telling;
> > for none can guess its grace,
> > till Love create a place
> wherein the Holy Spirit makes a dwelling.

Bianco da Siena (d. 1434?); tr. Richard Frederick Littledale (1833–1890), alt.

## 517

How lovely is thy dwelling-place,
    O Lord of hosts, to me!
My thirsty soul desires and longs
    within thy courts to be;
my very heart and flesh cry out,
    O living God, for thee.

Beside thine altars, gracious Lord,
    the swallows find a nest;
how happy they who dwell with thee
    and praise thee without rest,
and happy they whose hearts are set
    upon the pilgrim's quest.

They who go through the desert vale
    will find it filled with springs,
and they shall climb from height to height
    till Zion's temple rings
with praise to thee, in glory throned,
    Lord God, great King of kings.

One day within thy courts excels
    a thousand spent away;
how happy they who keep thy laws
    nor from thy precepts stray,
for thou shalt surely bless all those
    who live the words they pray.

Para. of Psalm 84; sts. 1–2, *The Psalms of David in Meeter*, 1650, alt.; sts. 3–4, Carl P. Daw, Jr. (b. 1944)

## 518

Christ is made the sure foundation,
 Christ the head and cornerstone,
chosen of the Lord, and precious,
 binding all the Church in one;
holy Zion's help for ever,
 and her confidence alone.

All that dedicated city,
 dearly loved of God on high,
in exultant jubilation
 pours perpetual melody;
God the One in Three adoring
 in glad hymns eternally.

To this temple, where we call thee,
 come, O Lord of Hosts, today;
with thy wonted loving-kindness
 hear thy servants as they pray,
and thy fullest benediction
 shed within its walls alway.

Here vouchsafe to all thy servants
 what they ask of thee to gain;
what they gain from thee, for ever
 with the blessèd to retain,
and hereafter in thy glory
 evermore with thee to reign.

Latin, ca. 7th cent.; tr. *Hymns Ancient and Modern*, 1861, after John Mason Neale (1818–1856), alt.

## 519, 520

Blessèd city, heavenly Salem,
    vision dear of peace and love,
who of living stones art builded
    in the height of heaven above,
and, with angel hosts encircled,
    as a bride dost earthward move;

from celestial realms descending,
    bridal glory round thee shed,
meet for him whose love espoused thee,
    to thy Lord shalt thou be led;
all thy streets and all thy bulwarks
    of pure gold are fashionèd.

Bright thy gates of pearl are shining;
    they are open evermore;
and by virtue of his merits
    thither faithful souls do soar,
who, for Christ's dear Name, in this world
    pain and tribulation bore.

Many a blow and biting sculpture
    polished well those stones elect,
in their places now compacted
    by the heavenly Architect,
who therewith hath willed for ever
    that his palace should be decked.

Laud and honor to the Father,
    laud and honor to the Son,
laud and honor to the Spirit,
    ever Three, and ever One,
consubstantial, co-eternal,
    while unending ages run.

Latin, ca. 7th cent.; *Hymns Ancient and Modern*, 1861, after John Mason Neale (1818–1866), alt.

## 521

Put forth, O God, thy Spirit's might
    and bid thy Church increase,
in breadth and length, in depth and height,
    her unity and peace.

Let works of darkness disappear
    before thy conquering light;
let hatred and tormenting fear
    pass with the passing night.

Let what apostles learned of thee
    be ours from age to age;
their steadfast faith our unity,
    their peace our heritage.

O Judge divine of human strife!
    O Vanquisher of pain!
To know thee is eternal life,
    to serve thee is to reign.

Howard Chandler Robbins (1876–1952)

## 522, 523

Glorious things of thee are spoken,
    Zion, city of our God;
he whose word cannot be broken
    formed thee for his own abode;
on the Rock of Ages founded,
    what can shake thy sure repose?
With salvation's walls surrounded,
    thou may'st smile at all thy foes.

See! the streams of living waters,
    springing from eternal love,
well supply thy sons and daughters
    and all fear of want remove.
Who can faint, when such a river
    ever will their thirst assuage?
Grace which, like the Lord, the giver
    never fails from age to age.

Round each habitation hovering,
    see the cloud and fire appear
for a glory and a covering,
    showing that the Lord is near.
Thus deriving from their banner,
    light by night, and shade by day,
safe they feed upon the manna
    which he gives them when they pray.

Blest inhabitants of Zion,
    washed in the Redeemer's blood!

Jesus, whom their souls rely on,
  makes them kings and priests to God.
'Tis his love his people raise
  over self to reign as kings:
and as priests, his solemn praises
  each for a thank-offering brings.

John Newton (1725–1807), alt.

**524**

I love thy kingdom, Lord,
  the house of thine abode,
the Church our blest Redeemer saved
  with his own precious blood.

For her my tears shall fall;
  for her my prayers ascend;
to her my cares and toils be given,
  till toils and cares shall end.

Beyond my highest joy
  I prize her heavenly ways,
her sweet communion, solemn vows,
  her hymns of love and praise.

Jesus, thou friend divine,
  our Savior and our King,
thy hand from every snare and foe
  shall great deliverance bring.

Sure as thy truth shall last,
    to Zion shall be given
the brightest glories earth can yield,
    and brighter bliss of heaven.

Timothy Dwight (1725–1817)

## 525

The Church's one foundation
    is Jesus Christ her Lord;
she is his new creation
    by water and the word:
from heaven he came and sought her
    to be his holy bride;
with his own blood he bought her,
    and for her life he died.

Elect from every nation,
    yet one o'er all the earth,
her charter of salvation,
    one Lord, one faith, one birth;
one holy Name she blesses,
    partakes one holy food,
and to one hope she presses,
    with every grace endued.

Though with a scornful wonder
    men see her sore oppressed,
by schisms rent asunder,
    by heresies distressed;
yet saints their watch are keeping,
    their cry goes up, "How long?"
and soon the night of weeping
    shall be the morn of song.

Mid toil and tribulation,
    and tumult of her war
she waits the consummation
    of peace for evermore;
till with the vision glorious
    her longing eyes are blessed,
and the great Church victorious
    shall be the Church at rest.

Yet she on earth hath union
    with God, the Three in One,
and mystic sweet communion
    with those whose rest is won.
O happy ones and holy!
    Lord, give us grace that we
like them, the meek and lowly,
    on high may dwell with thee.

Samuel John Stone (1839–1900)

## 526

Let saints on earth in concert sing
    with those whose work is done;
for all the servants of our King
    in heaven and earth are one.

One family we dwell in him,
    one Church, above, beneath,
though now divided by the stream,
    the narrow stream of death.

One army of the living God,
    to his command we bow;
part of the host have crossed the flood,
    and part are crossing now.

E'en now by faith we join our hands
    with those that went before,
and greet the ever-living bands
    on the eternal shore.

Jesus, be thou our constant Guide;
    then, when the word is given,
bid Jordan's narrow stream divide,
    and bring us safe to heaven.

Charles Wesley (1707–1788), alt.

## 527

Singing songs of expectation,
    onward goes the pilgrim band,
through the night of doubt and sorrow,
    marching to the promised land.
Clear before us through the darkness
    gleams and burns the guiding light:
trusting God we march together
    stepping fearless through the night.

One the light of God's own presence,
    o'er his ransomed people shed,
chasing far the gloom and terror,
    brightening all the path we tread:
one the object of our journey,
    one the faith which never tires,
one the earnest looking forward,
    one the hope our God inspires.

One the strain the lips of thousands
    lift as from the heart of one;
one the conflict, one the peril,
    one the march in God begun:
one the gladness of rejoicing
    on the far eternal shore,
where the one almighty Father
    reigns in love for evermore.

Bernard Severin Ingemann (1789–1862) tr. Sabine Baring-Gould (1834–1924), alt.

## 528

Lord, you give the great commission:
  "Heal the sick and preach the word."
Lest the Church neglect its mission
  and the Gospel go unheard,
help us witness to your purpose
with renewed integrity;

> *with the Spirit's gifts empower us*
> *for the work of ministry.*

Lord, you call us to your service:
  "In my name baptize and teach."
That the world may trust your promise,
  life abundant meant for each,
give us all new fervor, draw us
closer in community;

*Refrain*

Lord, you make the common holy:
  "This my body, this my blood."
Let your priests, for earth's true glory,
  daily lift life heavenward,
asking that the world around us
share your children's liberty;

*Refrain*

Lord, you show us love's true measure:
  "Father, what they do, forgive."
Yet we hoard as private treasure
  all that you so freely give.

May your care and mercy lead us
to a just society;

*Refrain*

Lord, you bless with words assuring:
    "I am with you to the end."
Faith and hope and love restoring,
    may we serve as you intend,
and, amid the cares that claim us,
hold in mind eternity;

*Refrain*

Jeffery Rowthorn (b. 1934)

**529**

In Christ there is no East or West,
    in him no South or North,
but one great fellowship of love
    throughout the whole wide earth.

Join hands, disciples of the faith,
    whate'er your race may be!
Who serves my Father as his child
    is surely kin to me.

In Christ now meet both East and West,
    in him meet South and North,
all Christly souls are one in him,
    throughout the whole wide earth.

John Oxenham (1852–1941), alt.

## 530

Spread, O spread, thou mighty word,
spread the kingdom of the Lord,
that to earth's remotest bound
all may heed the joyful sound;

word of how the Father's will
made the world, and keeps it, still;
how his only Son he gave,
earth from sin and death to save;

word of how the Savior's love
earth's sore burden doth remove;
how forever, in its need,
through his death the world is freed;

word of how the Spirit came
bringing peace in Jesus' name;
how his never-failing love
guides us on to heaven above.

Word of life, most pure and strong,
word for which the nations long,
spread abroad, until from night
all the world awakes to light.

Jonathan Friedrich Bahnmaier (1774–1841); tr. Arthur William Farlander (1898–1952) and Charles Winfred Douglas (1867–1944), alt. St. 4, F. Bland Tucker (1895–1984)

## 531

O Spirit of the living God,
   in all thy plenitude of grace,
where'er the foot of man hath trod,
   descend on our apostate race.

Give tongues of fire and hearts of love,
   to preach the reconciling word;
give power and unction from above,
   whene'er the joyful sound is heard.

Be darkness, at thy coming, light;
   confusion, order in thy path;
souls without strength inspire with might,
   bid mercy triumph over wrath.

Convert the nations! far and nigh
   the triumphs of the cross record;
the Name of Jesus glorify,
   till every people call him Lord.

James Montgomery (1771–1854), alt.

## 532, 533

How wondrous and great thy works, God of praise!
How just, King of saints, and true are thy ways!
O who shall not fear thee, and honor thy Name?
Thou only art holy, thou only supreme.

To nations of earth thy light shall be shown;
their worship and vows shall come to thy throne:
thy truth and thy judgments shall spread all abroad,
till earth's every people confess thee their God.

Henry Ustick Onderdonk (1759–1858), alt.; para. *The Song of the Redeemed*

## 534

God is working his purpose out
    as year succeeds to year:
God is working his purpose out,
    and the time is drawing near;
nearer and nearer draws the time,
    the time that shall surely be,
when the earth shall be filled with the glory of God
    as the waters cover the sea.

From utmost east to utmost west,
    wherever foot hath trod,
by the mouth of many messengers
    goes forth the voice of God;
give ear to me, ye continents,
    ye isles, give ear to me,
that the earth may be filled with the glory of God
    as the waters cover the sea.

March we forth in the strength of God,
    with the banner of Christ unfurled,

that the light of the glorious gospel of truth
    may shine throughout the world:
fight we the fight with sorrow and sin
    to set their captives free,
that the earth may be filled with the glory of God
    as the waters cover the sea.

All we can do is nothing worth
    unless God blesses the deed;
vainly we hope for the harvest-tide
    till God gives life to the seed;
yet nearer and nearer draws the time,
    the time that shall surely be,
when the earth shall be filled with the glory of God
    as the waters cover the sea.

Arthur Campbell Ainger (1841–1919), alt.

## 535

Ye servants of God, your Master proclaim,
and publish abroad his wonderful Name;
the Name all-victorious of Jesus extol:
his kingdom is glorious; he rules over all.

God ruleth on high, almighty to save;
and still he is nigh: his presence we have.
The great congregation his triumph shall sing,
ascribing salvation to Jesus our King.

Salvation to God who sits on the throne!
Let all cry aloud, and honor the Son.
The praises of Jesus the angels proclaim,
fall down on their faces, and worship the Lamb.

Then let us adore, and give him his right:
All glory and power, all wisdom and might,
and honor and blessing, with angels above,
and thanks never-ceasing and infinite love.

Charles Wesley (1707–1788), alt.

## 536

Open your ears, O faithful people,
open your ears and hear God's word.
Open your hearts, O royal priesthood,
God has come to you.

> *God has spoken to his people,\**
> *Hallelujah!*
> *And his words are words of wisdom,\**
> *Hallelujah!*

They who have ears to hear the message,
they who have ears, then let them hear.
They who would learn the way of wisdom,
let them hear God's word.

*Refrain*

Israel comes to greet the Savior,
Judah is glad to see his day.
From east and west the peoples travel,
he will show the way.

*Refrain*

\*Alternate line *"Torah ora, Tora ora"* (Hebrew for "The Law is our Light") may be used.

Willard F. Jabusch (b. 1930), alt.

## 537

Christ for the world we sing!
The world to Christ we bring
   with loving zeal;
the poor, and them that mourn,
the faint and overborne,
sin-sick and sorrow-worn,
   whom Christ doth heal.

Christ for the world we sing!
The world to Christ we bring
   with fervent prayer;
the wayward and the lost,
by restless passions tossed,
redeemed at countless cost
   from dark despair.

Christ for the world we sing!
The world to Christ we bring
   with one accord;
with us the work to share,

with us reproach to dare,
with us the cross to bear,
   for Christ our Lord.

Christ for the world we sing!
The world to Christ we bring
   with joyful song;
the new-born souls, whose days,
reclaimed from error's ways,
inspired with hope and praise,
   to Christ belong.

Samuel Wolcott (1813–1886)

# 538

God of mercy, God of grace,
show the brightness of thy face.
Shine upon us, Savior, shine,
fill thy Church with light divine,
and thy saving health extend
unto earth's remotest end.

Let thy people praise thee, Lord;
be by all that live adored.
Let the nations shout and sing
glory to their Savior King;
let all be, below, above,
one in joy, and light, and love.

Henry Francis Lyte (1793–1847), alt.

# 539

O Zion, haste, thy mission high fulfilling,
  to tell to all the world that God is Light;
that he who made all nations is not willing
  one soul should fail to know his love and might.

> *Publish glad tidings:*
>   *tidings of peace,*
> *tidings of Jesus,*
>   *redemption and release.*

Proclaim to every people, tongue, and nation
  that God, in whom they live and move, is Love:
tell how he stooped to save his lost creation,
  and died on earth that all might live above.

*Refrain*

Send heralds forth to bear the message glorious;
  give of thy wealth to speed them on their way;
pour out thy soul for them in prayer victorious
  till God shall bring his kingdom's joyful day.

*Refrain*

He comes again! O Zion, ere thou meet him,
  make known to every heart his saving grace;
let none whom he hath ransomed fail to greet him,
  through thy neglect, unfit to see his face.

*Refrain*

Mary Ann Thomson (1834–1923), alt.

## 540

Awake, thou Spirit of the watchmen
    who never held their peace by day or night,
contending from the walls of Zion
    against the foe, confiding in thy might.
Throughout the world their cry is ringing still,
and bringing peoples to thy holy will.

O Lord, now let thy fire enkindle
    our hearts, that everywhere its flame may go,
and spread the glory of redemption
    till all the world thy saving grace shall know.
O harvest Lord, look down on us and view
how white the fields; the laborers, how few!

Send forth, O Lord, thy strong Evangel
    by many messengers, all hearts to win;
make haste to help us in our weakness;
    break down the realm of Satan, death, and sin:
the circle of the earth shall then proclaim
thy kingdom, and the glory of thy Name.

Karl Heinrich von Bogatzky (1690–1774); tr. Arthur William
Farlander (1898–1952) and Charles Winfred Douglas (1867–
1944)

# 541

Come, labor on.
Who dares stand idle on the harvest plain,
while all around us waves the golden grain?
And to each servant does the Master say,
"Go work today."

Come, labor on.
The enemy is watching night and day,
to sow the tares, to snatch the seed away;
while we in sleep our duty have forgot,
he slumbered not.

Come, labor on.
Away with gloomy doubts and faithless fear!
No arm so weak but may do service here:
by feeblest agents may our God fulfill
his righteous will.

Come, labor on.
Claim the high calling angels cannot share–
to young and old the Gospel gladness bear:
redeem the time; its hours too swiftly fly.
The night draws nigh.

Come, labor on.
No time for rest, till glows the western sky,
till the long shadows o'er our pathway lie,
and a glad sound comes with the setting sun,
"Servants, well done."

Jane Laurie Borthwick (1813–1897), alt.

## 542

Christ is the world's true Light,
    its Captain of salvation,
the Daystar clear and bright
    of every race and nation;
new life, new hope awakes,
    for all who own his sway:
freedom her bondage breaks,
    and night is turned to day.

In Christ all races meet,
    their ancient feuds forgetting,
the whole round world complete,
    from sunrise to its setting:
when Christ is throned as Lord
    all shall forsake their fear,
to ploughshare beat the sword,
    to pruning-hook the spear.

One Lord, in one great Name
    unite us all who own thee;
cast out our pride and shame
    that hinder to enthrone thee;
the world has waited long,
    has travailed long in pain;
to heal its ancient wrong,
    come, Prince of Peace, and reign.

George Wallace Briggs (1875–1959), alt.

## 543

O Zion, tune thy voice,
   and raise thy hands on high;
tell all the earth thy joys,
   and boast salvation nigh.
      Cheerful in God,
         arise and shine,
         while rays divine
      stream all abroad.

He gilds thy morning face
   with beams that cannot fade;
his all-resplendent grace
   he pours around thy head;
      the nations round
         thy form shall view,
         with luster new
      divinely crowned.

In honor to his Name
   reflect that sacred light;
and loud that grace proclaim,
   which makes thy darkness bright;
      pursue his praise,
         till sovereign love
         in worlds above
      the glory raise.

There on his holy hill
  a brighter sun shall rise,
and with his radiance fill
  those fairer purer skies;
    while round his throne
      ten thousand stars
      in nobler spheres
    his influence own.

Philip Doddridge (1702–1751) alt.; based on *The Third Song of Isaiah*

## 544

Jesus shall reign where'er the sun
doth his successive journeys run;
his kingdom stretch from shore to shore,
till moons shall wax and wane no more.

To him shall endless prayer be made,
and praises throng to crown his head;
his Name like sweet perfume shall rise
with every morning sacrifice.

People and realms of every tongue
dwell on his love with sweetest song;
and infant voices shall proclaim
their early blessings on his Name.

Blessings abound where'er he reigns:
the prisoners leap to lose their chains,

the weary find eternal rest,
and all who suffer want are blest.

Let every creature rise and bring
peculiar honors to our King;
angels descend with songs again,
and earth repeat the loud amen.

Isaac Watts (1674–1748), alt.

**545**

Lo! what a cloud of witnesses
 encompass us around!
They, once like us with suffering tried,
 are now with glory crowned.

Let us, with zeal like theirs inspired,
 strive in the Christian race;
and, freed from every weight of sin,
 their holy footsteps trace.

Behold a Witness nobler still,
 who trod affliction's path:
Jesus, the author, finisher,
 rewarder of our faith.

He, for the joy before him set,
 and moved by pitying love,
endured the cross, despised the shame,
 and now he reigns above.

Thither, forgetting things behind,
    press we to God's right hand;
there, with the Savior and his saints,
    triumphantly to stand.

*Translations and Paraphrases*, 1745, alt.; para. of Hebrews 12: 1–3

## 546

Awake, my soul, stretch every nerve,
    and press with vigor on;
a heavenly race demands thy zeal,
    and an immortal crown.

A cloud of witnesses around
    hold thee in full survey;
forget the steps already trod
    and onward urge thy way.

'tis God's all-animating voice
    that calls thee from on high;
'tis his own hand presents the prize
    to thine aspiring eye.

Then wake, my soul, stretch every nerve,
    and press with vigor on;
a heavenly race demands thy zeal,
    and an immortal crown.

Philip Doddridge (1702–1751)

## 547

Awake, O sleeper, rise from death,
    and Christ shall give you light,
so learn his love—its length and breadth,
    its fullness, depth, and height.

To us on earth he came to bring
    from sin and fear release,
to give the spirit's unity,
    the very bond of peace.

There is one Body and one hope,
    one Spirit and one call,
one Lord, one Faith, and one Baptism,
    one Father of us all.

Then walk in love as Christ has loved,
    who died that he might save;
with kind and gentle hearts forgive
    as God in Christ forgave.

For us Christ lived, for us he died
    and conquered in the strife.
Awake, arise, go forth in faith,
    and Christ shall give you life.

F. Bland Tucker (1895–1984)

## 548

Soldiers of Christ, arise,
    and put your armor on,
strong in the strength which God supplies
    through his eternal Son;

strong in the Lord of hosts,
    and in his mighty power:
who in the strength of Jesus trusts
    is more than conqueror.

Stand then in his great might,
    with all his strength endued,
and take, to arm you for the fight,
    the panoply of God.

From strength to strength go on,
    wrestle, and fight, and pray:
tread all the power of darkness down,
    and win the well-fought day.

That, having all things done,
    and all your conflicts past,
ye may o'ercome, through Christ alone,
    and stand complete at last.

Charles Wesley (1707–1788)

**549, 550**

Jesus calls us; o'er the tumult
    of our life's wild, restless sea,
day by day his clear voice soundeth,
    saying, "Christian, follow me;"

as, of old, Saint Andrew heard it
    by the Galilean lake,
turned from home and toil and kindred,
    leaving all for his dear sake.

Jesus calls us from the worship
    of the vain world's golden store;
from each idol that would keep us,
    saying, "Christian, love me more."

In our joys and in our sorrows,
    days of toil and hours of ease,
still he calls, in cares and pleasures,
    "Christian, love me more than these."

Jesus calls us! By thy mercies,
    Savior, make us hear thy call,
give our hearts to thine obedience,
    serve and love thee best of all.

Cecil Frances Alexander (1818–1895), alt.

## 551

Rise up, ye saints of God!
  Have done with lesser things,
give heart and soul and mind and strength
  to serve the King of kings.

Rise up, ye saints of God!
  His kingdom tarries long:
Lord, bring the day of truth and love
  and end the night of wrong.

Lift high the cross of Christ!
  Tread where his feet have trod;
and quickened by the Spirit's power,
  rise up, ye saints of God!

William Pierson Merrill (1867–1954), alt.

## 552, 553

Fight the good fight with all thy might,
Christ is thy strength and Christ thy right;
lay hold on life, and it shall be
thy joy and crown eternally.

Run the straight race through God's good grace,
lift up thine eyes and seek his face;
life with its way before us lies,
Christ is the path and Christ the prize.

Cast care aside, lean on thy Guide;
his boundless mercy will provide;
trust, and thy trusting soul shall prove
Christ is its life and Christ its love.

Faint not nor fear, his arms are near;
he changeth not, and thou art dear;
only believe, and thou shalt see
that Christ is all in all to thee.

John Samuel Bewley Monsell (1811–1875)

## 554

'Tis the gift to be simple, 'tis the gift to be free,
'tis the gift to come down where we ought to be,
and when we find ourselves in the place just right,
'twill be in the valley of love and delight.
When true simplicity is gained
to bow and to bend we shan't be ashamed,
to turn, turn, will be our delight
till by turning, turning we come round right.

Joseph Brackett, Jr. (1797–1882)

## 555

Lead on, O King eternal,
    the day of march has come;
henceforth in fields of conquest
    thy tents shall be our home:
through days of preparation
    thy grace has made us strong,
and now, O King eternal,
    we lift our battle-song.

Lead on, O King eternal,
    till sin's fierce war shall cease,
and holiness shall whisper
    the sweet amen of peace;
for not with swords loud clashing,
    nor roll of stirring drums,
but deeds of love and mercy,
    the heavenly kingdom comes.

Lead on, O King eternal:
    we follow, not with fears;
for gladness breaks like morning
    where'er thy face appears.
Thy cross is lifted o'er us;
    we journey in its light:
the crown awaits the conquest;
    lead on, O God of might!

Ernest Warburton Shurtleff (1862–1917)

**556, 557**

Rejoice, ye pure in heart!
  Rejoice, give thanks, and sing!
Your glorious banner wave on high,
  the cross of Christ your King.

> *Rejoice, rejoice,*
>   *rejoice, give thanks, and sing.*

With all the angel choirs,
  with all the saints of earth,
pour out the strains of joy and bliss,
  true rapture, noblest mirth.

*Refrain*

Your clear hosannas raise,
  and alleluias loud;
while answering echoes upward float,
  like wreaths of incense cloud.

*Refrain*

Yes, on through life's long path,
  still chanting as ye go,
from youth to age, by night and day,
  in gladness and in woe.

*Refrain*

Still lift your standard high,
>   still march in firm array,
> as warriors through the darkness toil,
>   till dawns the golden day.

*Refrain*

At last the march shall end;
>   the wearied ones shall rest;
> the pilgrims find their Father's house,
>   Jerusalem the blest.

*Refrain*

Then on, ye pure in heart!
>   Rejoice, give thanks, and sing!
> Your glorious banner wave on high
>   the cross of Christ your King.

*Refrain*

Edward Hayes Plumptre (1821–1891)

The following refrain may be used:
>   *Hosanna, hosanna!*
>     *Rejoice, give thanks, and sing.*

## 558

Faith of our fathers! living still
   in spite of dungeon, fire and sword:
O how our hearts beat high with joy,
   whene'er we hear that glorious word:

> *Faith of our fathers, holy faith!*
> *We will be true to thee till death.*

Faith of our fathers! faith and prayer
   shall win all nations unto thee;
and through the truth that comes from God,
   mankind shall then indeed be free.

*Refrain*

Faith of our fathers! we will love
   both friend and foe in all our strife:
and preach thee, too, as love knows how,
   by kindly deeds and virtuous life.

*Refrain*

Frederick William Faber (1814–1863), alt.

## 559

Lead us, heavenly Father, lead us
   o'er the world's tempestuous sea;
guard us, guide us, keep us, feed us,
   for we have no help but thee,
yet possessing every blessing,
   if our God our Father be.

Savior, breathe forgiveness o'er us;
  all our weakness thou dost know;
thou didst tread this earth before us;
  thou didst feel its keenest woe;
yet unfearing, persevering,
  to thy passion thou didst go.

Spirit of our God, descending,
  fill our hearts with heavenly joy;
love with every passion blending,
  pleasure that can never cloy;
thus provided, pardoned, guided,
  nothing can our peace destroy.

James Edmeston (1791–1867), alt.

## 560

*Antiphon  Remember your servants, Lord,
  when you come in your kingly power.*

Blessèd are the poor in spirit;
  for theirs is the kingdom of heaven.

Blessèd are those who mourn;
  for they shall be comforted.

Blessèd are the meek;
  for they shall inherit the earth.

Blessèd are those who hunger and thirst
      after righteousness;
  for they shall be satisfied.

Blessèd are the merciful;
   for they shall obtain mercy.

Blessèd are the pure in heart;
   for they shall see God.

Blessèd are the peacemakers;
   for they shall be called the children of God.

Blessèd are those who are persecuted
            for righteousness' sake;
   for theirs is the kingdom of heaven.

Blessèd are you when the world reviles you
            and persecutes you;
   and utters all manner of evil against you falsely
            for my sake:

Rejoice and be exceeding glad;
   for great is your reward in heaven.

*Antiphon*

Russian Orthodox liturgy; Matthew 5:3–12

## 561

Stand up, stand up, for Jesus,
 ye soldiers of the cross;
lift high his royal banner,
 it must not suffer loss:
from victory unto victory
 his army shall be lead,
till every foe is vanquished
 and Christ is Lord indeed.

Stand up, stand up, for Jesus;
 the trumpet call obey;
forth to the mighty conflict
 in this his glorious day:
ye that are his now serve him
 against unnumbered foes;
let courage rise with danger,
 and strength to strength oppose.

Stand up, stand up, for Jesus;
 stand in this strength alone;
the arm of flesh will fail you,
 ye dare not trust your own:
put on the Gospel armor,
 and watching unto prayer,
when duty calls, or danger,
 be never wanting there.

Stand up, stand up, for Jesus:
    the strife will not be long:
this day, the noise of battle;
    the next, the victor's song.
To valiant hearts triumphant,
    a crown of life shall be;
they with the King of glory
    shall reign eternally.

George Duffield, Jr. (1818–1888), alt.

**562**

Onward, Christian soldiers,
    marching as to war,
with the cross of Jesus
    going on before!
Christ, the royal Master,
    leads against the foe;
forward into battle,
    see, his banners go.

> *Onward, Christian soldiers,*
> *marching as to war,*
> *with the cross of Jesus*
> *going on before!*

At the sign of triumph
 Satan's host doth flee;
on, then, Christian soldiers,
 on to victory!
Hell's foundations quiver
 at the shout of praise;
Christians, lift your voices,
 loud your anthems raise.

*Refrain*

Like a mighty army
 moves the Church of God;
Christians, we are treading
 where the saints have trod;
we are not divided,
 all one body we,
one in hope and doctrine,
 one in charity.

*Refrain*

Crowns and thrones may perish,
 kingdoms rise and wane,
but the Church of Jesus
 constant will remain;
gates of hell can never
 'gainst that Church prevail;
we have Christ's own promise,
 and that cannot fail.

*Refrain*

Onward, then, ye people,
   join our happy throng;
blend with ours your voices
   in the triumph song:
glory, laud, and honor,
   unto Christ the King;
this through countless ages
   we with angels sing.

*Refrain*

Sabine Baring-Gould (1834–1924), alt.

**563**

Go forward, Christian soldier,
   beneath his banner true:
the Lord himself, thy Leader,
   shall all thy foes subdue.
His love foretells thy trials;
   he knows thine hourly need;
he can with bread of heaven
   thy fainting spirit feed.

Go forward, Christian soldier,
   fear not the secret foe;
far more o'er thee are watching
   than human eyes can know:

trust only Christ, thy Captain;
   cease not to watch and pray;
heed not the treacherous voices
   that lure thy soul astray.

Go forward, Christian soldier,
   nor dream of peaceful rest,
till Satan's host is vanquished
   and heaven is all possessed;
till Christ himself shall call thee
   to lay thine armor by,
and wear in endless glory
   the crown of victory.

Go forward, Christian soldier,
   fear not the gathering night:
the Lord has been thy shelter;
   the Lord will be thy light.
When morn his face revealeth
   thy dangers all are past:
O pray that faith and virtue
   may keep thee to the last!

Laurence Tuttiett (1825–1895)

## 564, 565

He who would valiant be
   'gainst all disaster,
let him in constancy
   follow the Master.
There's no discouragement
shall make him once relent
his first avowed intent
   to be a pilgrim.

Who so beset him round
   with dismal stories,
do but themselves confound,
   his strength the more is.
No foes shall stay his might,
though he with giants fight;
he will make good his right
   to be a pilgrim.

Since, Lord, thou dost defend
   us with thy Spirit,
we know we at the end
   shall life inherit.
Then fancies flee away;
I'll fear not what men say,
I'll labor night and day
   to be a pilgrim.

Percy Dearmer (1867–1936), after John Bunyan (1628–1688)

## 566

From thee all skill and science flow,
  all pity, care, and love,
all calm and courage, faith and hope:
  O pour them from above!
Impart them, Lord, to each and all,
  as each and all shall need,
to rise, like incense, each to thee,
  in noble thought and deed.

And hasten, Lord, that perfect day
  when pain and death shall cease,
and thy just rule shall fill the earth
  with health and light and peace;
when ever-blue the sky shall gleam,
  and ever-green the sod,
and our rude work deface no more
  the handiwork of God.

Charles Kingsley (1819–1875), alt.

## 567

Thine arm, O Lord, in days of old
  was strong to heal and save;
it triumphed o'er disease and death,
  o'er darkness and the grave.
To thee they went, the blind, the deaf,
  the palsied, and the lame,
the leper set apart and shunned,
  the sick with fevered frame.

And lo! thy touch brought life and health,
    gave hearing, strength, and sight;
and youth renewed and frenzy calmed
    owned thee, the Lord of light:
and now, O Lord, be near to bless,
    almighty as of yore,
in crowded street, by restless couch,
    as by Gennesaret's shore.

Be thou our great deliverer still,
    thou Lord of life and death;
restore and quicken, soothe and bless,
    with thine almighty breath:
to hands that work and eyes that see,
    give wisdom's heavenly lore,
that whole and sick, and weak and strong,
    may praise thee evermore.

Edward Hayes Plumptre (1821–1891), alt.

## 568

Father all loving, who rulest in majesty,
    judgment is thine, and condemneth our pride;
stir up our leaders and peoples to penitence,
    sorrow for sins that for vengeance have cried.

Blessèd Lord Jesus, who camest in poverty,
    sharing a stable with beasts at thy birth,
stir us to work for thy justice and charity,
    truly to care for the poor of the earth.

Come, Holy Spirit, create in us holiness,
    lift up our lives to thy standard of right;
stir every will to new ventures of faithfulness,
    flood the whole Church with thy glorious light.

Holiest Trinity, perfect in unity,
    bind in thy love every nation and race;
may we adore thee for time and eternity,
    Father, Redeemer, and Spirit of grace.

Patrick Robert Norman Appleford (b. 1925), alt.

## 569

God the Omnipotent! King, who ordainest
    thunder thy clarion, the lightning thy sword;
show forth thy pity on high where thou reignest:
    give to us peace in our time, O Lord.

God the All-merciful! earth hath forsaken
    thy ways all holy, and slighted thy word;
bid not thy wrath in its terrors awaken:
    give to us peace in our time, O Lord.

God the All-righteous One! earth hath defied thee;
    yet to eternity standeth thy word,
falsehood and wrong shall not tarry beside thee:
    give to us peace in our time, O Lord.

God the All-provident! earth by thy chastening
 yet shall to freedom and truth be restored;
through the thick darkness thy kingdom is hastening:
 thou wilt give peace in thy time, O Lord.

Sts. 1-2, Henry Fothergill Chorley (1808-1872), alt.; sts. 3-4, John Ellerton (1826-1893), alt.

## 570, 571

All who love and serve your city,
 all who bear its daily stress,
all who cry for peace and justice,
 all who curse and all who bless,

in your day of loss and sorrow,
 in your day of helpless strife,
honor, peace and love retreating,
 seek the Lord, who is your life.

In your day of wealth and plenty,
 wasted work and wasted play,
call to mind the word of Jesus,
 "I must work while it is day."

For all days are days of judgment,
 and the Lord is waiting still,
drawing near a world that spurns him,
 offering peace from Calvary's hill.

Risen Lord! shall yet the city
  be the city of despair?
Come today, our Judge, our Glory;
  be its name, "The Lord is there!"

Erik Routley (1917–1982), rev.

## 572

Weary of all trumpeting,
  weary of all killing,
weary of all songs that sing
  promise, nonfulfilling,
we would raise, O Christ, one song;
  we would join in singing
that great music pure and strong,
  wherewith heaven is ringing.

Captain Christ, O lowly Lord,
  Servant King, your dying
bade us sheathe the foolish sword,
  bade us cease denying.
Trumpet with your Spirit's breath
  through each height and hollow;
into your self-giving death,
  call us all to follow.

To the triumph of your cross
  summon all the living;
summon us to love by loss,
  gaining all by giving,

suffering all, that we may see
    triumph in surrender;
leaving all, that we may be
    partners in your splendor.

Martin H. Franzmann (1907–1976), alt.

## 573

Father eternal, Ruler of creation,
    Spirit of life, which moved ere form was made,
through the thick darkness covering every nation,
    light to our blindness, O be thou our aid:

*thy kingdom come, O Lord,*
*thy will be done.*

Races and peoples, lo, we stand divided,
    and, sharing not our griefs, no joy can share;
by wars and tumults love is mocked, derided;
    his saving cross no nation yet will bear:

*Refrain*

Envious of heart, blind-eyed,
                with tongues confounded,
    nation by nation still goes unforgiven,
in wrath and fear, by jealousies surrounded,
    building proud towers which shall not
                reach to heaven:

*Refrain*

Lust of possession worketh desolations;
> there is no meekness in the powers of earth;
led by no star, the rulers of the nations
> still fail to bring us to the blissful birth:

*Refrain*

How shall we love thee, holy hidden Being,
> if we love not the world which thou hast made?
Bind us in thine own love for better seeing
> thy Word made flesh, and in a manger laid:

*Refrain*

Laurence Housman (1865–1959), alt.

## 574, 575

Before thy throne, O God, we kneel:
give us a conscience quick to feel,
a ready mind to understand
the meaning of thy chastening hand;
whate'er the pain and shame may be,
bring us, O Father, nearer thee.

Search out our hearts and make us true;
help us to give to all their due.
From love of pleasure, lust of gold,
from sins which make the heart grow cold,
wean us and train us with thy rod;
teach us to know our faults, O God.

For sins of heedless word and deed,
for pride ambitious to succeed,
for crafty trade and subtle snare
to catch the simple unaware,
for lives bereft of purpose high,
forgive, forgive, O Lord, we cry.

Let the fierce fires which burn and try,
our inmost spirits purify:
consume the ill; purge out the shame;
O God, be with us in the flame;
a new-born people may we rise,
more pure, more true, more nobly wise.

William Boyd Carpenter (1841–1918), alt.

## 576, 577

*God is love, and where true love is*
*God himself is there.*

Here in Christ we gather, love of Christ our calling.
Christ, our love, is with us, gladness be his greeting.
Let us fear and love him, holy God eternal.
Loving him, let each love Christ in one another.

*Refrain*

When we Christians gather, members of one Body,
let there be in us no discord but one spirit.

Banished now be anger, strife and every quarrel.
Christ, our God, be always present here among us.

*Refrain*

Grant us love's fulfillment, joy with all the blessèd,
when we see your face, O Savior, in its glory.
Shine on us, O purest Light of all creation,
be our bliss while endless ages sing your praises.

*Refrain*

Latin; tr. James Quinn (b. 1919), alt.

# 578

O God of love, O King of peace,
make wars throughout the world to cease;
the wrath of nations now restrain,
give peace, O God, give peace again!

Remember, Lord, thy works of old,
the wonders that thy people told;
remember not our sin's dark stain,
give peace, O God, give peace again!

Whom shall we trust but thee, O Lord?
Where rest but on thy faithful word?
None ever called on thee in vain,
give peace, O God, give peace again!

Henry Williams Baker (1821–1877), alt.

## 579

Almighty Father, strong to save,
whose arm hath bound the restless wave,
who bidd'st the mighty ocean deep
its own appointed limits keep:
O hear us when we cry to thee
for those in peril on the sea.

O Christ, the Lord of hill and plain
o'er which our traffic runs amain
by mountain pass or valley low;
wherever, Lord, thy people go,
protect them by thy guarding hand
from every peril on the land.

O Spirit, whom the Father sent
to spread abroad the firmament;
O Wind of heaven, by thy might
save all who dare the eagle's flight,
and keep them by thy watchful care
from every peril in the air.

O Trinity of love and power,
our people shield in danger's hour;
from rock and tempest, fire and foe,
protect them wheresoe're they go;
thus evermore shall rise to thee
glad praise from space, air, land, and sea.

Sts. 1 and 4, William Whiting (1825–1878), alt.; sts. 2–3, Robert Nelson Spencer (1877–1961), alt.

## 580

God, who stretched the spangled heavens
    infinite in time and place,
flung the suns in burning radiance
    through the silent fields of space:
we, your children in your likeness,
    share inventive powers with you;
Great Creator, still creating,
    show us what we yet may do.

Proudly rise our modern cities,
    stately buildings, row on row;
yet their windows, blank, unfeeling,
    stare on canyoned streets below,
where the lonely drift unnoticed
    in the city's ebb and flow,
lost to purpose and to meaning,
    scarcely caring where they go.

We have ventured worlds undreamed of
    since the childhood of our race;
known the ecstasy of winging
    through untraveled realms of space;
probed the secrets of the atom,
    yielding unimagined power,
facing us with life's destruction
    or our most triumphant hour.

As each far horizon beckons,
   may it challenge us anew,
children of creative purpose,
   serving others, honoring you.
May our dreams prove rich with promise,
   each endeavor well begun:
Great Creator, give us guidance
   till our goals and yours are one.

Catherine Cameron (b. 1927), alt.

**581**

Where charity and love prevail
   there God is ever found;
brought here together by Christ's love
   by love are we thus bound.

With grateful joy and holy fear
   his charity we learn;
let us with heart and mind and strength
   now love him in return.

Forgive we now each other's faults
   as we our faults confess;
and let us love each other well
   in Christian holiness.

Let strife among us be unknown,
   let all contention cease;

be his the glory that we seek,
    be ours his holy peace.

Let us recall that in our midst
    dwells God's begotten Son;
as members of his Body joined
    we are in him made one.

Love can exclude no race or creed
    if honored be God's Name;
our common life embraces all
    whose Father is the same.

Latin; tr. J. Clifford Evers (b. 1916)

## 582, 583

O holy city, seen of John,
    where Christ, the Lamb, doth reign,
within whose foursquare walls shall come
    no night, nor need, nor pain,
and where the tears are wiped from eyes
    that shall not weep again!

O shame to us who rest content
    while lust and greed for gain
in street and shop and tenement
    wring gold from human pain,
and bitter lips in blind despair
    cry, "Christ hath died in vain!"

Give us, O God, the strength to build
    the city that hath stood
too long a dream, whose laws are love,
    whose crown is servanthood,
and where the sun that shineth is
    God's grace for human good.

Already in the mind of God
    that city riseth fair:
lo, how its splendor challenges
    the souls that greatly dare—
yea, bids us seize the whole of life
    and build its glory there.

Walter Russell Bowie (1892–1969), alt.

**584**

God, you have given us power to sound
    depths hitherto unknown,
to probe earth's hidden mysteries,
    and make their might our own.

Great are your gifts; yet greater far
    this gift, O God, bestow:
that as to knowledge we attain
    we may in wisdom grow.

Let wisdom's godly fear dispel
  the fears that hate impart;
give understanding to the mind,
  and with new mind, new heart.

So for your glory and our good
  may we your gifts employ,
lest, maddened by the lust of power,
  we shall ourselves destroy.

George Wallace Briggs (1875–1959), alt.

## 585

Morning glory, starlit sky,
  soaring music, scholars' truth,
flight of swallows, autumn leaves,
  memory's treasure, grace of youth:

Open are the gifts of God,
  gifts of love to mind and sense;
hidden is love's agony,
  love's endeavor, love's expense.

Love that gives, gives ever more,
  gives with zeal, with eager hands,
spares not, keeps not, all outpours,
  ventures all, its all expends.

Drained is love in making full,
  bound in setting others free,

poor in making many rich,
  weak in giving power to be.

Therefore he who shows us God
  helpless hangs upon the tree;
and the nails and crown of thorns
  tell of what God's love must be.

Here is God: no monarch he,
  throned in easy state to reign;
here is God, whose arms of love
  aching, spent, the world sustain.

W. H. Vanstone (b. 1923)

**586**

Jesus, thou divine Companion,
  by thy lowly human birth
thou hast come to join the workers,
  burden-bearers of the earth.
Thou, the carpenter of Nazareth,
  toiling for thy daily food,
by thy patience and thy courage,
  thou hast taught us toil is good.

Where the many toil together,
  there art thou among thine own;
where the solitary labor,
  thou art there with them alone;

thou, the peace that passeth knowledge,
    dwellest in the daily strife;
thou, the Bread of heaven, art broken
    in the sacrament of life.

Every task, however simple,
    sets the soul that does it free;
every deed of human kindness
    done in love is done to thee.
Jesus, thou divine Companion,
    help us all to work our best;
bless us in our daily labor,
    lead us to our Sabbath rest.

Henry Van Dyke (1852–1933), alt.

## 587

Our Father, by whose Name
    all fatherhood is known,
who dost in love proclaim
    each family thine own,
bless thou all parents, guarding well,
with constant love as sentinel,
the homes in which thy people dwell.

O Christ, thyself a child
    within an earthly home,
with heart still undefiled,
    thou didst to manhood come;

our children bless, in every place,
that they may all behold thy face,
and knowing thee may grow in grace.

    O Spirit, who dost bind
        our hearts in unity,
    who teachest us to find
        the love from self set free,
in all our hearts such love increase,
that every home, by this release,
may be the dwelling place of peace.

F. Bland Tucker (1895–1984)

## 588, 589

Almighty God, your word is cast
    like seed upon the ground,
now let the dew of heaven descend
    and righteous fruits abound.

Let not our selfishness and hate
    this holy seed remove,
but give it root in every heart
    to bring forth fruits of love.

Let not the world's deceitful cares
    the rising plant destroy,
but let it yield a hundredfold
    the fruits of peace and joy.

John Cawood (1775–1852), alt.

## 590

O Jesus Christ, may grateful hymns be rising,
    in every city for your love and care;
inspire our worship, grant the glad surprising
    that your blest Spirit rouses everywhere.

Grant us new courage, sacrificial, humble,
    strong in your strength to venture and to dare;
to lift the fallen, guide the feet that stumble,
    seek out the lonely and God's mercy share.

Show us your Spirit, brooding o'er each city,
    as you once wept above Jerusalem,
seeking to gather all in love and pity,
    and healing those who touch your garment's hem.

Bradford Gray Webster (1898–1991), alt.

## 591

O God of earth and altar,
    bow down and hear our cry,
our earthly rulers falter,
    our people drift and die;
the walls of gold entomb us,
    the swords of scorn divide,
take not thy thunder from us,
    but take away our pride.

From all that terror teaches,
    from lies of tongue and pen,

from all the easy speeches
    that comfort cruel men,
from sale and profanation
    of honor, and the sword,
from sleep and from damnation,
    deliver us, good Lord!

Tie in a living tether
    the prince and priest and thrall,
bind all our lives together,
    smite us and save us all;
in ire and exultation
    aflame with faith, and free,
lift up a living nation,
    a single sword to thee.

Gilbert Keith Chesterton (1874–1936)

**592**

Teach me, my God and King,
    in all things thee to see;
and what I do in anything,
    to do it as for thee.

All may of thee partake;
    nothing can be so mean,
which with this tincture, "for thy sake,"
    will not grow bright and clean.

A servant with this clause
    makes drudgery divine:
who sweeps a room, as for thy laws,
    makes that and the action fine.

This is the famous stone
    that turneth all to gold;
for that which God doth touch and own
    cannot for less be told.

George Herbert (1593–1633)

## 593

Lord, make us servants of your peace:
where there is hate, may we sow love;
where there is hurt, may we forgive;
where there is strife, may we make one.

Where all is doubt, may we sow faith;
where all is gloom, may we sow hope;
where all is night, may we sow light;
where all is tears, may we sow joy.

Jesus, our Lord, may we not seek
to be consoled, but to console,
nor look to understanding hearts,
but look for hearts to understand.

May we not look for love's return,
but seek to love unselfishly,

for in our giving we receive,
and in forgiving are forgiven.

Dying, we live, and are reborn
through death's dark night to endless day:
Lord, make us servants of your peace,
to wake at last in heaven's light.

James Quinn (b. 1919), based on a prayer att. to St. Francis of
Assisi (1182–1226)

**594, 595**

God of grace and God of glory,
  on thy people pour thy power;
crown thine ancient Church's story;
  bring her bud to glorious flower.
Grant us wisdom, grant us courage,
  for the facing of this hour.

Lo! the hosts of evil round us
  scorn thy Christ, assail his ways!
From the fears that long have bound us
  free our hearts to faith and praise:
grant us wisdom, grant us courage
  for the living of these days.

Cure thy children's warring madness,
  bend our pride to thy control;
shame our wanton, selfish gladness,
  rich in things and poor in soul.

Grant us wisdom, grant us courage,
    lest we miss thy kingdom's goal.

Save us from weak resignation
    to the evils we deplore;
let the gift of thy salvation
    be our glory evermore.
Grant us wisdom, grant us courage,
    serving thee whom we adore.

Harry Emerson Fosdick (1878–1969), alt.

## 596

Judge eternal, throned in splendor,
    Lord of lords and King of kings,
with thy living fire of judgment
    purge this land of bitter things;
solace all its wide dominion
    with the healing of thy wings.

Still the weary folk are pining
    for the hour that brings release,
and the city's crowded clangor
    cries aloud for sin to cease;
and the homesteads and the woodlands
    plead in silence for their peace.

Crown, O God, thine own endeavor;
 cleave our darkness with thy sword;
feed all those who do not know thee
 with the richness of thy word;
cleanse the body of this nation
 through the glory of the Lord.

Henry Scott Holland (1847–1918), alt.

## 597

O day of peace that dimly shines
 through all our hopes and prayers and dreams,
guide us to justice, truth, and love,
 delivered from our selfish schemes.
May swords of hate fall from our hands,
 our hearts from envy find release,
till by God's grace our warring world
 shall see Christ's promised reign of peace.

Then shall the wolf dwell with the lamb,
 nor shall the fierce devour the small;
as beasts and cattle calmly graze,
 a little child shall lead them all.
Then enemies shall learn to love,
 all creatures find their true accord;
the hope of peace shall be fulfilled,
 for all the earth shall know the Lord.

Carl P. Daw, Jr. (b. 1944)

## 598

Lord Christ, when first thou cam'st to earth,
    upon a cross they bound thee,
and mocked thy saving kingship then
    by thorns with which they crowned thee:
and still our wrongs may weave thee now
new thorns to pierce that steady brow,
    and robe of sorrow round thee.

O aweful Love, which found no room
    in life where sin denied thee,
and, doomed to death, must bring to doom
    the powers which crucified thee,
till not a stone was left on stone,
and all those nations' pride, o'erthrown,
    went down to dust beside thee!

New advent of the love of Christ,
    shall we again refuse thee,
till in the night of hate and war
    we perish as we lose thee?
From old unfaith our souls release
to seek the kingdom of thy peace,
    by which alone we choose thee.

O wounded hands of Jesus, build
    in us thy new creation;
our pride is dust, our vaunt is stilled,
    we wait thy revelation:

O love that triumphs over loss,
we bring our hearts before thy cross,
   to finish thy salvation.

Walter Russell Bowie (1882–1969), alt.

**599**

Lift every voice and sing
till earth and heaven ring,
   ring with the harmonies of liberty.
Let our rejoicing rise
high as the listening skies;
   let it resound loud as the rolling sea.
Sing a song full of the faith that the dark past
              has taught us;
sing a song full of the hope that the present
              has brought us;
facing the rising sun
of our new day begun,
   let us march on, till victory is won.

Stony the road we trod,
bitter the chastening rod,
   felt in the days when hope unborn had died;
yet, with a steady beat,
have not our weary feet
   come to the place for which our parents sighed?

We have come over a way that with tears
    has been watered;
we have come, treading our path through the blood
    of the slaughtered,
out from the gloomy past,
till now we stand at last
 where the white gleam of our bright star is cast.

God of our weary years,
God of our silent tears,
 thou who hast brought us thus far on the way;
thou who hast by thy might
led us into the light;
 keep us for ever in the path, we pray.
Lest our feet stray from the places, our God,
    where we met thee;
lest, our hearts drunk with the wine of the world,
    we forget thee;
shadowed beneath thy hand
may we for ever stand,
 true to our God, true to our native land.

James Weldon Johnson (1871–1938)

## 600, 601

O day of God, draw nigh
  in beauty and in power,
come with thy timeless judgment now
  to match our present hour.

Bring to our troubled minds,
  uncertain and afraid,
the quiet of a steadfast faith,
  calm of a call obeyed.

Bring justice to our land,
  that all may dwell secure,
and finely build for days to come
  foundations that endure.

Bring to our world of strife
  thy sovereign word of peace,
that war may haunt the earth no more
  and desolation cease.

O day of God, draw nigh
  as at creation's birth,
let there be light again, and set
  thy judgments in the earth.

Robert Balgarnie Young Scott (1899–1987)

## 602

> *Jesu, Jesu, fill us with your love,*
> *show us how to serve the neighbors*
> *we have from you.*

Kneels at the feet of his friends,
silently washes their feet,
Master who acts as a slave to them.

*Chorus*

Neighbors are rich and poor,
neighbors are black and white,
neighbors are nearby and far away.

*Chorus*

These are the ones we should serve,
these are the ones we should love.
All are neighbors to us and you.

*Chorus*

Loving puts us on our knees,
serving as though we were slaves;
this is the way we should live with you.

*Chorus*

Ghanian; tr. Thomas Stephenson Colvin (b. 1925), alt.

## 603, 604

When Christ was lifted from the earth,
    his arms stretched out above
through every culture, every birth,
    to draw an answering love.

Still east and west his love extends
    and always, near or far,
he calls and claims us as his friends
    and loves us as we are.

Where generation, class, or race
    divide us to our shame,
he sees not labels but a face,
    a person, and a name.

Thus freely loved, though fully known,
    may I in Christ be free
to welcome and accept his own
    as Christ accepted me.

Brian A. Wren (b. 1936)

## 605

What does the Lord require
   for praise and offering?
What sacrifice desire,
   or tribute bid you bring?
     Do justly;
     love mercy;
   walk humbly with your God.

Rulers of earth, give ear!
   Should you not justice show?
Will God your pleading hear,
   while crime and cruelty grow?
     Do justly;
     love mercy;
   walk humbly with your God.

Still down the ages ring
   the prophet's stern commands.
To merchant, worker, king
   he brings God's high demands.
     Do justly;
     love mercy;
   walk humbly with your God.

How shall my soul fulfill
    God's law so hard and high?
Let Christ endue our will
    with grace to fortify.
        Then justly;
        in mercy
    we'll humbly walk with God.

Albert F. Bayly (1901–1984), alt.

# 606

*Antiphon:   Where true charity and love dwell,*
*God himself is there.*

Since the love of Christ has joined us in one body,
    let us all rejoice and be glad now and always.
And as we hear and love our Lord, the living God,
    so let us in sincerity love all people.

*Antiphon*

As we are all of one body, when we gather
    let no discord or enmity break our oneness.
May all our petty jealousies and hatred cease
    that Christ the Lord may be with us
                through all our days.

*Antiphon*

Now we pray that with the blessèd you grant us grace
   to see your exalted glory, O Christ our God,
our boundless source of joy and truth,
              of peace and love,
for ever and for evermore, world without end.

*Antiphon*

Latin; tr. Joyce M. Glover (b. 1923)

# 607

O God of every nation,
   of every, race and land,
redeem the whole creation
   with your almighty hand;
where hate and fear divide us
   and bitter threats are hurled,
in love and mercy guide us
   and heal our strife-torn world.

From search for wealth and power
   and scorn of truth and right,
from trust in bombs that shower
   destruction through the night,
from pride of race and nation
   and blindness to your way,
deliver every nation,
   eternal God, we pray!

Lord, strengthen all who labor
    that we may find release
from fear of rattling saber,
    from dread of war's increase;
when hope and courage falter,
    your still small voice be heard;
with faith that none can alter,
    your servants undergird.

Keep bright in us the vision
    of days when war shall cease,
when hatred and division
    give way to love and peace,
till dawns the morning glorious
    when truth and justice reign
and Christ shall rule victorious
    o'er all the world's domain.

William Watkins Reid, Jr. (b. 1923), alt.

**608**

Eternal Father, strong to save,
whose arm hath bound the restless wave,
who bidd'st the mighty ocean deep
its own appointed limits keep:
    O hear us when we cry to thee
    for those in peril on the sea.

O Christ, whose voice the waters heard
and hushed their raging at thy word,

who walkedst on the foaming deep,
and calm amid its rage didst sleep:
    O hear us when we cry to thee
    for those in peril on the sea.

Most Holy Spirit, who didst brood
upon the chaos dark and rude,
and bid its angry tumult cease,
and give, for wild confusion, peace;
    O hear us when we cry to thee
    for those in peril on the sea.

O Trinity of love and power,
thy children shield in danger's hour;
from rock and tempest, fire and foe,
protect them wheresoe'er they go;
    thus evermore shall rise to thee
    glad hymns of praise from land and sea.

William Whiting (1825–1878), alt.

## 609

Where cross the crowded ways of life,
    where sound the cries of race and clan,
above the noise of selfish strife,
    we hear thy voice, O Son of Man.

In haunts of wretchedness and need,
    on shadowed thresholds dark with fears,
from paths where hide the lures of greed,
    we catch the vision of thy tears.

The cup of water given for thee
    still holds the freshness of thy grace;
yet long these multitudes to see
    the true compassion of thy face.

O Master, from the mountain side,
    make haste to heal these hearts of pain;
among these restless throngs abide,
    O tread the city's streets again;

till all the world shall learn thy love,
    and follow where thy feet have trod;
till glorious from thy heaven above,
    shall come the city of our God.

Frank Mason North (1850–1935), alt.

## 610

Lord, whose love through humble service
    bore the weight of human need,
who upon the cross, forsaken,
    offered mercy's perfect deed,
we, your servants, bring the worship
    not of voice alone, but heart,
consecrating to your purpose
    every gift that you impart.

Still your children wander homeless;
    still the hungry cry for bread;
still the captives long for freedom;
    still in grief we mourn our dead.
As, O Lord, your deep compassion
    healed the sick and freed the soul,
use the love your Spirit kindles
    still to save and make us whole.

As we worship, grant us vision,
    till your love's revealing light,
in its height and depth and greatness,
    dawns upon our quickened sight,
making known the needs and burdens
    your compassion bids us bear,
stirring us to tireless striving,
    your abundant life to share.

Called by worship to your service,
    forth in your dear name we go,
to the child, the youth, the agèd
    love in living deeds to show;
hope and health, good will and comfort,
    counsel, aid, and peace we give,
that your servants, Lord, in freedom
    may your mercy know and live.

Albert F. Bayly (1901–1984), alt.

# 611

Christ the worker,
Christ the worker,
born in Bethlehem,
born to work and die for every one.

Blessèd manchild,
blessèd manchild,
boy of Nazareth,
grew in wisdom as he grew in skill.

Skillful craftsman,
skillful craftsman,
blessèd carpenter,
praising God by labor at his bench.

Yoke maker,
yoke maker,
fashioned by his hands,
easy yokes that made the labor less.

All who labor,
all who labor,
listen to his call,
he will make that heavy burden light.

Heavy laden,
heavy laden,
gladly come to him,
he will ease your load and give you rest.

Christ the worker,
Christ the worker,
Love alive for us,
teach us how to do all work for God.

Ghanian work song; tr. Thomas Stephenson Colvin (b. 1925), alt.

## 612

Gracious Spirit, Holy Ghost,
taught by thee we covet most,
of thy gifts at Pentecost,
    holy heavenly love.

Love is kind, and suffers long,
love is meek, and thinks no wrong,
love than death itself more strong;
    therefore, give us love.

Prophecy will fade away,
melting in the light of day;
love will ever with us stay;
    therefore, give us love.

Faith and hope and love we see,
joining hand in hand, agree,
but the greatest of the three,
    and the best, is love.

Christopher Wordsworth (1807–1885)

## 613

Thy kingdom come, O God!
   Thy rule, O Christ, begin!
Break with thine iron rod
   the tyrannies of sin!

Where is thy reign of peace,
   and purity, and love?
When shall all hatred cease,
   as in the realms above?

When comes the promised time
   that war shall be no more,
oppression, lust, and crime
   shall flee thy face before?

We pray thee, Lord, arise,
   and come in thy great might;
revive our longing eyes,
   which languish for thy sight.

Wherever near or far
   thick darkness broodeth yet:
arise, O Morning Star,
   arise, and never set!

Lewis Hensley (1824–1905), alt.

## 614

Christ is the King! O friends upraise
anthems of joy and holy praise
for his brave saints of ancient days,
who with a faith for ever new
followed the King, and round him drew
thousands of servants brave and true.

O Christian women, Christian men,
all the world over, seek again
the Way disciples followed then.
Christ through all ages is the same:
place the same hope in his great Name,
with the same faith his word proclaim.

Let Love's unconquerable might
your scattered companies unite
in service to the Lord of light:
so shall God's will on earth be done,
new lamps be lit, new tasks begun,
and the whole Church at last be one.

George Kennedy Allen Bell (1883–1958), alt.

## 615

"Thy kingdom come!" on bended knee
    the passing ages pray;
and faithful souls have yearned to see
    on earth that kingdom's day.

But the slow watches of the night
    not less to God belong;
and for the everlasting right
    the silent stars are strong.

And lo, already on the hills
    the flags of dawn appear;
gird up your loins, ye prophet souls,
    proclaim the day is near:

the day to whose clear-shining light
    all wrong shall stand revealed,
when justice shall be throned in might,
    and every hurt be healed;

when knowledge, hand in hand with peace,
    shall walk the earth abroad;
the day of perfect righteousness,
    the promised day of God.

Frederick Lucian Hosmer (1840–1929)

## 616

Hail to the Lord's Anointed,
    great David's greater Son!
Hail, in the time appointed,
    his reign on earth begun!
He comes to break oppression,
    to set the captive free;
to take away transgression,
    and rule in equity.

He comes with succor speedy
    to those who suffer wrong,
to help the poor and needy,
    and bid the weak be strong;
to give them songs for sighing,
    their darkness turn to light,
whose souls, condemned and dying,
    were precious in his sight.

He shall come down like showers
    upon the fruitful earth,
and love, joy, hope, like flowers,
    spring in his path to birth:
before him on the mountains
    shall peace, the herald, go;
and righteousness in fountains
    from hill to valley flow.

Kings shall bown before him,
    and gold and incense bring;

all nations shall adore him,
>   his praise all people sing;
> to him shall prayer unceasing
>   and daily vows ascend;
> his kingdom still increasing,
>   a kingdom without end.

O'er every foe victorious,
>   he on his throne shall rest;
> from age to age more glorious,
>   all-blessing and all-blest:
> the tide of time shall never
>   his covenant remove;
> his Name shall stand for ever,
>   his changeless Name of Love.

James Montgomery (1771–1854); para. of Psalm 72

## 617

Eternal Ruler of the ceaseless round
>   of circling planets singing on their way,
> guide of the nations from the night profound
>   into the glory of the perfect day;
> rule in our hearts, that we may ever be
>   guided and strengthened and upheld by thee.

We would be one in hatred of all wrong,
>   one in the love of all things sweet and fair,
> one with the joy that breaketh into song,
>   one with the grief that trembleth into prayer;

one in the power that makes thy children free
   to follow truth, and thus to follow thee.

Oh, clothe us with thy heavenly armor, Lord,
   thy trusty shield, thy word of love divine;
our inspiration be thy constant word,
   we ask no victories that are not thine;
give or withhold, let pain or pleasure be;
   enough to know that we are serving thee.

John White Chadwick (1840–1904), alt.

## 618

Ye watchers and ye holy ones,
bright seraphs, cherubim, and thrones,
   raise the glad strain, Alleluia!
Cry out, dominions, princedoms, powers,
virtues, archangels, angels' choirs,
   Alleluia, alleluia, alleluia, alleluia, alleluia!

O higher than the cherubim,
more glorious than the seraphim,
   lead their praises, Alleluia!
Thou bearer of the eternal Word,
most gracious, magnify the Lord,
   Alleluia, alleluia, alleluia, alleluia, alleluia!

Respond, ye souls in endless rest,
ye patriarchs and prophets blest,
   Alleluia, alleluia!

Ye holy twelve, ye martyrs strong,
all saints triumphant, raise the song,
 Alleluia, alleluia, alleluia, alleluia, alleluia!

O friends, in gladness let us sing,
supernal anthems echoing,
 Alleluia, alleluia!
To God the Father, God the Son,
and God the Spirit, Three in One,
 Alleluia, alleluia, alleluia, alleluia, alleluia!

John Athelstan Laurie Riley (1858–1945)

**619**

Sing alleluia forth in duteous praise,
ye citizens of heaven, O sweetly raise
 an endless alleluia.

Ye powers who stand before the eternal Light,
let all your choirs re-echo to the height
 an endless alleluia.

Then let the holy city raise the strain,
and with glad songs resounding wake again
 an endless alleluia.

Ye who have fought and joined the starry throng,
ye victors, now take up the eternal song,
 an endless alleluia.

Your songs of triumph shall for ever ring,
the hymns which tell the honor of your King,
    an endless alleluia.

Such song is rest and food and deep delight
to saints forgiven; let them unite
    in endless alleluia.

Almighty Christ, to thee our voices sing
glory for evermore; to thee we bring
    an endless alleluia.

Latin, 5th–8th cent.; ver. *Hymnal 1940*

# 620

Jerusalem, my happy home,
    when shall I come to thee?
When shall my sorrows have an end?
    Thy joys when shall I see?

Thy saints are crowned with glory great;
    they see God face to face;
they triumph still, they still rejoice
    in that most happy place.

There David stands with harp in hand
    as master of the choir:
ten thousand times would one be blest
    who might this music hear.

Our Lady sings Magnificat
>   with tune surpassing sweet,
and blessèd martyrs' harmony
>   doth ring in every street.

Jerusalem, Jerusalem,
>   God grant that I may see
thine endless joy, and of the same
>   partaker ever be!

F. B. P. (ca. 16th cent.), alt.

## 621, 622

Light's abode, celestial Salem,
>   vision whence true peace doth spring,
brighter than the heart can fancy,
>   mansion of the highest King;
O how glorious are the praises
>   which of thee the prophets sing!

There for ever and for ever
>   alleluia is outpoured;
for unending, for unbroken
>   is the feast-day of the Lord;
all is pure and all is holy
>   that within thy walls is stored.

There no cloud nor passing vapor
>   dims the brightness of the air;

endless noonday, glorious noonday,
   from the Sun of suns is there;
there no night brings rest from labor,
   for unknown are toil and care.

O how glorious and resplendent,
   fragile body, shalt thou be,
when endued with heavenly beauty,
   full of health, and strong, and free,
full of vigor, full of pleasure
   that shall last eternally!

Now with gladness, now with courage,
   bear the burden on thee laid,
that hereafter these thy labors
   may with endless gifts be paid,
and in everlasting glory
   thou with brightness be arrayed.

Latin, 15th cent.; tr. John Mason Neale (1818–1866), alt.

## 623

O what their joy and their glory must be,
those endless Sabbaths the blessèd ones see;
crown for the valiant, to weary ones rest:
God shall be all, and in all ever blest.

Truly "Jerusalem" name we that shore,
city of peace that brings joy evermore;

wish and fulfillment are not severed there,
nor do things prayed for come short of the prayer.

There, where no troubles distraction can bring,
we the sweet anthems of Zion shall sing;
while for thy grace, Lord, their voices of praise
thy blessed people eternally raise.

Now, in the meanwhile, with hearts raised on high,
we for that country must yearn and must sigh,
seeking Jerusalem, dear native land,
through our long exile on Babylon's strand.

Low before him with our praises we fall,
of whom, and in whom, and through whom are all;
of whom, the Father; and in whom, the Son;
through whom, the Spirit, with them ever One.

Peter Abelard (1079–1142); tr. John Mason Neale (1818–1866), alt.

## 624

Jerusalem the golden,
   with milk and honey blest,
beneath thy contemplation
   sink heart and voice oppressed:
I know not, oh, I know not,
   what joys await us there;
what radiancy of glory,
   what bliss beyond compare!

They stand, those halls of Zion
    all jubilant with song,
and bright with many an angel,
    and all the martyr throng:
the Prince is ever in them,
    the daylight is serene;
the pastures of the blessèd
    are decked in glorious sheen.

There is the throne of David;
    and there, from care released,
the shout of them that triumph,
    the song of them that feast;
and they who with their Leader
    have conquered in the fight,
for ever and for ever
    are clad in robes of white.

Oh, sweet and blessèd country,
    the home of God's elect!
Oh, sweet and blessèd country
    that eager hearts expect!
Jesus, in mercy bring us
    to that dear land of rest,
who art with God the Father,
    and Spirit, ever blest.

Bernard of Cluny (12th cent.); tr. John Mason Neale (1818–1866). alt.

## 625

Ye holy angels bright,
 who wait at God's right hand,
or through the realms of light
 fly at your Lord's command,
  assist our song,
   for else the theme
   too high doth seem
  for mortal tongue.

Ye blessèd souls at rest,
 who ran this earthly race
and now, from sin released,
 behold the Savior's face,
  God's praises sound,
   as in his sight
   with sweet delight
  ye do abound.

Ye saints, who toil below,
 adore your heavenly King,
and onward as ye go
 some joyful anthem sing;
  take what he gives
   and praise him still,
   through good or ill,
  who ever lives!

My soul, bear thou thy part,
   triumph in God above:
and with a well-tuned heart
   sing thou the songs of love!
     Let all thy days
       till life shall end,
       whate'er he send,
     be filled with praise.

Richard Baxter (1615–1691); rev. John Hampden Gurney (1802–1862)

## 626

Lord, be thy word my rule;
   in it may I rejoice;
thy glory be my aim,
   thy holy will my choice;

thy promises my hope;
   thy providence my guard;
thine arm my strong support;
   thyself my great reward.

Christopher Wordsworth (1807–1885)

# 627

Lamp of our feet, whereby we trace
    our path when wont to stray;
stream from the fount of heavenly grace,
    brook by the traveler's way;

bread of our souls, whereon we feed,
    true manna from on high;
our guide and chart, wherein we read
    of realms beyond the sky;

pillar of fire, through watches dark,
    and radiant cloud by day;
when waves would whelm our tossing bark,
    our anchor and our stay;

word of the ever-living God,
    will of his glorious Son;
without thee how could earth be trod,
    or heaven itself be won?

Lord, grant us all aright to learn
    the wisdom it imparts;
and to its heavenly teaching turn,
    with simple, childlike hearts.

Bernard Barton (1784–1849)

## 628

Help us, O Lord, to learn
    the truths your word imparts:
to study, that your laws may be
    inscribed upon our hearts.

Help us, O Lord, to live
    the faith which we proclaim,
that all our thoughts and words and deeds
    may glorify your Name.

Help us, O Lord, to teach
    the beauty of your ways,
that yearning souls may find the Christ
    and live a life of praise.

William Watkins Reid, Jr. (b. 1923), alt.

## 629

We limit not the truth of God
    to our poor reach of mind,
to notions of our day and place,
    crude, partial, and confined;
no, let a new and better hope
    within our hearts be stirred;
the Lord has yet more light and truth
    to break forth from his word.

Who dares to bind to one's own sense
    the oracles of heaven,
for all the nations, tongues, and climes
    and all the ages given?
That universe, how much unknown!
    The ocean unexplored!
The Lord has yet more light and truth
    to break forth from his word.

O Father, Son, and Spirit, send
    us increase from above;
enlarge, expand all living souls
    to comprehend your love;
and make us all go on to know
    with nobler powers conferred—
the Lord has yet more light and truth
    to break forth from his word.

George Rawson (1807–1889), alt.

## 630

Thanks to God whose Word was spoken
    in the deed that made the earth.
His the voice that called a nation;
    his the fires that tried her worth.
        God has spoken:
    praise God for his open word.

Thanks to God whose Word Incarnate
   heights and depths of life did share.
Deeds and words and death and rising,
   grace in human form declare.
      God has spoken:
   praise God for his open word.

Thanks to God whose word was written
   in the Bible's sacred page,
record of the revelation
   showing God to every age.
      God has spoken:
   praise God for his open word.

Thanks to God whose word is published
   in the tongues of every race.
See its glory undiminished
   by the change of time or place.
      God has spoken:
   praise God for his open word.

Thanks to God whose Word is answered
   by the Spirit's voice within.
Here we drink of joy unmeasured,
   life redeemed from death and sin.
      God is speaking:
   praise God for his open word.

R. T. Brooks (b. 1918), alt.

# 631

Book of books, our people's strength,
    statesman's, teacher's, hero's treasure,
bringing freedom, spreading truth,
    shedding light that none can measure:
        wisdom comes to those who know thee,
        all the best we have we owe thee.

Thank we those who toiled in thought,
    many diverse scrolls completing,
poets, prophets, scholars, saints,
    each a word from God repeating;
        till they came, who told the story
        of the Word, and showed his glory.

Praise we God, who hath inspired
    those whose wisdom still directs us;
praise him for the Word made flesh,
    for the Spirit which protects us.
        Light of knowledge, ever burning,
        shed on us thy deathless learning.

Percy Dearmer (1867–1936)

## 632

O Christ, the Word Incarnate,
 O Wisdom from on high,
O Truth, unchanged, unchanging,
 O Light of our dark sky;
we praise thee for the radiance
 that from the scripture's page,
a lantern to our footsteps,
 shines on from age to age.

The Church from our dear Master
 received the word divine,
and still that light is lifted
 o'er all the earth to shine.
It is the chart and compass
 that o'er life's surging sea,
mid mists and rocks and quicksands,
 still guides, O Christ, to thee.

O make thy Church, dear Savior,
 a lamp of purest gold,
to bear before the nations
 thy true light as of old;
O teach thy wandering pilgrims
 by this their path to trace,
till, clouds and darkness ended,
 they see thee face to face.

William Walsham How (1823–1897), alt.

**633**

Word of God, come down on earth,
    living rain from heaven descending;
touch our hearts and bring to birth
    faith and hope and love unending.
Word almighty, we revere you;
Word made flesh, we long to hear you.

Word eternal, throned on high,
    Word that brought to life creation,
Word that came from heaven to die,
    crucified for our salvation,
saving Word, the world restoring,
speak to us, your love outpouring.

Word that caused blind eyes to see,
    speak and heal our mortal blindness;
deaf we are: our healer be;
    loose our tongues to tell your kindness.
Be our Word in pity spoken;
heal the world, by our sin broken.

Word that speaks your Father's love,
    one with him beyond all telling,
Word that sends us from above
    God the Spirit, with us dwelling,
Word of truth, to all truth lead us,
Word of life, with one Bread feed us.

James Quinn (b. 1919)

## 634

    I call on thee, Lord Jesus Christ,
        I have none other help but thee.
    My heart is never set at rest
        till thy sweet word have comforted me.
    And steadfast faith grant me therefore,
    to hold by thy word evermore,
        above all thing,
        never resisting
    but to increase in faith more and more.

Miles Coverdale (1487–1568)

## 635

    If thou but trust in God to guide thee,
        and hope in him through all thy ways,
    he'll give thee strength whate'er betide thee,
        and bear thee through the evil days.
    Who trusts in God's unchanging love
    builds on a rock that nought can move.

    Sing, pray, and keep his ways unswerving;
        so do thine own part faithfully,
    and trust his word, though undeserving;
        thou yet shalt find it true for thee;
    God never yet forsook in need
    the soul that trusted him indeed.

Georg Neumark (1621–1681); tr. Catherine Winkworth (1829–1878), alt.

## 636, 637

How firm a foundation, ye saints of the Lord,
is laid for your faith in his excellent word!
What more can he say than to you he hath said,
to you that for refuge to Jesus have fled?

"Fear not, I am with thee; O be not dismayed!
For I am thy God, and will still give thee aid;
I'll strengthen thee, help thee, and cause thee
                to stand,
upheld by my righteous, omnipotent hand.

"When through the deep waters I call thee to go,
the rivers of woe shall not thee overflow;
for I will be with thee, thy troubles to bless,
and sanctify to thee thy deepest distress.

"When through fiery trials thy pathway shall lie,
my grace, all-sufficient, shall be thy supply;
the flame shall not hurt thee; I only design
thy dross to consume, and thy gold to refine.

"The soul that to Jesus hath fled for repose,
I will not, I will not desert to its foes;
that soul, though all hell shall endeavor to shake,
I'll never, no, never, no, never forsake."

K. in John Rippon's *Selection*, 1787, alt.

## 638, 639

Come, O thou Traveler unknown,
    whom still I hold, but cannot see;
my company before is gone,
    and I am left alone with thee.
With thee all night I mean to stay,
and wrestle till the break of day.

I need not tell thee who I am,
    my misery or sin declare;
thyself hast called me by my name,
    look on thy hands, and read it there.
But who, I ask thee, who art thou?
Tell me thy name, and tell me now.

Yield to me now, for I am weak
    but confident in self-despair;
speak to my heart, in blessings speak,
    be conquered by my instant prayer.
Speak, or thou never hence shalt move,
and tell me, if thy name is Love.

'Tis Love, 'tis Love!  Thou diedst for me!
    I hear thy whisper in my heart:
the morning breaks, the shadows flee.
    Pure Universal Love thou art;
thy mercies never shall remove,
thy nature and thy name is Love.

Charles Wesley (1707–1788), alt.

# 640

Watchman, tell us of the night,
    what its signs of promise are.
Traveler, o'er yon mountain's height,
    see that glory-beaming star.
Watchman, does its beauteous ray
    aught of joy or hope foretell?
Traveler, yes; it brings the day,
    promised day of Israel.

Watchman, tell us of the night;
    higher yet that star ascends.
Traveler, blessedness and light,
    peace and truth its course portends.
Watchman, will its beams alone
    gild the spot that gave them birth?
Traveler, ages are its own;
    see, it bursts o'er all the earth.

Watchman, tell us of the night,
    for the morning seems to dawn.
Traveler, darkness takes its flight,
    doubt and terror are withdrawn.
Watchman, let thy wanderings cease;
    hie thee to thy quiet home.
Traveler, lo! the Prince of Peace,
    lo! the Son of God is come!

John Bowring (1792–1872)

# 641

Lord Jesus, think on me,
    and purge away my sin;
from harmful passions set me free,
    and make me pure within.

Lord Jesus, think on me,
    with care and woe oppressed;
let me thy loving servant be,
    and taste thy promised rest.

Lord Jesus, think on me,
    nor let me go astray;
through darkness and perplexity
    point thou the heavenly way.

Lord Jesus, think on me,
    that, when the flood is passed,
I may the eternal brightness see,
    and share thy joy at last.

Synesius of Cyrene (375?–414?); tr. Allen William Chatfield (1808–1896), alt.

# 642

Jesus, the very thought of thee
    with sweetness fills the breast;
but sweeter far thy face to see,
    and in thy presence rest.

No voice can sing, no heart can frame,
    nor can the memory find,
a sweeter sound than Jesus' Name,
    the Savior of mankind.

O hope of every contrite heart,
    O joy of all the meek,
to those who fall, how kind thou art:
    how good to those who seek!

But what to those who find? Ah, this
    nor tongue nor pen can show;
the love of Jesus, what it is,
    none but who love him know.

Jesus, our only joy be thou,
    as thou our prize wilt be;
in thee be all our glory now,
    and through eternity.

Latin, 12th cent.; st. 5, Latin, 15th cent.; tr. Edward Caswall (1814–1878), alt.

## 643

My God, how wonderful thou art,
    thy majesty how bright,
how beautiful thy mercy-seat,
    in depths of burning light!

How dread are thine eternal years,
    O everlasting Lord,
by prostrate spirits day and night
    incessantly adored!

How wonderful, how beautiful,
    the sight of thee must be,
thine endless wisdom, boundless power,
    and awful purity!

O how I fear thee, living God,
    with deepest, tenderest fears,
and worship thee with trembling hope
    and penitential tears!

Yet I may love thee too, O Lord,
    almighty as thou art,
for thou hast stooped to ask of me
    the love of my poor heart.

Frederick William Faber (1814–1863)

## 644

How sweet the Name of Jesus sounds
  in a believer's ear!
It soothes our sorrows, heals our wounds,
  and drives away our fear.

It makes the wounded spirit whole,
  and calms the troubled breast;
'tis manna to the hungry soul,
  and to the weary, rest.

Dear Name, the rock on which I build,
  my shield and hiding-place,
my never-failing treasury, filled
  with boundless stores of grace!

O Jesus! Shepherd, Guardian, Friend,
  O Prophet, Priest, and King,
my Lord, my Life, my Way, my End,
  accept the praise I bring.

Weak is the effort of my heart,
  and cold my warmest thought;
but when I see thee as thou art,
  I'll praise thee as I ought.

John Newton (1725–1807), alt.

## 645, 646

The King of love my shepherd is,
    whose goodness faileth never;
I nothing lack if I am his,
    and he is mine for ever.

Where streams of living water flow,
    my ransomed soul he leadeth,
and where the verdant pastures grow,
    with food celestial feedeth.

Perverse and foolish oft I strayed,
    but yet in love he sought me,
and on his shoulder gently laid,
    and home, rejoicing, brought me.

In death's dark vale I fear no ill
    with thee, dear Lord, beside me;
thy rod and staff my comfort still,
    thy cross before to guide me.

Thou spread'st a table in my sight;
    thy unction grace bestoweth;
and oh, what transport of delight
    from thy pure chalice floweth!

And so through all the length of days
    thy goodness faileth never:
Good Shepherd, may I sing thy praise
    within thy house for ever.

Henry Williams Baker (1821–1877); para. Psalm 23

# 647

I know not where the road will lead
I follow day by day,
or where it ends: I only know
I walk the King's highway.
I know not if the way is long,
and no one else can say;
but rough or smooth, up hill or down,
I walk the King's highway.

And some I love have reached the end,
but some with me may stay,
their faith and hope still guiding me,
I walk the King's highway.
The way is truth, the way is love,
for light and strength I pray,
and through the years of life, to God
I walk the King's highway.

The countless hosts lead on before,
I must not fear nor stray;
with them, the pilgrims of the faith,
I walk the Kings highway.
Through light and dark the road leads on
till dawns the endless day,
when I shall know why in this life
I walk the King's highway.

Evelyn Atwater Cummins (1891–1971)

## 648

When Israel was in Egypt's land,
   let my people go;
oppressed so hard they could not stand,
   let my people go.

> *Go down, Moses, way down in*
>    *Egypt's land;*
> *tell old Pharaoh to let my*
>    *people go.*

The Lord told Moses what to do,
   let my people go;
to lead the children of Israel through,
   let my people go.

*Refrain*

They journeyed on at his command,
   let my people go;
and came at length to Canaan's land,
   let my people go.

*Refrain*

Oh, let us all from bondage flee,
   let my people go;
and let us all in Christ be free,
   let my people go.

*Refrain*

African-American spiritual

## 649, 650

O Jesus, joy of loving hearts,
   the fount of life and our true light,
we seek the peace your love imparts,
   and stand rejoicing in your sight.

We taste in you our living bread,
   and long to feast upon you still;
we drink of you, the fountainhead,
   our thirsting souls to quench and fill.

For you our restless spirits yearn
   where'er our changing lot is cast;
glad, when your presence we discern,
   blest, when our faith can hold you fast.

O Jesus, ever with us stay;
   make all our moments calm and bright;
oh, chase the night of sin away,
   shed o'er the world your holy light.

Att. Bernard of Clairvaux (1091-1153), tr. and para. Ray Palmer (1808–1887), alt.

## 651

This is my Father's world,
    and to my listening ears
        all nature sings
        and round me rings
    the music of the spheres.
This is my Father's world:
    I rest me in the thought
        of rocks and trees,
        of skies and seas,
    his hand the wonders wrought.

This is our Father's world,
    oh, let us not forget
        that though the wrong
        is great and strong,
    God is our Father yet.
He trusts us with his world,
    to keep it clean and fair,
        all earth and trees,
        all skies and seas,
    all creatures everywhere.

St. 1, Maltbie D. Babcock (1858–1901); st. 2, Mary Babcock Crawford (b. 1909)

## 652, 653

Dear Lord and Father of mankind,
    forgive our foolish ways!
Reclothe us in our rightful mind,
in purer lives thy service find,
    in deeper reverence, praise.

In simple trust like theirs who heard,
    beside the Syrian sea,
the gracious calling of the Lord,
let us, like them, without a word,
    rise up and follow thee.

O Sabbath rest by Galilee!
    O calm of hills above,
where Jesus knelt to share with thee
the silence of eternity
    interpreted by love!

Drop thy still dews of quietness,
    till all our strivings cease;
take from our souls the strain and stress,
and let our ordered lives confess
    the beauty of thy peace.

Breathe through the heats of our desire
    thy coolness and thy balm;
let sense be dumb, let flesh retire;
speak through the earthquake, wind, and fire,
    O still, small voice of calm.

John Greenleaf Whittier (1807–1892), alt.

## 654

>Day by day,
>dear Lord, of thee three things I pray:
>to see thee more clearly,
>love thee more dearly,
>follow thee more nearly,
>day by day.

Att. Richard of Chichester (1197–1253)

## 655

>O Jesus, I have promised
>>to serve thee to the end:
>be thou for ever near me,
>>my Master and my friend;
>I shall not fear the battle,
>>if thou art by my side,
>nor wander from the pathway,
>>if thou wilt be my guide.
>
>O let me hear thee speaking
>>in accents clear and still,
>above the storms of passion,
>>the murmurs of self-will;
>O speak to reassure me,
>>to hasten or control;
>O speak, and make me
>>listen, thou guardian of my soul.

O Jesus, thou hast promised
    to all who follow thee,
that where thou art in glory
    there shall thy servant be;
and, Jesus, I have promised
    to serve thee to the end;
O give me grace to follow,
    my Master and my friend.

John Ernest Bode (1816–1874), alt.

**656**

Blest are the pure in heart,
    for they shall see our God;
the secret of the Lord is theirs,
    their soul is Christ's abode.

The Lord, who left the heavens
    our life and peace to bring,
to dwell in lowliness with us,
    our pattern and our King;

he to the lowly soul
    will still himself impart
and for his dwelling and his throne
    will choose the pure in heart.

Lord, we thy presence seek;
    may ours this blessing be;
give us a pure and lowly heart,
    a temple fit for thee.

Sts. 1 and 3, John Keble (1792–1866), alt.; sts. 2 and 4, William John Hall (1793–1861), alt.

## 657

Love divine, all loves excelling,
    joy of heaven, to earth come down,
fix in us thy humble dwelling,
    all thy faithful mercies crown.
Jesus, thou art all compassion,
    pure, unbounded love thou art;
visit us with thy salvation,
    enter every trembling heart.

Come, almighty to deliver,
    let us all thy life receive;
suddenly return, and never,
    nevermore thy temples leave.
Thee we would be alway blessing,
    serve thee as thy hosts above,
pray, and praise thee without ceasing,
    glory in thy perfect love.

Finish then thy new creation;
    pure and spotless let us be;
let us see thy great salvation
    perfectly restored in thee:
changed from glory into glory,
    till in heaven we take our place,
till we cast our crowns before thee,
    lost in wonder, love, and praise.

Charles Wesley (1707–1788)

## 658

As longs the deer for cooling streams
   in parched and barren ways,
so longs my soul, O God, for thee
   and thy refreshing grace.

For thee, my God, the living God,
   my thirsty soul doth pine:
O when shall I behold thy face,
   thou Majesty divine?

Why restless, why cast down, my soul?
   Hope still, and thou shalt sing
the praise of him who is thy God,
   thy health's eternal spring.

To Father, Son, and Holy Ghost,
   the God whom we adore,
be glory, as it was, is now,
   and shall be evermore.

*New Version of the Psalms of David*, 1696, alt.; para. of Psalm 42

## 659, 660

O Master, let me walk with thee
in lowly paths of service free;
tell me thy secret; help me bear
the strain of toil, the fret of care.

Help me the slow of heart to move
by some clear, winning word of love;

teach me the wayward feet to stay,
and guide them in the homeward way.

Teach me thy patience; still with thee
in closer, dearer company,
in work that keeps faith sweet and strong,
in trust that triumphs over wrong,

in hope that sends a shining ray
far down the future's broadening way,
in peace that only thou canst give,
with thee, O Master, let me live.

Washington Gladden (1836–1918)

## 661

They cast their nets in Galilee
   just off the hills of brown;
such happy, simple fisherfolk,
   before the Lord came down.

Contented, peaceful fishermen,
   before they ever knew
the peace of God that filled their hearts
   brimful, and broke them too.

Young John who trimmed the flapping sail,
   homeless, in Patmos died.
Peter, who hauled the teeming net,
   head-down was crucified.

The peace of God, it is no peace,
> but strife closed in the sod.
Yet let us pray for but one thing—
> the marvelous peace of God.

William Alexander Percy (1885–1942), alt.

**662**

Abide with me: fast falls the eventide;
the darkness deepens; Lord, with me abide:
when other helpers fail and comforts flee,
help of the helpless, O abide with me.

I need thy presence every passing hour;
what but thy grace can foil the tempter's power?
Who, like thyself, my guide and stay can be?
Through cloud and sunshine, Lord, abide with me.

I fear no foe, with thee at hand to bless;
ills have no weight, and tears no bitterness.
Where is death's sting? Where, grave, thy victory?
I triumph still, if thou abide with me.

Hold thou thy cross before my closing eyes;
shine through the gloom, and point me to the skies;
heaven's morning breaks, and earth's
> vain shadows flee;
in life, in death, O Lord, abide with me.

Henry Frances Lyte (1793–1847)

## 663

The Lord my God my shepherd is;
   how could I want or need?
In pastures green, by streams serene,
   he safely doth me lead.

To wholeness he restores my soul
   and doth in mercy bless,
and helps me take for his Name's sake
   the paths of righteousness.

Yea, even when I must pass through
   the valley of death's shade,
I will not fear, for thou art here,
   to comfort and to aid.

Thou hast in grace my table spread
   secure in all alarms,
and filled my cup, and borne me up
   in everlasting arms.

Then surely I can trust thy love
   for all the days to come,
that I may tell thy praise, and dwell
   for ever in thy home.

F. Bland Tucker (1895–1984); para. of Psalm 23

# 664

My Shepherd will supply my need,
   Jehovah is his Name;
in pastures fresh he makes me feed
   beside the living stream.
He brings my wandering spirit back
   when I forsake his ways,
and leads me, for his mercy's sake,
   in paths of truth and grace.

When I walk through the shades of death,
   thy presence is my stay;
one word of thy supporting breath
   drives all my fears away.
Thy hand, in sight of all my foes,
   doth still my table spread;
my cup with blessings overflows,
   thy oil anoints my head.

The sure provisions of my God
   attend me all my days;
oh, may thy house be mine abode
   and all my work be praise.
There would I find a settled rest,
   while others go and come;
no more a stranger or a guest,
   but like a child at home.

Isaac Watts (1674-1748); para. of Psalm 23

## 665

All my hope on God is founded;
    he doth still my trust renew,
me through change and chance he guideth,
    only good and only true.
        God unknown,
        he alone
calls my heart to be his own.

Mortal pride and earthly glory,
    sword and crown betray our trust;
though with care and toil we build them,
    tower and temple fall to dust.
        But God's power,
        hour by hour,
is my temple and my tower.

God's great goodness e'er endureth,
    deep his wisdom passing thought:
splendor, light, and life attend him,
    beauty springeth out of nought.
        Evermore
        from his store
newborn worlds rise and adore.

Daily doth the almighty Giver
   bounteous gifts on us bestow;
his desire our soul delighteth,
   pleasure leads us where we go.
      Love doth stand
      at his hand;
   joy doth wait on his command.

Still from earth to God eternal
   sacrifice of praise be done,
high above all praises praising
   for the gift of Christ, his Son.
      Christ doth call
      one and all:
   ye who follow shall not fall.

Robert Seymour Bridges (1844–1930), alt.; after Joachim Neander (1650–1680)

**666**

Out of the depths I call,
   to God I send my cry;
Lord, hear my supplicating voice
   and graciously reply.

My soul with patience waits
   for thee, the living Lord,
my hopes are on thy promise built,
   thy never-failing word.

My longing eyes look out
    for thy enlivening ray,
more duly than the morning watch
    to spy the dawning day.

Let Israel trust in God;
    no bounds his mercy knows;
the plenteous source and spring from whence
    redemption ever flows.

Tate and Brady, *New Version of the Psalms*, 1698, alt.; para. of Psalm 130

## 667

Sometimes a light surprises
    the Christian while he sings;
it is the Lord who rises
    with healing in his wings:
when comforts are declining,
    he grants the soul again
a season of clear shining,
    to cheer it after rain.

In holy contemplation
    we sweetly then pursue
the theme of God's salvation,
    and find it ever new;
set free from present sorrow,
    we cheerfully can say,
let the unknown tomorrow
    bring with it what it may.

It can bring with it nothing
    but he will bear us through:
who gives the lilies clothing
    will clothe his people, too:
beneath the spreading heavens
    no creature but is fed;
and he who feeds the ravens
    will give his children bread.

Though vine nor fig tree neither
    their wonted fruit should bear,
though all the fields should wither,
    nor flocks nor herds be there;
yet, God the same abiding,
    his praise shall tune my voice;
for, while in him confiding,
    I cannot but rejoice.

William Cowper (1731–1800)

## 668

I to the hills will lift mine eyes;
    from whence shall come my aid?
My help is from the Lord above
    who heaven and earth hath made.

He will not let thy foot be moved,
    his own he safely keeps;
with watchful and untiring eye
    he slumbers not, nor sleeps.

Thy faithful guardian is the Lord,
    thy shelter and thy shade;
nor sun by day, nor moon by night,
    need make thy soul afraid.

From evil he shall keep thee safe
    and shall thy strength restore
and guard thy going out and in,
    both now and evermore.

*The Psalms of David in Meter,* 1650, alt.; st. 4, F. Bland Tucker (1895–1984); para. of Psalm 121

## 669

Commit thou all that grieves thee
    and fills thy heart with care
to him whose faithful mercy
    the skies above declare,
who gives the winds their courses,
    who points the clouds their way;
'tis he will guide thy footsteps
    and be thy staff and stay.

O trust the Lord then wholly,
    if thou wouldst be secure;
his work must thou consider
    for thy work to endure.

What profit doth it bring thee
    to pine in grief and care?
God ever sends his blessing
    in answer to thy prayer.

Thy lasting truth and mercy,
    O Father, see aright
the needs of all thy children,
    their anguish or delight:
what loving wisdom chooseth,
    redeeming might will do,
and bring to sure fulfillment
    thy counsel good and true.

Hope on, then, broken spirit;
    hope on, be not afraid:
fear not the griefs that plague thee
    and keep thy heart dismayed:
thy God, in his great mercy,
    will save thee, hold thee fast,
and in his own time grant thee
    the sun of joy at last.

Paulus Gerhardt (1607–1676); tr. Arthur William Farlander
(1898–1952) and Charles Winfred Douglas (1867–1944), alt.

## 670

Lord, for ever at thy side
  let my place and portion be,
strip me of the robe of pride,
  clothe me with humility.

When I come before thy Word,
  quiet my anxiety;
teach me thou alone art Lord,
  let my heart find rest in thee.

What thy Spirit doth reveal,
  that may I in faith receive;
though my doubts I sorely feel,
  thy sure promise I believe.

Israel, now and evermore
  in the Lord Almighty trust;
him, in all his ways, adore,
  wise, and wonderful, and just.

Sts. 1 and 4, James Montgomery (1771–1854), alt.; sts. 2–3, Charles P. Price (b. 1920)

## 671

Amazing grace! how sweet the sound,
  that saved a wretch like me!
I once was lost but now am found,
  was blind but now I see.

'Twas grace that taught my heart to fear,
  and grace my fears relieved;

how precious did that grace appear
    the hour I first believed!

The Lord has promised good to me,
    his word my hope secures;
he will my shield and portion be
    as long as life endures.

Through many dangers, toils, and snares,
    I have already come;
'tis grace that brought me safe thus far,
    and grace will lead me home.

When we've been there ten thousand years,
    bright shining as the sun,
we've no less days to sing God's praise
    than when we'd first begun.

John Newton (1725–1807), alt.; st. 5, from *A Collection of Sacred ballads*, 1790; compiled by Richard Broaddus and Andrew Broaddus

## 672

O very God of very God,
    and very Light of Light,
whose feet this earth's dark valley trod
    that so it might be bright:

Our hopes are weak, our fears are strong,
    thick darkness blinds our eyes;
cold is the night; thy people long
    that thou, their Sun, wouldst rise.

And even now, though dull and gray,
    the east is brightening fast,
and kindling to the perfect day
    that never shall be past.

O guide us till our path is done,
    and we have reached the shore
where thou, our everlasting Sun,
    art shining evermore!

We wait in faith, and turn our face
    to where the daylight springs,
till thou shalt come our gloom to chase,
    with healing in thy wings.

John Mason Neale (1818–1866)

## 673

The first one ever, oh, ever to know
of the birth of Jesus, was the maid Mary,
was Mary the maid of Galilee,
and blessèd is she,
    is she who believes.
Oh, blessèd is she who believes in the Lord,
oh, blessèd is she who believes.
She was Mary the maid of Galilee,
and blessèd is she,
    is she who believes.

The first one ever, oh, ever to know
of Messiah, Jesus, when he said, "I am he,"

was the Samaritan woman who drew from the well,
and is blessèd she,
>  is she who perceives.
Oh, blessèd is she who perceives the Lord,
oh, blessèd is she who perceives.
'Twas the Samaritan woman who drew from the well,
and blessèd is she,
>  is she who perceives.

The first ones ever, oh, ever to know
of the rising of Jesus, his glory to be,
they were Mary, Joanna, and Magdalene,
and blessèd are they,
>  are they who see.
Oh, blessèd are they who see the Lord,
oh, blessèd are they who see.
They were Mary, Joanna, and Magdalene,
and blessèd are they,
>  are they who see.

Linda Wilberger Egan (b. 1946), alt.

## 674

"Forgive our sins as we forgive"
>  you taught us, Lord, to pray;
but you alone can grant us grace
>  to live the words we say.

How can your pardon reach and bless
>  the unforgiving heart

that broods on wrongs and will not let
   old bitterness depart?

In blazing light your cross reveals
   the truth we dimly knew,
how small the debts men owe to us,
   how great our debt to you.

Lord, cleanse the depths within our souls,
   and bid resentment cease;
then, reconciled to God and man,
   our lives will spread your peace.

Rosamond E. Herklots (1905–1987)

## 675

Take up your cross, the Savior said,
   if you would my disciple be;
take up your cross with willing heart,
   and humbly follow after me.

Take up your cross, let not its weight
   fill your weak spirit with alarm;
his strength shall bear your spirit up,
   and brace your heart, and nerve your arm.

Take up your cross, heed not the shame,
   and let your foolish heart be still;
the Lord for you accepted death
   upon a cross, on Calvary's hill.

Take up your cross, then, in his strength,
    and calmly every danger brave:
it guides you to abundant life
    and leads to victory o'er the grave.

Take up your cross, and follow Christ,
    nor think till death to lay it down;
for only those who bear the cross
    may hope to wear the glorious crown.

Charles William Everest (1814–1877), alt.

**676**

*There is a balm in Gilead,*
    *to make the wounded whole,*
*there is a balm in Gilead,*
    *to heal the sin-sick soul.*

Sometimes I feel discouraged,
    and think my work's in vain,
but then the Holy Spirit
    revives my soul again.

*Refrain*

If you cannot preach like Peter,
    if you cannot pray like Paul,
you can tell the love of Jesus,
    and say, "He died for all."

*Refrain*

African-American spiritual

## 677

God moves in a mysterious way
    his wonders to perform:
he plants his footsteps in the sea,
    and rides upon the storm.

Deep in unfathomable mines,
    with never-failing skill,
he treasures up his bright designs,
    and works his sovereign will.

Ye fearful saints, fresh courage take;
    the clouds ye so much dread
are big with mercy, and shall break
    in blessings on your head.

Judge not the Lord by feeble sense,
    but trust him for his grace;
behind a frowning providence
    he hides a smiling face.

His purposes will ripen fast,
    unfolding every hour:
the bud may have a bitter taste,
    but sweet will be the flower.

Blind unbelief is sure to err,
    and scan his work in vain;
God is his own interpreter,
    and he will make it plain.

William Cowper (1731–1800)

## 678, 679

Surely it is God who saves me;
    trusting him, I shall not fear.
For the Lord defends and shields me
    and his saving help is near.
So rejoice as you draw water
    from salvation's living spring;
in the day of your deliverance
    thank the Lord, his mercies sing.

Make his deeds known to the peoples;
    tell out his exalted Name.
Praise the Lord, who has done great things;
    all his works his might proclaim.
Zion, lift your voice in singing;
    for with you has come to dwell,
in your very midst, the great and
    Holy One of Israel.

Carl P. Daw, Jr. (b. 1944); para. of *The First Song of Isaiah*

## 680

O God, our help in ages past,
    our hope for years to come,
our shelter from the stormy blast,
    and our eternal home:

under the shadow of thy throne
    thy saints have dwelt secure;
sufficient is thine arm alone,
    and our defense is sure.

Before the hills in order stood,
    or earth received her frame,
from everlasting thou art God,
    to endless years the same.

A thousand ages in thy sight
    are like an evening gone;
short as the watch that ends the night
    before the rising sun.

Time, like an ever-rolling stream,
    bears all our years away;
they fly, forgotten, as a dream
    dies at the opening day.

O God, our help in ages past,
    our hope for years to come,
be thou our guide while life shall last,
    and our eternal home.

Isaac Watts (1674–1748), alt.; para. of Psalm 90

## 681

Our God, to whom we turn
    when weary with illusion,
whose stars serenely burn
    above this earth's confusion,
thine is the mighty plan,
    the steadfast order sure
in which the world began,
    endures, and shall endure.

Thou art thyself the truth;
    though we who seek to find thee
have tried, with thoughts uncouth,
    in feeble words to bind thee,
it is because thou art
    we're driven to the quest;
till truth from falsehood part,
    our hearts can find no rest.

All beauty speaks of thee:
    the mountains and the rivers,
the line of lifted sea,
    where spreading moonlight quivers,
the hymns thy people raise,
    the psalms and anthems strong,
hint at the glorious praise
    of thy eternal song.

Where goodness comes to light
    we glimpse thy plan unfolding;

where justice wins its fight
    thou art the Kingdom molding;
the blood of friend as sign
    of love for comrade spilt,
reflects the vast design
    by which thy house is built.

Thou hidden fount of love,
    of peace, and truth, and beauty,
inspire us from above
    with joy and strength for duty.
May thy fresh light arise
    within each clouded heart,
and give us open eyes
    to see thee as thou art.

Edward Grubb (1854–1939), alt.

## 682

I love thee, Lord, but not because
    I hope for heaven thereby,
nor yet for fear that loving not
    I might for ever die;

but for that thou didst all the world
    upon the cross embrace;
for us didst bear the nails and spear,
    and manifold disgrace,

and griefs and torments numberless,
    and sweat of agony;

e'en death itself; and all for one
    who was thine enemy.

Then why, most loving Jesus Christ,
    should I not love thee well,
not for the sake of winning heaven,
    nor any fear of hell;

not with the hope of gaining aught,
    not seeking a reward;
but as thyself hast lovèd me,
    O ever-loving Lord!

E'en so I love thee, and will love,
    and in thy praise will sing,
solely because thou art my God
    and my eternal King.

Spanish, 17th cent.; tr. Edward Caswall (1814–1878); adapt. Percy Dearmer (1867–1936), alt.

## 683, 684

O for a closer walk with God,
a calm and heavenly frame,
a light to shine upon the road
that leads me to the Lamb!

Where is the blessedness I knew
when first I saw the Lord?
Where is the soul-refreshing view
of Jesus and his word?

Return, O holy Dove, return,
sweet messenger of rest;
I hate the sins that made thee mourn,
and drove thee from my breast.

The dearest idol I have known,
whate'er that idol be,
help me to tear it from thy throne,
and worship only thee.

So shall my walk be close with God,
calm and serene my frame;
so purer light shall mark the road
that leads me to the Lamb.

William Cowper (1731–1800), alt.

# 685

Rock of ages, cleft for me,
let me hide myself in thee;
let the water and the blood
from thy wounded side that flowed,
be of sin the double cure,
cleanse me from its guilt and power.

Should my tears for ever flow,
should my zeal no languor know,
all for sin could not atone:
thou must save, and thou alone;

in my hand no price I bring,
simply to thy cross I cling.

While I draw this fleeting breath,
when mine eyelids close in death,
when I rise to worlds unknown
and behold thee on thy throne,
Rock of ages, cleft for me,
let me hide myself in thee.

Augustus Montague Toplady (1740–1778), alt.

**686**

Come, thou fount of every blessing,
    tune my heart to sing thy grace!
Streams of mercy never ceasing,
    call for songs of loudest praise.
Teach me some melodious sonnet,
    sung by flaming tongues above.
Praise the mount! Oh, fix me on it,
    mount of God's unchanging love.

Here I find my greatest treasure;
    hither, by thy help, I've come;
and I hope, by thy good pleasure,
    safely to arrive at home.
Jesus sought me when a stranger
    wandering from the fold of God;

he, to rescue me from danger,
    interposed his precious blood.

Oh, to grace how great a debtor
    daily I'm constrained to be!
Let thy goodness, like a fetter,
    bind my wandering heart to thee:
prone to wander, Lord, I feel it,
    prone to leave the God I love;
here's my heart, oh, take and seal it,
    seal it for thy courts above.

Robert Robinson (1735–1790), alt.

## 687, 688

A mighty fortress is our God,
    a bulwark never failing;
our helper he amid the flood
    of mortal ills prevailing:
for still our ancient foe
doth seek to work us woe;
his craft and power are great,
and, armed with cruel hate,
    on earth is not his equal.

Did we in our own strength confide,
    our striving would be losing;
were not the right man on our side,
    the man of God's own choosing:
dost ask who that may be?

Christ Jesus, it is he;
Lord Sabaoth his Name,
from age to age the same,
    and he must win the battle.

And though this world, with devils filled,
    should threaten to undo us;
we will not fear, for God hath willed
    his truth to triumph through us;
the prince of darkness grim,
we tremble not for him;
his rage we can endure,
for lo! his doom is sure,
    one little word shall fell him.

That word above all earthly powers,
    no thanks to them, abideth;
the Spirit and the gifts are ours
    through him who with us sideth:
let goods and kindred go,
this mortal life also;
the body they may kill:
God's truth abideth still,
    his kingdom is for ever.

Martin Luther (1483–1546); tr. Frederic Henry Hedge (1805–1890); based on Psalm 46

## 689

I sought the Lord, and afterward I knew
    he moved my soul to seek him, seeking me;
it was not I that found, O Savior true;
    no, I was found of thee.

Thou didst reach forth thy hand and mine enfold;
    I walked and sank not on the storm-vexed sea;
'twas not so much that I on thee took hold,
    as thou, dear Lord, on me.

I find, I walk, I love, but oh, the whole
    of love is but my answer, Lord, to thee:
for thou wert long beforehand with my soul,
    always thou lovedst me.

Anon., *Pilgrim Hymnal*, 1904

## 690

Guide me, O thou great Jehovah,
    pilgrim through this barren land;
I am weak, but thou art mighty;
    hold me with thy powerful hand;
        bread of heaven,
    feed me now and evermore.

Open now the crystal fountain,
    whence the healing stream doth flow;

let the fire and cloudy pillar
 lead me all my journey through;
  strong deliverer,
 be thou still my strength and shield.

When I tread the verge of Jordan,
 bid my anxious fears subside;
death of death, and hell's destruction,
 land me safe on Canaan's side;
  songs of praises,
 I will ever give to thee.

William Williams (1717–1791); tr. Peter Williams (1722–1796), alt.

## 691

My faith looks up to thee,
 thou Lamb of Calvary,
Savior divine!
 Now hear me while I pray,
 take all my guilt away;
 O let me from this day
be wholly thine.

May thy rich grace impart
 strength to my fainting heart,
my zeal inspire;
 as thou hast died for me,
 O may my love to thee
 pure, warm, and changeless be,
a living fire.

While life's dark maze I tread,
    and griefs around me spread,
be thou my guide;
    bid darkness turn to day;
    wipe sorrow's tears away,
    nor let me ever stray
from thee aside.

Ray Palmer (1808–1887)

## 692

I heard the voice of Jesus say,
    "Come unto me and rest;
and in your weariness lay down
    your head upon my breast."
I came to Jesus as I was,
    so weary, worn, and sad;
I found in him a resting place,
    and he has made me glad.

I heard the voice of Jesus say,
    "Behold, I freely give
the living water; thirsty one,
    stoop down and drink, and live."
I came to Jesus, and I drank
    of that life-giving stream;
my thirst was quenched, my soul revived,
    and now I live in him.

I heard the voice of Jesus say,
 "I am this dark world's light;
look unto me, your morn shall rise,
 and all your day be bright."
I looked to Jesus, and I found
 in him my Star, my Sun;
and in that light of life I'll walk
 till pilgrim days are done.

Horatius Bonar (1808–1889), alt.

**693**

Just as I am, without one plea,
 but that thy blood was shed for me,
and that thou bidd'st me come to thee,
 O Lamb of God, I come.

Just as I am, though tossed about
 with many a conflict, many a doubt;
fightings and fears within, without,
 O Lamb of God, I come.

Just as I am, poor, wretched, blind;
 sight, riches, healing of the mind,
yea, all I need, in thee to find,
 O Lamb of God, I come.

Just as I am: thou wilt receive;
 wilt welcome, pardon, cleanse, relieve,
because thy promise I believe,
 O Lamb of God, I come.

Just as I am, thy love unknown
    has broken every barrier down;
now to be thine, yea, thine alone,
    O Lamb of God, I come.

Just as I am, of thy great love
    the breadth, length, depth, and height to prove,
here for a season, then above:
    O Lamb of God, I come.

Charlotte Elliott (1789–1871)

## 694

God be in my head,
    and in my understanding;

God be in mine eyes,
    and in my looking;

God be in my mouth,
    and in my speaking;

God be in my heart,
    and in my thinking;

God be at mine end,
    and at my departing.

*Sarum Primer*, 1514

## 695, 696

By gracious powers so wonderfully sheltered,
    and confidently waiting come what may,
we know that God is with us night and morning,
    and never fails to greet us each new day.

Yet is this heart by its old foe tormented,
    still evil days bring burdens hard to bear;
O give our frightened souls the sure salvation,
    for which, O Lord, you taught us to prepare.

And when this cup you give is filled to brimming
    with bitter suffering, hard to understand,
we take it thankfully and without trembling,
    out of so good and so beloved a hand.

Yet when again in this same world you give us
    the joy we had, the brightness of your Sun,
we shall remember all the days we lived through,
    and our whole life shall then be yours alone.

F. Pratt Green (b. 1903); from Dietrich Bonhoeffer (1906–1945)

## 697

My God, accept my heart this day,
    and make it always thine,
that I from thee no more may stray,
    no more from thee decline.

Before the cross of him who died,
    behold, I prostrate fall;

let every sin be crucified,
    and Christ be all in all.

Anoint me with thy heavenly grace
    and seal me for thine own,
that I may see thy glorious face,
    and worship near thy throne.

Let every thought and work and word,
    to thee be ever given;
then life shall be thy service, Lord,
    and death the gate of heaven.

Matthew Bridges (1800–1894), alt.

## 698

Eternal Spirit of the living Christ,
    I know not how to ask or what to say;
I only know my need, as deep as life,
    and only you can teach me how to pray.

Come, pray in me the prayer I need this day;
    help me to see your purpose and your will–
where I have failed, what I have done amiss;
    held in forgiving love, let me be still.

Come with the vision and the strength I need
    to serve my God, and all humanity;
fulfillment of my life in love outpoured–
    my life in you, O Christ, your love in me.

Frank von Christierson (1900–1996), rev.

# 699

Jesus, Lover of my soul,
    let me to thy bosom fly,
while the nearer waters roll,
    while the tempest still is high:
hide me, O my Savior, hide,
    till the storm of life be past;
safe into the haven guide,
    O receive my soul at last.

Other refuge have I none,
    hangs my helpless soul on thee;
leave, ah! leave me not alone,
    still support and comfort me!
All my trust on thee is stayed;
    all my help from thee I bring;
cover my defenseless head
    with the shadow of thy wing.

Plenteous grace with thee is found,
    grace to cleanse from every sin;
let the healing streams abound,
    make and keep me pure within.
Thou of life the fountain art,
    freely let me take of thee:
spring thou up within my heart,
    rise to all eternity.

Charles Wesley (1707–1783), alt.

## 700

O love that casts out fear,
  O love that casts out sin,
tarry no more without,
  but come and dwell within.

True sunlight of the soul,
  surround us as we go;
so shall our way be safe,
  our feet no straying know.

Great love of God, come in!
  Wellspring of heavenly peace;
thou Living Water, come!
  Spring up, and never cease.

Love of the living God,
  of Father and of Son;
love of the Holy Ghost,
  fill thou each needy one.

Horatius Bonar (1808–1889)

## 701

Jesus, all my gladness,
my repose in sadness,
  Jesus, heaven to me,
ah, my heart long plaineth,
ah, my spirit straineth,
  longeth after thee!

Thine I am, O holy Lamb;
   only where thou art is pleasure,
   thee alone I treasure.

Hence with earthly treasure:
thou art all my pleasure,
   Jesus, my desire!
Hence, for pomps I care not,
e'en as though they were not
   rank and fortune's hire.
Want and gloom, cross, death and tomb;
   nought that I may suffer ever
   shall from Jesus sever.

Flee, dark clouds that lower,
for my joy-bestower,
   Jesus, enters in!
Joy from tribulation,
hope from desolation,
   they who love God win.
Be it blame or scorn or shame,
   thou art with me in earth's sadness,
   Jesus, all my gladness!

Johann Franck (1618–1677); tr. Arthur Wellesley Wotherspoon (1853–1936), alt.

## 702

Lord, thou has searched me and dost know
where'er I rest, where'er I go;
thou knowest all that I have planned,
and all my ways are in thy hand.

My words from thee I cannot hide;
I feel thy power on every side;
oh, wondrous knowledge, awful might,
unfathomed depth, unmeasured height!

Where can I go apart from thee,
or whither from thy presence flee?
In heaven? It is thy dwelling fair;
in death's abode? Lo, thou art there.

If I the wings of morning take,
and far away my dwelling make,
the hand that leadeth me is thine,
and my support thy power divine.

If deepest darkness cover me,
the darkness hideth not from thee;
to thee both night and day are bright,
the darkness shineth as the light.

*The Psalter Hymnal*, 1927; para. of Psalm 139:1–11

## 703

Lead us, O Father, in the paths of peace;
    without thy guiding hand we go astray,
and doubts appall, and sorrows still increase;
    lead us through Christ, the true and living Way.

Lead us, O Father, in the paths of right;
    blindly we stumble when we walk alone,
involved in shadows of a darksome night;
    only with thee we journey safely on.

Lead us, O Father, to thy heavenly rest,
    however rough and steep thy path may be;
through joy or sorrow, as thou deemest best,
    until our lives are perfected in thee.

William Henry Burleigh (1812–1871), alt.

## 704

O thou who camest from above
    the fire celestial to impart,
kindle a flame of sacred love
    upon the altar of my heart.

There let it for thy glory burn
    with ever-bright, undying blaze,
and trembling to its source return
    in humble prayer and fervent praise.

Jesus, confirm my heart's desire
    to work, and speak, and think for thee;
still let me guard the holy fire
    and still stir up the gift in me.

Still let me prove thy perfect will,
    my acts of faith and love repeat,
till death thy endless mercies seal,
    and make the sacrifice complete.

Charles Wesley (1707–1788), alt.

## 705

As those of old their first fruits brought
    of vineyard, flock, and field
to God, the giver of all good,
    the source of bounteous yield;
so we today our first fruits bring,
    the wealth of this good land,
of farm and market, shop and home,
    of mind, and heart, and hand.

A world in need now summons us
    to labor, love, and give;
to make our life an offering
    to God that all may live;
the Church of Christ is calling us
    to make the dream come true:
a world redeemed by Christ-like love;
    all life in Christ made new.

With gratitude and humble trust
    we bring our best to thee
to serve thy cause and share thy love
    with all humanity.
O thou who gavest us thyself
    in Jesus Christ thy Son,
help us to give ourselves each day
    until life's work is done.

Frank von Christierson (1900–1996), alt.

**706**

In your mercy, Lord, you called me,
    taught my sin-filled heart and mind,
else this world had still enthralled me,
    and to glory kept me blind.

Lord, I did not freely choose you
    till by grace you set me free;
for my heart would still refuse you
    had your love not chosen me.

Now my heart sets none above you,
    for your grace alone I thirst,
knowing well, that if I love you,
    you, O Lord, have loved me first.

Josiah Conder (1789–1855); alt. Charles P. Price (b. 1920)

## 707

Take my life, and let it be
consecrated, Lord, to thee;
take my moments and my days,
let them flow in ceaseless praise.
Take my hands, and let them move
at the impulse of thy love;
take my heart, it is thine own;
it shall be thy royal throne.

Take my voice, and let me sing
always, only, for my King;
take my intellect, and use
every power as thou shalt choose.
Take my will, and make it thine;
it shall be no longer mine.
Take myself, and I will be
ever, only, all for thee.

Francis Ridley Havargal (1836–1879), alt.

## 708

Savior, like a shepherd lead us;
    much we need thy tender care;
in thy pleasant pastures feed us;
    for our use thy folds prepare.
        Blessèd Jesus!
    Thou hast bought us, thine we are.

Early let us seek thy favor,
    early let us learn thy will;
do thou, Lord, our only Savior,
    with thy love our bosoms fill.
        Blessèd Jesus!
    Thou hast loved us: love us still.

*Hymns for the Young*, ca. 1830, alt.

## 709

O God of Bethel, by whose hand
    thy people still are fed;
who through this earthly pilgrimage
    hast all thine Israel led:

Our vows, our prayers, we now present
    before thy throne of grace:
O God of Israel, be the God
    of this succeeding race.

Through each perplexing path of life
    our wandering footsteps guide;
give us each day our daily bread,
    and raiment fit provide.

O spread thy sheltering wings around,
    till all our wanderings cease,
and at our Father's loved abode
    our souls arrive in peace!

Such blessings from thy gracious hand
    our humble prayers implore;
and thou shalt be our covenant God
    and portion evermore.

Philip Doddridge (1702–1751), alt.

## 710

Make a joyful noise unto the Lord,
O sing the honor of his holy Name,
give him glory evermore.

*Singt dem Herren!*
*Singet ihm und jubilieret alle samt in dieser*
    *Morgenstunde,*
*kommt herbei und danket ihm!*

German; adapt. Ann M. Gilman (b. 1932) and Lawrence Gilman (b. 1930)

## 711

Seek ye first the kingdom of God
and its righteousness,
and all these things shall be added unto you;
Allelu, alleluia!

> *Alleluia, alleluia, alleluia!*
> *Allelu, alleluia!*

Ask, and it shall be given unto you,
seek, and ye shall find,
knock, and the door shall be opened unto you;
Allelu, alleluia!

*Refrain*

St. 1, Matthew 6:33; adapt. Karen Lafferty (20th cent.). St. 2, Matthew 7:7

## 712

*Dona nobis pacem, pacem.*
  *Dona nobis pacem.*
*Dona nobis pacem.*
  *Dona nobis pacem.*
*Dona nobis pacem.*
  *Dona nobis pacem.*

Traditional Latin

## 713

    Christ is arisen.
    Alleluia, alleluia!
    Alleluia, alleluia!
    Christ is arisen.
    Christ is arisen.
    *Christ ist erstanden.*
    Alleluia, alleluia!
    Alleluia, alleluia!
    *Christ ist erstanden.*
    *Christ ist erstanden.*

German, ca. 1529; adapt.

## 714

    Shalom, my friends,
   shalom, my friends,
       shalom, shalom.
    Shalom my friends, shalom my friends.
       Shalom, shalom.
    *Shalom chaverim,*
   *shalom chaverim,*
       shalom, shalom.
    *Shalom chaverim, shalom chaverim.*
       *Shalom, shalom.*

Israeli round

## 715

When Jesus wept, the falling tear
  in mercy flowed beyond all bound;
when Jesus groaned, a trembling fear
  seized all the guilty world around.

*The New England Psalm Singer,* 1770

## 716

God bless our native land;
firm may she ever stand
  through storm and night:
when the wild tempests rave,
ruler of wind and wave,
do thou our country save
  by thy great might.

For her our prayers shall rise
to God, above the skies;
  on him we wait;
thou who art ever nigh,
guarding with watchful eye,
to thee aloud we cry,
  God save the state!

Siegfried August Mahlmann (1771–1826); tr. Charles Timothy
Brooks (1813–1883) and John Sullivan Dwight (1812–1893), alt.

## 717

My country, 'tis of thee,
sweet land of liberty,
   of thee I sing;
land where my fathers died,
land of the pilgrim's pride,
from every mountain side
   let freedom ring.

My native country, thee,
land of the noble free,
   thy name I love;
I love thy rocks and rills,
thy woods and templed hills;
my heart with rapture thrills
   like that above.

Let music swell the breeze,
and ring from all the trees
   sweet freedom's song;
let mortal tongues awake,
let all that breathe partake,
let rocks their silence break,
   the sound prolong.

Our fathers' God, to thee,
author of liberty,
    to thee we sing;
long may our land be bright
with freedom's holy light;
protect us by thy might,
    great God, our King.

Samuel Francis Smith (1808–1895)

# 718

God of our fathers, whose almighty hand
leads forth in beauty all the starry band
of shining worlds in splendor through the skies,
our grateful songs before thy throne arise.

Thy love divine hath led us in the past,
in this free land by thee our lot is cast;
be thou our ruler, guardian, guide, and stay
thy word our law, thy paths our chosen way.

From war's alarms, from deadly pestilence,
be thy strong arm our ever sure defense;
thy true religion in our hearts increase,
thy bounteous goodness nourish us in peace.

Refresh thy people on their toilsome way,
lead us from night to never-ending day;
fill all our lives with love and grace divine,
and glory, laud, and praise be ever thine.

Daniel Crane Roberts (1841–1907)

## 719

O beautiful for spacious skies,
    for amber waves of grain,
for purple mountain majesties
    above the fruited plain!
America! America!
    God shed his grace on thee,
and crown thy good with brotherhood
    from sea to shining sea.

O beautiful for heroes proved
    in liberating strife,
who more than self their country loved,
    and mercy more than life!
America! America!
    God mend thine every flaw,
confirm thy soul in self-control,
    thy liberty in law.

O beautiful for patriot dream
    that sees beyond the years
thine alabaster cities gleam,
    undimmed by human tears!
America! America!
    God shed his grace on thee,
and crown thy good with brotherhood
    from sea to shining sea.

Katherine Lee Bates (1859–1929), alt.

# 720

O say can you see, by the dawn's early light,
what so proudly we hailed at the twilight's
                last gleaming,
whose broad stripes and bright stars, through
                the perilous fight,
o'er the ramparts we watched, were so gallantly
                streaming?
And the rockets' red glare, the bombs bursting in air,
gave proof through the night that our flag
                was still there.
O say does that star-spangled banner yet wave
o'er the land of the free and the home
                of the brave?

O thus be it ever, when freemen shall stand
between their loved homes and the war's desolation!
Blest with victory and peace, may
                the heaven-rescued land
praise the Power that hath made and preserved
                us a nation!
Then conquer we must, when our cause
                it is just,
and this be our motto, "In God is our trust."
And the star-spangled banner in triumph shall wave
o'er the land of the free and the home of the brave!

Francis Scott Key (1779–1843)

# Copyrights

| | |
|---|---|
| 3, 4 | ©1972, sts. 2,3,4 Peter J. Scagnelli. From *Catholic Liturgy Book*. Used by Permission. |
| 8 | ©By permission of David Higham Associates Ltd., London. |
| 12, 13 | ©1982, Charles P. Price |
| 14, 15 | ©1982, st. 3 James Waring McCrady |
| 16, 17 | ©1982, st. 4 Anne LeCroy; sts. 1-3 Church Pension Fund |
| 18 | ©Church Pension Fund |
| 19, 20 | ©Sts. 1-2 Church Pension Fund; 1982, st. 3 James Waring McCrady |
| 21, 22 | ©1982, st. 3 James Waring McCrady |
| 23 | ©1982, Charles P. Price |
| 25, 26 | ©Church Pension Fund |
| 27, 28 | ©1982, Anne LeCroy |
| 31, 32 | ©1982, Anne LeCroy |
| 33, 34, 35 | ©1982, Anne LeCroy |
| 38, 39 | ©1982, st. 5 Anne LeCroy; sts. 1-4 Church Pension Fund |
| 40, 41 | ©1982, st. 5 Charles P. Price; sts. 1-4 Church Pension Fund |
| 44, 45 | ©1982, st. 4 James Waring McCrady; sts. 1-3 Church Pension Fund |
| 48 | ©1982, st. 3 Charles P. Price; st. 4 Church Pension Fund |
| 51 | ©By permission of John E. Bowers |

| | |
|---|---|
| 54 | ©1982, sts. 3-4 James Waring McCrady |
| 55 | ©1982, Charles P. Price |
| 56 | ©Church Pension Fund |
| 60 | ©Church Pension Fund |
| 61, 62 | ©1982, for Carl P. Daw Jr., Hope Publishing Company, Carol Stream, IL 60188. All Rights Reserved. Used by Permission. |
| 63, 64 | ©Church Pension Fund |
| 65 | ©1982, Charles P. Price |
| 69 | ©1971, Carol C. Stone |
| 70 | ©By permission of Margaret Waters |
| 74 | ©1974, Hope Publishing Company, Carol Stream, IL 60188. All Rights Reserved. Used by Permission. |
| 80 | ©Trans. 1978, *Lutheran Book of Worship*. Used by permission of Augsburg Publishing House |
| 81 | ©St. 3 Church Pension Fund |
| 85, 86 | ©1978, *Lutheran Book of Worship*. Used by permission of Augsburg Publishing House |
| 91 | ©Church Pension Fund |
| 92 | ©G. Schirmer Inc. Reprinted by permission |
| 102 | ©1982, st. 3 James Waring McCrady |
| 103 | ©1964, G.I.A. Publications, Inc. |
| 104 | ©1961, from *Advice to a Prophet and other Poems* by Richard Wilburby, permission of Harcourt Brace Jovanovich, Inc. |
| 113 | ©1954, University of New Mexico Press. Used by permission. |
| 114 | ©Used by permission of The Frederick Harris Music Co. Ltd. |
| 120 | ©From *English Praise*. By permission of Oxford University Press |

| | |
|---|---|
| 121 | ©Church Pension Fund |
| 129, 130 | ©1977, Hope Publishing Company, Carol Stream, IL 60188. All Rights Reserved. Used by Permission. |
| 131, 132 | ©Reprinted from *The Hymn Book of the Anglican Church of Canada and the United Church of Canada.* Used by permission. |
| 135 | ©St. 4 Church Pension Fund |
| 139 | ©Church Pension Fund |
| 143 | ©By permission of Oxford University Press |
| 144 | ©1982, Anne LeCroy |
| 145 | ©By permission of Oxford University Press |
| 146, 147 | ©James Quinn, SJ. Printed by permission of Geoffrey Chapman Publishers, a division of Cassell, Ltd. |
| 148 | ©By permission of Donald P. Hughes |
| 149 | ©1982, Thomas H. Cain |
| 152 | ©Church Pension Fund |
| 153 | ©Church Pension Fund |
| 159 | ©Church Pension Fund |
| 161 | ©1971, John Webster Grant |
| 162 | ©Church Pension Fund |
| 164 | ©Church Pension Fund |
| 165, 166 | ©Church Pension Fund |
| 170 | ©1973, Hope Publishing Company, Carol Stream, IL 60188. All Rights Reserved. Used by Permission. |
| 173 | ©Sts. 1,4 Church Pension Fund; 1982, sts. 2-3 James Waring McCrady |
| 175 | ©By permission of Oxford University Press |
| 176 & 177 | ©St. 3 Church Pension Fund; 1976 sts. 1-2 from *A Monastic Breviary.* Holy Cross Publications. All rights reserved. |

| | |
|---|---|
| 178 | ©1978, Word of God. admin. by the Copyright Company, Nashville, TN 37203. All Rights Reserved. |
| 182 | ©1975, Hope Publishing Company, Carol Stream, IL 60188. All Rights Reserved. Used by Permission. |
| 187 | ©By permission of Burns & Oates |
| 192 | ©from *The Cowley Carol Book* by G.R. Woodward and C. Wood. By permission of A. R. Mowbray & Co. Ltd. |
| 193 | ©Church Pension Fund |
| 196, 197 | ©1980, John Bennett |
| 201 | ©By permission of Oxford University Press |
| 204 | ©1964, From *Oxford Book of Carols*. Oxford University Press |
| 205 | ©By permission of Hymns Ancient & Modern admin. by Hope Publishing Company, Carol Stream, IL 60188. All Rights Reserved; 1971, st. 5 Walton Music Corporation admin. by Plymouth Music Corporation, Ft. Lauderdale, FL 33307. Used by permission. |
| 211 | ©1964, From *Oxford Book of Carols*. Oxford University Press |
| 220, 221 | ©Church Pension Fund |
| 222 | ©1979, Albert F. Bayly. Used by permission of Oxford University Press |
| 223, 224 | ©By permission of Burns & Oates |
| 226, 227 | ©1982, Charles P. Price |
| 228 | ©1971, John Webster Grant |
| 230 | ©By permission of Oxford University Press |
| 231, 232 | ©Church Pension Fund |
| 233, 234 | ©Church Pension Fund |
| 236 | ©1971, John Webster Grant |

| | |
|---|---|
| 243 | ©By permission of Oxford University Press |
| 245 | ©1983, F. Samuel Janzow. From *Sing Glorias for All His Saints*. Used by permission. |
| 246 | ©By permission of Oxford University Press |
| 250 | ©1969, Concordia Publishing House |
| 256 | ©1993, Selah Publishing Company, Kingston, NY 12401 |
| 260 | ©1979, Hymn Society of America admin. by Hope Publishing Company, Carol Stream, IL 60188. All Rights Reserved. Used by Permission. |
| 261, 262 | ©Church Pension Fund |
| 262 | ©Church Pension Fund |
| 263, 264 | ©Sts. 1,3,4 Hymns Ancient & Modern Limited admin. by Hope Publishing Company, Carol Stream, IL 60188. All Rights Reserved. Used by Permission; 1982, st. 2 Anne LeCroy |
| 266 | ©1982, Carl P. Daw, Jr. |
| 268 | ©St. 4 Church Pension Fund |
| 273, 274 | ©1982, Anne LeCroy |
| 277 | ©Used by permission of the Reverend Roland F. Palmer |
| 278 | ©By permission of Oxford University Press |
| 282, 283 | ©Church Pension Fund |
| 284 | ©1982, st. 4 Charles P. Price |
| 294 | ©1982, Michael Saward |
| 295 | ©1962, World Library Publications; 3815 N. Willow Rd., Schiller Park, IL 60175. All Rights Reserved. Used by Permission. |
| 296 | ©Used by permission of the author |

| | |
|---|---|
| 297 | ©1972, Reprinted from *The Worshipbook-Services and Hymns*, The Westminster Press |
| 299 | ©By permission of Mary Arthur |
| 302, 303 | ©Church Pension Fund |
| 304 | ©1971, Hope Publishing Company, Carol Stream, IL 60188. All Rights Reserved. Used by Permission. |
| 305, 306 | ©By permission of Oxford University Press |
| 308, 309 | ©By permission of Oxford University Press |
| 314 | ©Sts. 1-3 Church Pension Fund |
| 315 | ©Hymns Ancient & Modern Limited admin. by Hope Publishing Company, Carol Stream, IL 60188. All Rights Reserved. Used by Permission |
| 319 | ©Church Pension Fund |
| 320 | ©Church Pension Fund |
| 329, 330, 331 | ©Church Pension Fund |
| 333 | ©1969, Hope Publishing Company, Carol Stream, IL 60188. All Rights Reserved. Used by Permission. |
| 334 | ©H.C.A. Gaunt. By permission of Oxford University Press |
| 335 | ©1971, G.I.A. Publications, Inc. |
| 336 | ©1982, sts. 2,3 Charles P. Price |
| 340, 341 | ©By Louis F. Benson. Used by permission of Robert F. Jeffery |
| 342 | ©By permission of the Estate of Frank W. Price |
| 346 | ©By permission of the Executor of Mrs. V.M. Pocknee, deceased |
| 347 | ©By permission of the Estate of Mildred E. Peacey |
| 348 | ©1979, Hope Publishing Company, Carol Stream, IL 60188. All Rights Reserved. Used by Permission. |

| | |
|---|---|
| 352 | ©1982, sts. 1,3 Charles P. Price |
| 353 | ©Church Pension Fund |
| 354 | ©by permission of Theodore Marier |
| 356 | ©Church Pension Fund |
| 358 | ©1982, Carl P. Daw, Jr. |
| 359 | ©1982, st. 3 Carl P. Daw, Jr. |
| 364 | ©Sts. 6-8 Church Pension Fund |
| 366 | ©Church Pension Fund |
| 375 | ©Church Pension Fund |
| 381 | ©1969, From *Worship Supplement.* Concordia Publishing House. Used by permission. |
| 390 | ©Church Pension Fund |
| 394, 395 | ©1979, Hymn Society of America admin. by Hope Publishing Company, Carol Stream, IL 60188. All Rights Reserved. Used by Permission |
| 399 | ©1992, Selah Publishing Company, Kingston, NY 12401 |
| 404 | ©Reproduced with the kind permission of T & T Clark Ltd., Edinburgh |
| 412 | ©Augsburg Publishing House. Used by permission. |
| 413 | ©1974, Hope Publishing Company, Carol Stream, IL 60188. All Rights Reserved. Used by Permission. |
| 418 | ©1978, From *Lutheran Book of Worship.* On behalf of the publishers and copyright holders Augsburg Publishing House |
| 420 | ©1972, Hope Publishing Company, Carol Stream, IL 60188. All Rights Reserved. Used by Permission. |
| 421 | ©Church Pension Fund |
| 422 | ©1982, George B. Caird |

| | |
|---|---|
| 424 | ©1970, Hope Publishing Company, Carol Stream, IL 60188. All Rights Reserved. Used by Permission. |
| 428 | ©Church Pension Fund |
| 431 | ©1981, Hope Publishing Company, Carol Stream, IL 60188. All Rights Reserved. Used by Permission. |
| 437, 438 | ©1962, Hope Publishing Company, Carol Stream, IL 60188. All Rights Reserved. Used by Permission. |
| 443 | ©Church Pension Fund |
| 444 | ©1973, Michael A. Perry. Jubilate Hymns Ltd., Southampton, England. |
| 447 | ©Australian Hymn Book Company. Used by permission. |
| 452 | ©1969, Hope Publishing Company, Carol Stream, IL 60188. All Rights Reserved. Used by Permission. |
| 459 | ©Reprinted by permission of Morehouse-Barlow Co., Inc. |
| 463, 464 | ©Reprinted by permission of Faber and Faber Ltd.from *Collected Poems* by W.H. Auden. |
| 465, 466 | ©1982, Christopher Idle |
| 472 | ©1954, Renewal 1982; The Hymn Society of America admin. by Hope Publishing Company, Carol Stream, IL 60188. All Rights Reserved. Used by Permission |
| 473 | ©Hymns Ancient & Modern admin. by Hope Publishing Company, Carol Stream, IL 60188. All Rights Reserved. Used by Permission |
| 475 | ©Sts. 1,2,4 Church Pension Fund: st. 3 by permission of David D. Coffin |
| 476 | ©1980, Elizabeth J. Cosnett |
| 477 | ©Church Pension Fund |
| 478 | ©Church Pension Fund |

| | |
|---|---|
| 481 | ©By permission of Oxford University Press |
| 482 | ©By permission of Oxford University Press |
| 489 | ©Church Pension Fund |
| 490 | ©1970, 1975 Celebration admin. by the Copyright Company, Nashville, TN 37203. All Rights Reserved. Used by Permission. |
| 499 | ©Church Pension Fund |
| 501, 502 | ©1971, John Webster Grant |
| 505 | ©1917 & 1918, From *The Common Service Book of the Lutheran Church*, United Lutheran Church in America, a predecessor of the Lutheran Church in America. |
| 506, 507 | ©By permission of Oxford University Press |
| 511 | ©Copyright held by A. R. Mowbray & Co. Ltd. |
| 513 | ©1982, Carl P. Daw, Jr. |
| 517 | ©1982, sts. 3,4 Carl P. Daw, Jr. |
| 528 | ©1978, Jeffery W. Rowthorn |
| 530 | ©Church Pension Fund |
| 536 | ©1966, 1984 by Willard F. Jabusch |
| 540 | ©Church Pension Fund |
| 542 | ©By permission of Oxford University Press |
| 547 | ©1980, Augsburg Publishing House |
| 551 | ©Used by permission of The Presbyterian Outlook, Richmond, VA. |
| 568 | ©By permission of the United Society for the Progation of the Gospel |
| 570 | ©1969, Hope Publishing Company, Carol Stream, IL 60188. All Rights Reserved. Used by Permission. |
| 571 | ©1969 by Galliard Ltd. All Rights Reserved. Used by Permission. |

| | |
|---|---|
| 572 | ©By permission of the Inter-Lutheran Commission on Worship |
| 573 | ©By permission of Oxford University Press |
| 576, 577 | ©1992, Selah Publishing Company, Kingston, NY 12401 |
| 579 | ©Sts. 2,3 Church Pension Fund |
| 580 | ©1967, Hope Publishing Company, Carol Stream, IL 60188. All Rights Reserved. Used by Permission. |
| 581 | ©1961-62, World Library Publications; 3815 N. Willow Rd Schiller Park, IL 60175. All Rights Reserved. Used by Permission. |
| 582, 583 | ©1910, From *Hymns of the Christian Life*, ed. by M. S. Littlefield. Harper & Row, Publishers, Inc. Courtesy of the publishers. |
| 584 | ©By permission of Oxford University Press |
| 585 | ©By permission of J. W. Shore |
| 587 | ©Church Pension Fund |
| 590 | ©1954, Renewal 1982 The Hymn Society of America admin. by Hope Publishing Company, Carol Stream, IL 60188. All Rights Reserved. Used by Permission |
| 591 | ©By permission of Oxford University Press |
| 593 | ©1992, Selah Publishing Company, Kingston, NY 12401 |
| 594 | ©By permission of the author |
| 597 | ©1982, Carl P. Daw, Jr. |
| 598 | ©By permission of the family of Walter Russell Bowie |
| 599 | ©1921, Edward B. Marks Music Company. Copyright renewed. International copyright secured. |

| | |
|---|---|
| 600, 601 | ©Emmanuel College, Toronto. Used by permission. |
| 602 | ©1969, Hope Publishing Company, Carol Stream, IL 60188. All Rights Reserved. Used by Permission. |
| 603, 604 | ©1980, Hope Publishing Company, Carol Stream, IL 60188. All Rights Reserved. Used by Permission. |
| 605 | ©1949, Albert F. Bayly. Used by permission of Oxford University Press |
| 606 | ©1982, Joyce M. Glover |
| 607 | ©1958, The Hymn Society of America admin. by Hope Publishing Company, Carol Stream, IL 60188. All Rights Reserved. Used by Permission |
| 610 | ©1961, Albert F. Bayly. Used by permission of Oxford University Press |
| 611 | ©1969, Hope Publishing Company, Carol Stream, IL 60188. All Rights Reserved. Used by Permission. |
| 614 | ©By permission of Oxford University Press |
| 618 | ©By permission of Oxford University Press |
| 619 | ©Church Pension Fund |
| 628 | ©1959, The Hymn Society of America admin. by Hope Publishing Company, Carol Stream, IL 60188. All Rights Reserved. Used by Permission |
| 630 | ©1954, renewed 1982, Hope Publishing Company, Carol Stream, IL 60188. All Rights Reserved. Used by Permission. |
| 631 | ©By permission of Oxford University Press |
| 633 | ©1992, Selah Publishing Company, Kingston, NY 12401 |
| 647 | ©Church Pension Fund |

| | |
|---|---|
| 649, 650 | ©1981, adapted text from ICEL Resource Collection of *Hymns & Service Music for the Liturgy*. International Committee on English in the Liturgy. |
| 651 | ©St. 2, Used by permission of Mary Babcock Crawford |
| 661 | ©Edward B. Marks Music Company. Used by permission. |
| 663 | ©Church Pension Fund |
| 668 | ©St. 4 Church Pension Fund |
| 669 | ©Church Pension Fund |
| 670 | ©1982, sts. 2-3 Charles P. Price |
| 673 | ©1983, Linda Wilberger Egan |
| 674 | ©By permission of Oxford University Press |
| 678, 679 | ©1982, Carl P. Daw, Jr. |
| 681 | ©By permission of Heckford, Norton & Co., Solicitors |
| 682 | ©By permission of Oxford University Press |
| 695, 696 | ©1974, Hope Publishing Company, Carol Stream, IL 60188. All Rights Reserved. Used by Permission. |
| 698 | ©1976, The Hymn Society of America admin. by Hope Publishing Company, Carol Stream, IL 60188. All Rights Reserved. Used by Permission |
| 705 | ©1961, The Hymn Society of America admin. by Hope Publishing Company, Carol Stream, IL 60188. All Rights Reserved. Used by Permission |
| 706 | ©1982, Charles P. Price |
| 710 | ©1976, Council for Religion in Independant Schools. Adaption from *Song and Spirit.* |

711 ©1972, st. 1 Maranatha! admin. by the Copyright Company, Nashville, TN 37203. All Rights Reserved. Used by Permission.

# Index of First Lines

| | |
|---|---|
| A child is born in Bethlehem, Alleluia! | 103 |
| A hymn of glory let us sing | 217, 218 |
| A light from heaven shone around | 256 |
| A mighty fortress is our God | 687, 688 |
| A mighty sound from heaven | 230 |
| A stable lamp is lighted | 104 |
| Abide with me: fast falls the eventide | 662 |
| Ah, holy Jesus, how hast thou offended | 158 |
| All creatures of our God and King | 400 |
| All glory be to God on high | 421 |
| All glory, laud, and honor | 154, 155 |
| All hail the power of Jesus' Name! | 450, 451 |
| All my hope on God is founded | 665 |
| All people that on earth do dwell | 377, 378 |
| All praise to thee, for thou, O King divine | 477 |
| All praise to thee, my God, this night | 43 |
| All praise to you, O Lord | 138 |
| All things bright and beautiful | 405 |
| All who believe and are baptized | 298 |
| All who love and serve your city | 570, 571 |
| Alleluia! sing to Jesus! | 460, 461 |
| Alleluia, alleluia! Give thanks to the risen Lord | 178 |

| | |
|---|---:|
| Alleluia, alleluia! Hearts and voices heavenward raise | 191 |
| Alleluia, song of gladness | 122, 123 |
| Almighty Father, strong to save | 579 |
| Almighty God, your word is cast | 588, 589 |
| Alone thou goest forth, O Lord | 164 |
| Amazing grace! how sweet the sound | 671 |
| Ancient of Days, who sittest throned in glory | 363 |
| And have the bright immensities | 459 |
| And now, O Father, mindful of the love | 337 |
| Angels, from the realms of glory | 93 |
| Angels we have heard on high | 96 |
| As Jacob with travel was weary one day | 453 |
| As longs the deer for cooling streams | 658 |
| As now the sun shines down at noon | 18 |
| As those of old their first fruits brought | 705 |
| As with gladness men of old | 119 |
| At the cross her vigil keeping | 159 |
| At the Lamb's high feast we sing | 174 |
| At the Name of Jesus | 435 |
| Awake and sing the song | 181 |
| Awake, arise, lift up your voice | 212 |
| Awake, my soul, and with the sun | 11 |
| Awake, my soul, stretch every nerve | 546 |
| Awake, O sleeper, rise from death | 547 |
| Awake, thou Spirit of the watchmen | 540 |
| Away in a manger, no crib for his bed | 101 |
| Baptized in water | 294 |
| Be thou my vision, O Lord of my heart | 488 |
| Before the Lord's eternal throne | 391 |
| Before thy throne, O God, we kneel | 574, 575 |
| Beneath the cross of Jesus | 498 |
| Blessèd are the poor in spirit | 560 |
| Blessed be the God of Israel | 444 |

| | |
|---|---|
| Blessèd city, heavenly Salem | 519, 520 |
| Blessèd feasts of blessèd martyrs | 238, 239 |
| Blessed is the King who comes | 153 |
| Blessèd Jesus, at thy word | 440 |
| Blest are the pure in heart | 656 |
| Blest be the King whose coming | 74 |
| Book of books, our people's strength | 631 |
| Bread of heaven, on thee we feed | 323 |
| Bread of the world, in mercy broken | 301 |
| Break forth, O beauteous heavenly light | 91 |
| Breathe on me, Breath of God | 508 |
| Brightest and best of the stars of the morning | 117, 118 |
| By all your saints still striving | 231, 232 |
| By gracious powers so wonderfully sheltered | 695, 696 |
| By the Creator, Joseph was appointed | 261, 262 |
| Can we by searching find out God | 476 |
| Christ for the world we sing! | 537 |
| Christ is alive! Let Christians sing | 182 |
| Christ is arisen (Christ ist erstanden) | 713 |
| Christ is made the sure foundation | 518 |
| Christ is the King! O friends upraise | 614 |
| Christ is the world's true Light | 542 |
| Christ Jesus lay in death's strong bands | 185, 186 |
| Christ, mighty Savior, Light of all creation | 33, 34, 35 |
| Christ, the fair glory of the holy angels | 282, 283 |
| Christ the Lord is risen again! | 184 |
| Christ the Victorious, give to your servants | 358 |
| Christ the worker | 611 |
| Christ upon the mountain peak | 129, 130 |
| Christ, when for us you were baptized | 121 |
| Christ, whose glory fills the skies | 6, 7 |
| Christians, awake, salute the happy morn | 106 |

| | |
|---|---:|
| Christians, to the Paschal victim | 183 |
| Come away to the skies | 213 |
| Come down, O Love divine | 516 |
| Come, gracious Spirit, heavenly Dove | 512 |
| Come, Holy Ghost, our souls inspire | 503, 504 |
| Come, Holy Spirit, heavenly Dove | 510 |
| Come, labor on | 541 |
| Come, let us join our cheerful songs | 374 |
| Come, let us with our Lord arise | 49 |
| Come, my Way, my Truth, my Life | 487 |
| Come now, and praise the humble saint | 260 |
| Come, O come, our voices raise | 430 |
| Come, O thou Traveler unknown | 638, 639 |
| Come, pure hearts, in joyful measure | 244 |
| Come, risen Lord, and deign to be our guest | 305, 30 |
| Come sing, ye choirs exultant | 235 |
| Come, thou almighty King | 365 |
| Come, thou fount of every blessing | 686 |
| Come, thou Holy Spirit bright | 226, 227 |
| Come, thou long-expected Jesus | 66 |
| Come, we that love the Lord | 392 |
| Come with us, O blessèd Jesus | 336 |
| Come, ye faithful, raise the strain | 199, 200 |
| Come, ye thankful people, come | 290 |
| Comfort, comfort ye my people | 67 |
| Commit thou all that grieves thee | 669 |
| Completed, Lord, the Holy Mysteries | 346 |
| Creating God, your fingers trace | 394, 395 |
| Creator of the earth and skies | 148 |
| Creator of the stars of night | 60 |
| Creator Spirit, by whose aid | 500 |
| Cross of Jesus, cross of sorrow | 160 |
| Crown him with many crowns | 494 |

| | |
|---|---:|
| Day by day | 654 |
| Dear Lord and Father of mankind | 652, 653 |
| Deck thyself, my soul, with gladness | 339 |
| Descend, O Spirit, purging flame | 297 |
| Dona nobis pacem, pacem. | 712 |
| Dost thou in a manger lie | 97 |
| Draw nigh and take the Body of the Lord | 327, 328 |
| Duérmete, Níno lindo (Oh, sleep now, holy baby) | 113 |
| | |
| Earth and all stars | 412 |
| Earth has many a noble city | 127 |
| Eternal Father, strong to save | 608 |
| Eternal light, shine in my heart | 465, 466 |
| Eternal Lord of love, behold your Church | 149 |
| Eternal Ruler of the ceaseless round | 617 |
| Eternal Spirit of the living Christ | 698 |
| Fairest Lord Jesus | 383, 384 |
| Faith of our fathers! living still | 558 |
| Father all loving, who rulest in majesty | 568 |
| Father eternal, Ruler of creation | 573 |
| Father, we praise thee, now the night is over | 1, 2 |
| Father, we thank thee who hast planted | 302, 303 |
| Fight the good fight with all thy might | 552, 553 |
| For all the saints, who from their labors rest | 287 |
| For the beauty of the earth | 416 |
| For the bread which you have broken | 340, 341 |
| For the fruit of all creation | 424 |
| For thy blest saints, a noble throng | 276 |
| For thy dear saints, O Lord | 279 |
| "Forgive our sins as we forgive" | 674 |
| Forty days and forty nights | 150 |
| From all that dwell below the skies | 380 |

| | |
|---|---:|
| From deepest woe I cry to thee | 151 |
| From east to west, from shore to shore | 77 |
| From glory to glory advancing, we praise thee, O Lord | 326 |
| From God Christ's deity came forth | 443 |
| From heaven above to earth I come | 80 |
| From thee all skill and science flow | 566 |
| | |
| Gabriel's message does away | 270 |
| Give praise and glory unto God | 375 |
| Give rest, O Christ | 355 |
| Give us the wings of faith to rise | 253 |
| Glorious the day when Christ was born | 452 |
| Glorious things of thee are spoken | 522, 523 |
| Glory be to Jesus | 479 |
| Glory, love, and praise, and honor | 300 |
| Go forth for God; go to the world in peace | 347 |
| Go forward, Christian soldier | 563 |
| Go tell it on the mountain | 99 |
| Go to dark Gethsemane | 171 |
| God be in my head | 694 |
| God bless our native land | 716 |
| God has spoken to his people | 536 |
| God himself is with us | 475 |
| God is love, and where true love is | 576, 577 |
| God is Love, let heaven adore him | 379 |
| God is working his purpose out | 534 |
| God moves in a mysterious way | 677 |
| God of grace and God of glory | 594, 595 |
| God of mercy, God of grace | 538 |
| God of our fathers, whose almighty hand | 718 |
| God of saints, to whom the number | 280 |
| God of the prophets, bless the prophets' heir | 359 |
| God rest you merry, gentlemen | 105 |

| | |
|---|---|
| God the Omnipotent! King, who ordainest | 569 |
| God, my King, thy might confessing | 414 |
| God, who stretched the spangled heavens | 580 |
| God, you have given us power to sound | 584 |
| Good Christian friends, rejoice | 107 |
| Good Christians all, rejoice and sing! | 205 |
| Gracious Spirit, Holy Ghost | 612 |
| Guide me, O thou great Jehovah | 690 |
| Hail the day that sees him rise, Alleluia! | 214 |
| Hail thee, festival day! *Ascension* | 216 |
| Hail thee, festival day! *Easter* | 175 |
| Hail thee, festival day! *Pentecost* | 225 |
| Hail this joyful day's return | 223, 224 |
| Hail, thou once despisèd Jesus! | 495 |
| Hail to the Lord who comes | 259 |
| Hail to the Lord's Anointed | 616 |
| Hark! a thrilling voice is sounding | 59 |
| Hark! the glad sound! the Savior comes | 71, 72 |
| Hark! the herald angels sing | 87 |
| Hark! the sound of holy voices | 275 |
| He is risen, he is risen! | 180 |
| He is the Way | 463, 464 |
| He sat to watch o'er customs paid | 281 |
| He who would valiant be | 564, 565 |
| Hearken to the anthem glorious | 240, 241 |
| Help us, O Lord, to learn | 628 |
| Herald, sound the note of judgment | 70 |
| Here, O my Lord, I see thee face to face | 318 |
| Holy Father, great Creator | 368 |
| Holy Ghost, dispel our sadness | 515 |
| Holy God, we praise thy Name | 366 |
| Holy, holy, holy! Lord God Almighty! | 362 |
| Holy Spirit, ever living | 511 |
| Holy Spirit, font of light | 228 |

| | |
|---|---:|
| Holy Spirit, Lord of love | 349 |
| Hope of the world, thou Christ | 472 |
| Hosanna in the highest | 157 |
| Hosanna to the living Lord! | 486 |
| How bright appears the Morning Star | 496, 497 |
| How firm a foundation, ye saints of the Lord | 636, 637 |
| How lovely is thy dwelling-place | 517 |
| How oft, O Lord, thy face hath shone | 242 |
| How sweet the Name of Jesus sounds | 644 |
| How wondrous and great thy works, God of Praise | 532, 533 |
| How wondrous great, how glorious bright | 369 |
| Humbly I adore thee, Verity unseen | 314 |
| I am the bread of life | 335 |
| I bind unto myself today | 370 |
| I call on thee, Lord Jesus Christ | 634 |
| "I come," the great Redeemer cries | 116 |
| I come with joy to meet my Lord | 304 |
| I heard the voice of Jesus say | 692 |
| I know not where the road will lead | 647 |
| I love thee, Lord, but not because | 682 |
| I love thy kingdom, Lord | 524 |
| I sing a song of the saints of God | 293 |
| I sing the almighty power of God | 398 |
| I sought the Lord, and afterward I knew | 689 |
| I to the hills will lift mine eyes | 668 |
| I want to walk as a child of the light | 490 |
| If thou but trust in God to guide thee | 635 |
| I'll praise my Maker while I've breath | 429 |
| Immortal, invisible, God only wise | 423 |
| In Bethlehem a newborn boy | 246 |
| In Christ there is no East or West | 529 |
| In the bleak midwinter | 112 |

| | |
|---|---|
| In the cross of Christ I glory | 441, 442 |
| In your mercy, Lord, you called me | 706 |
| Into paradise may the angels lead you | 354 |
| It came upon the midnight clear | 89. 90 |
| It was poor little Jesus | 468 |
| | |
| Jerusalem, my happy home | 620 |
| Jerusalem the golden | 624 |
| Jesu, Jesu, fill us with your love | 602 |
| Jesus, all my gladness | 701 |
| Jesus calls us; o'er the tumult | 549, 550 |
| Jesus came, adored by angels | 454 |
| Jesus Christ is risen today, Alleluia! | 207 |
| Jesus is Lord of all the earth. | 178 |
| Jesus lives! thy terrors now | 194, 195 |
| Jesus, Lover of my soul | 699 |
| Jesus! Name of wondrous love! | 252 |
| Jesus, our mighty Lord | 478 |
| Jesus, Redeemer of the world | 38, 39 |
| Jesus shall reign where'er the sun | 544 |
| Jesus, Son of Mary | 357 |
| Jesus, the very thought of thee | 642 |
| Jesus, thou divine Companion | 586 |
| Joy to the world! the Lord is come | 100 |
| Joyful, joyful, we adore thee | 376 |
| Judge eternal, throned in splendor | 596 |
| Just as I am, without one plea | 693 |
| | |
| Kind Maker of the world, O hear | 152 |
| King of glory, King of peace | 382 |
| King of the martyrs' noble band | 236 |
| | |
| Lamp of our feet, whereby we trace | 627 |
| Lead on, O King eternal | 555 |
| Lead us, heavenly Father, lead us | 559 |
| Lead us, O Father, in the paths of peace | 703 |

| | |
|---|---:|
| Let all mortal flesh keep silence | 324 |
| Let all the world in every corner sing | 402, 403 |
| Let saints on earth in concert sing | 526 |
| Let thy Blood in mercy poured | 313 |
| Let us break bread together on our knees | 325 |
| Let us now our voices raise | 237 |
| Let us, with a gladsome mind | 389 |
| Lift every voice and sing | 599 |
| Lift high the cross | 473 |
| Lift up your heads, ye mighty gates | 436 |
| Lift your voice rejoicing, Mary | 190 |
| Light's abode, celestial Salem | 621, 622 |
| Like the murmur of the dove's song | 513 |
| Lo! he comes, with clouds descending | 57, 58 |
| Lo! what a cloud of witnesses | 545 |
| Lo, how a Rose e'er blooming | 81 |
| Look there! the Christ, our Brother, comes | 196, 197 |
| Lord, be thy word my rule | 626 |
| Lord Christ, when first thou cam'st to earth | 598 |
| Lord, dismiss us with thy blessing | 344 |
| Lord, enthroned in heavenly splendor | 307 |
| Lord, for ever at thy side | 670 |
| Lord God, you now have set your servant free | 499 |
| Lord Jesus, Sun of Righteousness | 144 |
| Lord Jesus, think on me | 641 |
| Lord, make us servants of your peace | 593 |
| Lord of all being, throned afar | 419 |
| Lord of all hopefulness, Lord of all joy | 482 |
| Lord, thou has searched me and dost know | 702 |
| Lord, we have come at your own invitation | 348 |
| Lord, who throughout these forty days | 142 |
| Lord, whose love through humble service | 610 |
| Lord, you give the great commission | 528 |

| | |
|---|---:|
| Love came down at Christmas | 84 |
| Love divine, all loves excelling | 657 |
| Love's redeeming work is done | 188, 189 |
| Lully, lullay, thou little tiny child | 247 |
| | |
| Make a joyful noise unto the Lord | 710 |
| Many and great, O God, are thy works (Singt dem Herren!) | 385 |
| May choirs of angels lead you | 356 |
| May the grace of Christ our Savior | 351 |
| Morning glory, starlit sky | 585 |
| Morning has broken | 8 |
| Most High, omnipotent, good Lord | 406, 407 |
| Most Holy God, the Lord of heaven | 31, 32 |
| My country, 'tis of thee | 717 |
| My faith looks up to thee | 691 |
| My God, accept my heart this day | 697 |
| My God, how wonderful thou art | 643 |
| My God, thy table now is spread | 321 |
| My Shepherd will supply my need | 664 |
| My song is love unknown | 458 |
| | |
| Nature with open volume stands | 434 |
| New every morning is the love | 10 |
| New songs of celebration render | 413 |
| Not far beyond the sea, nor high | 422 |
| Not here for high and holy things | 9 |
| Nova, nova | 266 |
| Now greet the swiftly changing year | 250 |
| Now Holy Spirit, ever One | 19, 20 |
| Now let us all with one accord | 146, 147 |
| Now let us sing our praise to God | 16, 17 |
| Now, my tongue, the mystery telling | 329, 330, 331 |
| Now quit your care | 145 |
| Now thank we all our God | 396, 397 |
| Now that the daylight fills the sky | 3, 4 |

| | |
|---|---|
| Now the day is over | 42 |
| Now the green blade riseth from the buried grain | 204 |
| Now the silence | 333 |
| Now yield we thanks and praise | 108 |
| | |
| O all ye works of God, now come | 428 |
| O beautiful for spacious skies | 719 |
| O bless the Lord, my soul! | 411 |
| O blest Creator, source of light | 27, 28 |
| O Bread of life, for sinners broken | 342 |
| O brightness of the immortal Father's face | 37 |
| O Christ, the Word Incarnate | 632 |
| O Christ, you are both light and day | 40, 41 |
| O come, all ye faithful | 83 |
| O come, O come, Emmanuel | 56 |
| O day of God, draw nigh | 600, 601 |
| O day of peace that dimly shines | 597 |
| O day of radiant gladness | 48 |
| O Food to pilgrims given | 308, 309 |
| O for a closer walk with God | 683, 684 |
| O for a thousand tongues to sing | 493 |
| O gladsome Light, O grace | 36 |
| O God, creation's secret force | 14, 15 |
| O God of Bethel, by whose hand | 709 |
| O God of earth and altar | 591 |
| O God of every nation | 607 |
| O God of love, O King of peace | 578 |
| O God of love, to thee we bow | 350 |
| O God of truth, O Lord of might | 21, 22 |
| O God, our help in ages past | 680 |
| O God, to those who here profess | 352 |
| O God, unseen yet ever near | 332 |
| O God, we praise thee, and confess | 364 |
| O God, whom neither time nor space | 251 |

| | |
|---|---|
| O gracious Light, Lord Jesus Christ | 25, 26 |
| O heavenly Word, eternal Light | 63, 64 |
| O holy city, seen of John | 582, 583 |
| O Holy Spirit, by whose breath | 501, 502 |
| O Jesus Christ, may grateful hymns be rising | 590 |
| O Jesus, crowned with all renown | 292 |
| O Jesus, I have promised | 655 |
| O Jesus, joy of loving hearts | 649, 650 |
| O Light of Light, Love given birth | 133, 134 |
| O little town of Bethlehem | 78, 79 |
| O Lord Most High, eternal King | 220, 221 |
| O love, how deep, how broad, how high | 448, 449 |
| O Love of God, how strong and true | 455, 45 |
| O love that casts out fear | 700 |
| O Master, let me walk with thee | 659, 660 |
| O praise ye the Lord! Praise him in the height | 432 |
| O sacred head, sore wounded | 168, 169 |
| O saving Victim, opening wide | 310, 311 |
| O Savior of our fallen race | 85, 86 |
| O say can you see, by the dawn's early light | 720 |
| O sons and daughters, let us sing! *Easter* | 203 |
| O sons and daughters, let us sing! *Second Sunday of Easter and Saint Tomas' Day* | 206 |
| O sorrow deep! | 173 |
| O Spirit of Life, O Spirit of God | 505 |
| O Spirit of the living God | 531 |
| O splendor of God's glory bright | 5 |
| O thou who camest from above | 704 |
| O Trinity of blessèd light | 29, 30 |
| O very God of very God | 672 |
| O what their joy and their glory must be | 623 |
| O wondrous type! O vision fair | 136, 137 |
| O worship the King, all glorious above! | 388 |

| | |
|---|---|
| O ye immortal throng | 284 |
| O Zion, haste, thy mission high fulfilling | 539 |
| O Zion, open wide thy gates | 257 |
| O Zion, tune thy voice | 543 |
| Of the Father's love begotten | 82 |
| Oh, sleep now, holy baby (Duèrmete, Niño liñdo) | 113 |
| On earth has dawned this day of days | 201 |
| On Jordan's bank the Baptist's cry | 76 |
| On this day earth shall ring | 92 |
| On this day, the first of days | 47 |
| Once he came in blessing | 53 |
| Once in royal David's city | 102 |
| Only-begotten, Word of God eternal | 360, 361 |
| Onward, Christian soldiers | 562 |
| Our Father, by whose Name | 587 |
| Our Father, by whose servants | 289 |
| Our God, to whom we turn | 681 |
| Out of the depths I call | 666 |
| Over the chaos of the empty waters | 176, 177 |
| | |
| Praise God for John, evangelist | 245 |
| Praise, my soul, the King of heaven | 410 |
| Praise our great and gracious Lord | 393 |
| Praise the Lord, rise up rejoicing | 334 |
| Praise the Lord through every nation | 484, 485 |
| Praise the Lord! ye heavens adore him | 373 |
| Praise the Spirit in creation | 506, 507 |
| Praise to God, immortal praise | 288 |
| Praise to the Holiest in the height | 445, 446 |
| Praise to the living God! | 372 |
| Praise to the Lord, the Almighty | 390 |
| Praise we the Lord this day | 267 |
| Prepare the way, O Zion | 65 |
| Put forth, O God, thy Spirit's might | 521 |

| | |
|---|---|
| Redeemer of the nations, come | 55 |
| Rejoice! rejoice, believers | 68 |
| Rejoice, the Lord is King! | 481 |
| Rejoice, the Lord of life ascends | 222 |
| Rejoice, ye pure in heart! | 556, 557 |
| Remember your servants, Lord | 560 |
| Ride on! ride on in majesty! | 156 |
| Rise up, ye saints of God! | 551 |
| Rock of ages, cleft for me | 685 |
| Round the Lord in glory seated | 367 |
| Savior, again to thy dear Name we raise | 345 |
| Savior, like a shepherd lead us | 708 |
| Savior of the nations, come! | 54 |
| See the Conqueror mounts in triumph | 215 |
| Seek ye first the kingdom of God | 711 |
| Shalom, my friends | 714 |
| Shepherd of souls, refresh and bless | 343 |
| Silent night, holy night | 111 |
| Sing alleluia forth in duteous praise | 619 |
| Sing, my soul, his wondrous love | 467 |
| Sing, my tongue, the glorious battle | 165, 166 |
| Sing now with joy unto the Lord | 425 |
| Sing, O sing, this blessèd morn | 88 |
| Sing of Mary, pure and lowly | 277 |
| Sing praise to God who reigns above | 408 |
| Sing praise to our Creator | 295 |
| Sing we of the blessèd Mother | 278 |
| Sing, ye faithful, sing with gladness | 492 |
| Singing songs of expectation | 527 |
| "Sleepers, wake!" A voice astounds us | 61, 62 |
| Soldiers of Christ, arise | 548 |
| Sometimes a light surprises | 667 |
| Songs of praise the angels sang | 426 |
| Songs of thankfulness and praise | 135 |

| | |
|---|---|
| Spirit divine, attend our prayers | 509 |
| Spirit of God, unleashed on earth | 299 |
| Spirit of mercy, truth, and love | 229 |
| Spread, O spread, thou mighty word | 530 |
| Stand up, stand up, for Jesus | 561 |
| Strengthen for service, Lord | 312 |
| Sunset to sunrise changes now | 163 |
| Surely it is God who saves me | 678, 679 |
| | |
| Take my life, and let it be | 707 |
| Take up your cross, the Savior said | 675 |
| Teach me, my God and King | 592 |
| Tell out, my soul, the greatness of the Lord! | 437, 438 |
| Thanks to God whose Word was spoken | 630 |
| That Easter day with joy was bright | 193 |
| The angel Gabriel from heaven came | 265 |
| The Christ who died but rose again | 447 |
| The Church's one foundation | 525 |
| The day of resurrection! | 210 |
| The day thou gavest, Lord, is ended | 24 |
| The duteous day now closeth | 46 |
| The eternal gifts of Christ the King | 233, 234 |
| The first Nowell the angel did say | 109 |
| The first one ever, oh, ever to know | 673 |
| The flaming banners of our King | 161 |
| The fleeting day is nearly gone | 23 |
| The glory of these forty days | 143 |
| The God of Abraham praise | 401 |
| The golden sun lights up the sky | 12, 13 |
| The great Creator of the worlds | 489 |
| The great forerunner of the morn | 271, 272 |
| The head that once was crowned with thorns | 483 |
| The King of love my shepherd is | 645, 646 |
| The King shall come when morning dawns | 73 |

| | |
|---|---:|
| The Lamb's high banquet called to share | 202 |
| The Lord ascendeth up on high | 219 |
| The Lord my God my shepherd is | 663 |
| The Lord will come and not be slow | 462 |
| The people who in darkness walked | 125, 126 |
| The royal banners forward go | 162 |
| The sinless one to Jordan came | 120 |
| The snow lay on the ground | 110 |
| The spacious firmament on high | 409 |
| The stars declare his glory | 431 |
| The strife is o'er, the battle done | 208 |
| The whole bright world rejoices now | 211 |
| The Word whom earth and sea and sky | 263, 264 |
| There is a balm in Gilead | 676 |
| There is a green hill far away | 167 |
| There's a voice in the wilderness crying | 75 |
| There's a wideness in God's mercy | 469, 470 |
| They cast their nets in Galilee | 661 |
| Thine arm, O Lord, in days of old | 567 |
| This day at thy creating word | 52 |
| This is my Father's world | 651 |
| This is the day the Lord hath made | 50 |
| This is the feast of victory for our God | 417, 418 |
| This is the hour of banquet and of song | 316, 317 |
| This joyful Eastertide | 192 |
| Thou art the Way, to thee alone | 457 |
| Thou hallowed chosen morn of praise | 198 |
| Thou, who at thy first Eucharist didst pray | 315 |
| Thou, whose almighty word | 371 |
| Through the Red Sea brought at last, Alleluia! | 187 |
| Thy kingdom come, O God! | 613 |
| "Thy kingdom come!" on bended knee | 615 |
| Thy strong word did cleave the darkness | 381 |
| 'Tis the gift to be simple | 554 |

| | |
|---|---|
| To God with gladness sing | 399 |
| To mock your reign, O dearest Lord | 170 |
| To the Name of our salvation | 248, 249 |
| To thee, O Comforter divine | 514 |
| To you before the close of day | 44, 45 |
| 'Twas in the moon of wintertime | 114 |
| Two stalwart trees both rooted | 273, 274 |
| | |
| Unto us a boy is born! | 98 |
| | |
| Virgin-born, we bow before thee | 258 |
| | |
| Watchman, tell us of the night | 640 |
| We gather together to ask the Lord's blessing | 433 |
| We know that Christ is raised and dies no more | 296 |
| We limit not the truth of God | 629 |
| We plow the fields, and scatter | 291 |
| We sing of God, the mighty source | 386, 387 |
| We sing the glorious conquest | 255 |
| We sing the praise of him who died | 471 |
| We the Lord's people, heart and voice uniting | 51 |
| We three kings of Orient are | 128 |
| We walk by faith, and not by sight | 209 |
| We will extol you, ever-blessèd Lord | 404 |
| Weary of all trumpeting | 572 |
| "Welcome, happy morning!" age to age shall say | 179 |
| Were you there when they crucified my Lord? | 172 |
| What child is this, who, laid to rest | 115 |
| What does the Lord require | 605 |
| What is the crying at Jordan? | 69 |
| What star is this, with beams so bright | 124 |
| What thanks and praise to thee we owe | 285 |
| What wondrous love is this | 439 |
| When all thy mercies, O my God | 415 |

| | |
|---|---|
| When Christ was lifted from the earth | 603, 604 |
| When Christ's appearing was made known | 131, 132 |
| When I survey the wondrous cross | 474 |
| When in our music God is glorified | 420 |
| When Israel was in Egypt's land | 648 |
| When Jesus died to save us | 322 |
| When Jesus left his Father's throne | 480 |
| When Jesus went to Jordan's stream | 139 |
| When Jesus wept, the falling tear | 715 |
| When morning gilds the skies | 427 |
| When Stephen, full of power and grace | 243 |
| Where charity and love prevail | 581 |
| Where cross the crowded ways of life | 609 |
| Where is this stupendous stranger? | 491 |
| Where true charity and love dwell | 606 |
| Wherefore, O Father, we thy humble servants | 338 |
| While shepherds watched their flocks by night | 94, 95 |
| Who are these like stars appearing | 286 |
| Wilt thou forgive that sin, where I begun | 140, 141 |
| Word of God, come down on earth | 633 |
| Ye holy angels bright | 625 |
| Ye servants of God, your Master proclaim | 535 |
| Ye watchers and ye holy ones | 618 |
| Ye who claim the faith of Jesus | 268, 269 |
| You are the Christ, O Lord | 254 |
| You, Lord, we praise in songs of celebration | 319 |
| Your love, O God, has called us here | 353 |
| Zion, praise thy Savior, singing | 320 |

www.ingramcontent.com/pod-product-compliance
Lightning Source LLC
Chambersburg PA
CBHW071230300426
44116CB00008B/979